Your book is definitely unique in its approach. You did a great job on the book.
—Nancy Tawney, Director of Planned and Major Giving, Florentine Opera of Milwaukee

The impact of the time I spent with you continues to multiply. It has really helped me stay on top of deadlines. I am saving time because I have the tools to move through my paperwork more quickly. Thanks for your ideas, coaching and advice!
—Terry Preuit, Training Director

Thank you for your book. Even the title is an inspiration to get started. In addition to providing a wealth of information, it is also well written and enjoyable to read.
—Patricia L. Stewart, AT&T Marketing Manager, New Jersey

From advice on managing time, to assistance on creating efficient work space, *Organized to Be Your Best!* has it all. It showed me how to tame my chaotic schedule, clear the clutter from my home office and generally bring order to my life...the most helpful book on the subject that I've come across.
—Elane Osborn, Novelist, *Skylark*, Reno, Nevada

Finally...a book on organizational techniques that I can use to help coach my clients toward peak performance! Your straightforward, immediately applicable book fills a critical gap in my coaching library.
—Lois P. Frankel, Ph.D., President of Corporate Coaching International

Concise, easy to read and so appropriate for today's work environment.
—Dave Webb, Supplier Standards Manager, Purchasing, Finning Ltd., Vancouver, British Columbia, Canada

As an attorney in a solo practice, I'm trying to make the office more efficient. The book was helpful for my legal assistant and me to organize our work and our office. It gets right down to the brass tacks.
—Shirley A. Bass, Attorney at Law, Portland, Oregon

What a pleasure to tell you how much I enjoyed reading *Organized to Be Your Best!* I'm very excited about the useful information it contains; it has given me the inspiration to actually put your ideas into use, right now!
—Eadye Martinson, Executive Secretary, Everett, Washington

Two hours with Susan changed my lift myself.
wonderful working environment. I ha
Wrong! Her guidance was what I neec
—Sharon Bloom, Ph.D., Psychothera   *nued...*

D1505008

We all felt the opportunities presented by you for organizing our daily life in the office were without equal. Thank you for increasing our office's efficiency, positively! Your sessions were a catalyst to which our entire staff responded so enthusiastically that we are still buzzing over your presentation, discussions and the projects you inspired. And I have a new "bible"—your book!
—Robert Aronoff, Former Controller, Weight Watchers of Southern California

Organized to Be Your Best! is concisely comprehensive, giving insight into the overall organizational plan while focusing in on its components—an excellent guide through the organizational maze!
—Meryl Perloff, ASID, Dina P Purses

I have just finished your book and found it terrific! I believe that the basics in an office library are: (1) a good dictionary, (2) a good grammar book and (3) a copy of *Organized to Be Your Best!*
—Sharon Leahy, Vice President, Tri-United Realty Development & Management Associates, Skokie, Illinois

Thanks for a great book!
—Bonnie P. Humphrey, Attorney at Law, North Dakota

It's amazing! Your book worked! I work for an electrical utility in a small town in Northern Ontario, Canada. We inherited a young manager a couple of years ago and haven't seen the top of his desk since then. Last week I gave him your book opened at Mastering Your Desk and the Paper Jungle and mentioned he might find some useful ideas. I saw results the next day. All his notes were in one pile and by the end of the week, his desk was completely cleared. Thank you, thank you, thank you.
—Peggy Wikiruk, Billing & Accounting Clerk, Ontario, Canada

Organized

To Be Your
Best!

Transforming
How You Work

SUSAN SILVER

ADAMS-HALL PUBLISHING

www.adams-hall.com

Library of Congress Cataloging-in-Publication Data

Silver, Susan
    Organized to be your best! : transforming how you work / Susan Silver.
        p.   cm.
    Includes index.
    ISBN-13: 978-0-944708-77-4 (hardback)
    ISBN-10: 0-944708-77-3 (hardback)
    ISBN-13: 978-0-944708-81-1 (pbk.)
    ISBN-10: 0-944708-81-1 (pbk.)

    1. Business Records--Management--Data Processing.   2. Information resources management.   3. Time management.   I. Title.

HF5736.S543 2006
650.1--dc22

                                                2006010818

Cover design by Hespenheide Design, www.hespenheide.com

Adams-Hall books are available at special, quantity discounts for bulk purchases, sales promotions, premiums, fund-raising or educational use. For details, contact Adams-Hall Publishing at **800.888.4452** or **www.adams-hall.com**.

First printing 2006
Printed in the United States of America
20 19 18 17 16 15 14 13 12 11 10 9 8 7 6 5 4 3 2 1

Printed on recycled paper

Contents

Part 3 *cont.*

Part 4
Positively Organized! Computing
Organizing, Finding and Protecting Digital Info

Part 5
Positively Organized! Collaboration
Working, Communicating and Computing with Others

Part 1

Positively Organized!
Change for the Best

Designing a Program for Positive
Action and Transformation

1

How to Best Use This Book to Transform How You Work

This book could be the answer for you if any of the following questions are true. Are you

- Overwhelmed with today's instant communication overload—email, instant or text messages, phone calls and voice mails?

- Struggling with too many priorities and projects and always in a time crunch?

- On overload with your workload and/or working 24-7?

- Swamped with paperwork or inundated with information?

- Suffering from excess stress every day?

- Out of balance with little or no personal time?

- Working in a chaotic or cluttered environment?

- Lacking real teamwork and collaboration with others?

- Juggling multiple offices or traveling extensively?

- Just looking for more ideas to help you grow professionally and personally and experience a real sense of accomplishment?

Why You Need This Book Now More Than Ever

If you answered "yes" to even one question, this is the right book at the right time.

Even if you've read other books on productivity or organization (including a prior edition of *Organized to Be Your Best!*), you need this new edition because as the "bible of organization," it has the latest advice on how to survive and thrive in a fast-paced, high-demand world that's big on information, communication, technology, stress and *change.*

This fifth edition comes to the rescue, combining **essential organization, time management and people skills** to transform how you work in a time of change. You'll see how to work more effectively using technology as well as time-tested, lower-tech tools. You'll discover the power of people in **communicating and collaborating**—whether you manage yourself or others. You'll appreciate more strategies on **improving your work environment** (including a mobile or home office)—as well as how to deal with paper and other "collectibles."

You'll get the benefit of my 20-plus years' experience as a recognized organizing expert and a business trainer on supervision, management, leadership and communication skills. I'm the president of a training and management consulting firm called Positively Organized! (which, I might add, is a positive approach to organization and is *not* to be confused with being compulsively organized).

Whatever work you do, organization can help you do it—and help you be the *best* that you can be. That's always been the goal for each edition of this book—to inspire you to do your *best work*, be your *best self* and have the *best time* in your life. Being organized is merely the means to make it happen, not an end in itself. Hopefully, in the process, you'll discover your own personal sense of achievement—what it really means to be *your best*. And if you share this information with colleagues and/or staff, you have a chance to experience the best quality, service and teamwork with others so they can be *their best*.

What's in It for You

This book will help you transform how you work so you can make time for your most important activities and achieve more of your goals.

And my goal for you is not only to get many good ideas from this book but to apply those ideas in your work and your life. Take what you read in this book and translate it into action. Use the Positively Organized! Plan of Action form in this chapter to help plan and tackle your goals, email, computer, projects, paperwork, desk, filing cabinet or mobile office.

Or maybe you and your colleagues will all read this book and together you'll create a joint plan of action to design a computer folder system for your department, improve a communication feedback system, establish a fail-safe method for follow-up, revamp an office filing system or simplify work flow procedures.

How the New, Fifth Edition is Organized and Why

Just as I encourage my clients to be their best, I also make each edition of my book the best it can be. And it's working: you're reading an award-winning book with more than one-quarter million copies in print that's been selected by more than ten book clubs.

I know "reorganization" is a bad word these days but I've done just that in this new edition. I've reorganized the chapters (which are all revised) into the following five parts:

Part 1 Positively Organized! Change for the Best
Designing a Program for Positive Action and Transformation

Part 2 Positively Organized! Essentials
Managing Your Time, Info and Communications

Part 3 Positively Organized! Workspaces
Working Productively and Ergonomically with Equipment, Files, Paper, and Other "Collectibles" in an Office and on the Go

Part 4 Positively Organized! Computing
Organizing, Finding and Protecting Digital Info

Part 5 Positively Organized! Collaboration
Communicating and Working Collaboratively with Others

Parts 1 and 2

In these "required reading" sections, you'll find out how to create your own **personal organization systems** that fit your work style to manage your **time, tasks, priorities, goals, work, projects, information** and **communications**. You'll learn how to customize systems that work for you because there's no one right way to get organized. You'll discover how to apply right away what you've read using my Positively Organized® Plan of Action form.

Part 3

If your office is a "jungle in there," Part 3 will help you dig out from under, deal with **paper** logjams, set up **filing systems**, design your **workspace** and **work ergonomically** so you can **stay healthy** while you're working—wherever you're working. Part 3 is helpful, too, for readers who telecommute, work out in the field, travel extensively for work or have multiple, mobile or virtual offices. You'll see the value of **mobile devices** and accessories and **Web solutions**.

Part 4

This part is "highly recommended reading" if you use a computer or mobile device extensively and especially, if you don't have access to an IT (Information Technology) department. You'll learn about **organizing your computer, backing it up, finding files and protecting your information and yourself while online.**

Part 5

Because most people today are highly connected and are communicating like crazy, Part 5 is also "highly recommended reading." **Connectivity** is simply how we work today; **collaboration** brings all the connectivity to a purposeful, productive level. Also, as a management trainer and an organization expert, I believe we can work most effectively and efficiently through and with others. You'll cover such topics as **teamwork, customer service, leadership, face-to-face/online meetings, document/information sharing and project management.**

Throughout the book I provide all kinds of helpful tips as well as info on specific tools, products and websites including a resource guide at the end of almost every chapter for easy reference.

How to Save Time
When Reading This Book

I've specially designed this book so it's instantly accessible and usable and will save you time. There are brief "Quick Scan" summaries at the beginning of each chapter and plentiful subheads and boldfaced words in the chapters to help you read more quickly,

And what's more, you don't have to read the whole book! Read only those chapters that apply to you (along with the recommended chapters).

The "Quick Survey" in Chapter 2 will let you see immediately where to fine tune and where to do a complete overhaul. After the survey, go to the table of contents and mark those chapters that relate most directly to the items you marked that need improvement. The "Quick Scan" summary at the beginning of a chapter will help confirm whether you should read the chapter. Whichever chapters you select, be sure to actually put key ideas from this book into action as soon as possible using the plan of action form in this chapter.

An Action Orientation

Tropophobia, the fear of change, is the biggest stumbling block to action for most people. Once you accept and initiate change in your life, you'll have more control over it.

Now's the time to act. While organization is a process that evolves over time, you can facilitate this process by taking action and using this book as a springboard for action.

As you read a chapter, skim the headings and subheads. Use a pen, pencil, highlighter, or some Post-it Flags to indicate key points for you. Be aware of what jumps out.

Find a small change you can make that will make a big difference. It might be changing a work habit or using a new system. Many clients find, for example, that setting aside five minutes a day to plan the next day is helpful. Some clients decide to set up and use a "Daily Paperwork System" (as described in Chapter 4 and 8) or to put their paper-based system on computer or a mobile handheld device. Others work together jointly to create or streamline an office system or procedure.

Write and Implement Action Plans

How much you read is not important; how much you do to transform
how you work is what really counts.

I have my clients write a plan of action at the conclusion of every
seminar or consultation. The plan can take a number of different
formats—it can be a simple but sincere written note to yourself or a
completed form such as the Positively Organized!® Plan of Action on the
next page. Feel free to make copies of this form and use them as you
read selected chapters.

Dare to put your intentions in writing

As soon as you've completed one chapter or section in which you've
identified a change you'd like to make, write down your intention. When
you write an intention, especially in handwriting, you're reinforcing that
intention and making it concrete.

Writing also helps you clarify your thinking so that you're better
prepared to take action. Many, if not most people, though, are afraid that
if they write something down, they'll forget about it. These people need
to combine the act of writing with reading and doing what has been
written. If you make a daily to-do list, for example, read it over several
times during the day and do the listed activities.

Commit to yourself, commit to a deadline

The plan of action is basically a written commitment to yourself. Ideally,
your first plan should focus on an organizational habit, tool, project or
system that can be put into action in a one- to four-week maximum block
of time. Create an experience of success. Don't overwhelm yourself with
a six-month project where you may become discouraged or disinterested.

Use a specific, small-step, short-term approach

Instead of the general "improving my time management skills," for your
project, select something more specific, such as "I will take five minutes
to plan and write tomorrow's to-do list at the end of each day." Instead
of cleaning out all your file cabinets from the last 12 years, complete one
file drawer in one week.

Your Positively Organized!® Plan of Action

Today's Date: _____

Organization Project or Activity:

_____

Benefits or Results:

_____

Ideas/Sketch/Brainstorm/Mind Map:

Action Steps   How long/often?   Calendared?

_____
_____
_____
_____
_____
_____
_____
_____

Reward yourself with:

_____
_____
_____

Completion Date (no longer than 30 days out):

_____

Follow-up with _____

What's in it for you?

Besides some hard work, you better be able to rattle off a whole list of benefits or results you hope to gain. Better yet, pick the most important benefit. Underline and star that benefit.

Benefits are the key

Just why is listing benefits so crucial? A benefit is the reason why you do something. It's the motivation behind an action or activity and it should be connected to at least one of your major goals. You need a compelling benefit to justify spending the time and effort required to organize anything. If there's no real payoff to getting more organized, you won't.

Organization gets put on the back burner because it doesn't appear to be a top priority. Your benefit has to be strong enough to make organization a top priority and to counteract all the reasons and excuses that justify this "back burner syndrome."

Once you've identified at least one top benefit, keep it uppermost in your mind as you're doing your plan of action.

Plan step by step

If your project has more than two or three steps, try "Mind Mapping" your steps before you put them in linear order. Mind Mapping is a way to pour out your thoughts and ideas in a visual, picture outline. Once you can "see" your ideas, then you can determine their sequential relationship to one another. (See Chapter 4 for a discussion of Mind Mapping and other idea organization tools.)

Make appointments with yourself

Once you've charted out your steps, schedule blocks of time to complete these steps. Schedule appointments with yourself and don't break them! Have calls screened (or let your voice mail take them), go off by yourself where no one can find you or pick a time when you won't be disturbed. Your plan of action should indicate how long steps will take—total time or time per day/week. Then write appointments in your calendar or planner based on your plan of action projections.

Reward Yourself!

Make your plan of action more enjoyable and more likely to be implemented by building in any or all of the three main types of rewards—tangible, psychological and experiential.

Tangible rewards include physical things you give yourself—for example, new clothes or a new mobile device.

Psychological rewards are positive messages you tell yourself—stating positive affirmations and giving yourself little mental "pats on the back."

Experiential rewards are a cross between tangible and psychological—getting a massage, taking a trip, dining out in a special restaurant are examples.

Getting others involved in your organization project can be a rewarding process in and of itself. Whether you engage a buddy who will offer positive reinforcement or you actually share the work with another, you'll more likely increase your accountability and success rate as well as lighten your load. Encourage others to support you in your goals and do the same for them.

How to Change Habits

Getting more organized almost always involves habit-changing behavior. But don't worry—it doesn't take a lifetime to change a habit. Actually it takes 21 to 30 days, provided you do the following:

1. Decide what new habit or behavior you intend to practice.

2. Write it down (or print it out) on paper. List how, when and why you're going to do it.

3. Share your new habit with someone else.

4. Reward yourself. Psychological affirmations before, during and after you practice a behavior can be particularly helpful.

5. Practice, practice, practice. You need to repeat the behavior, preferably every day, to create the habit.

Commitment to Be Your Best

You will succeed with your plan of action and habit changes and get the maximum value out of this book only if you are truly *committed to being your best*.

But what does being your best mean? For some, it's beating out the competition. For others, it's doing *your* best—being in competition with yourself. It's fine tuning what you're already good at. Award-winning athletes, such as world champion whitewater canoeist Jon Lugbill, are always fine tuning, looking for a better way. See if you can relate Lugbill's whitewater canoeing description to your work or life:

> I love the sport and I love being good at it. The challenge is that you constantly have to search out all the little advantages: techniques in the boat, types of boats, what you eat, how much sleep you get, everything down the line— you've got to learn to get the most out of everything you can. The combination of physical and mental goals, that's what's exciting about the sport for me.

Define it for yourself. After all, the way you live your life makes a statement about you. Why not make the best statement?

According to author David Viscott, we each have at least one special gift to give the world. I believe that those gifts should extend beyond yourself in some way to make a better world. What are your gifts and how are you making the *best* use of them?

Being Positively Organized! will help you *use* those gifts so you can indeed be your best. In the next chapter we'll explore just what it means to be Positively Organized!

2

How to Be
Positively Organized!

Quick Scan: This chapter is "required reading" because it helps you assess your organizational skills as well as your life balance. Through the Quick Survey, you'll identify your organizational strengths and weaknesses at work. Next, you'll pinpoint your work and personal goals and values.

Take a deep breath and relax. Positively Organized! does not mean being compulsively or perfectly organized. It's being **only as organized as you need to be.**

Being Positively Organized is *not* just having your stuff such as your papers in order; more important is having your life priorities and goals in order. It's also **a question of balance** between: (a) work and personal, (b) yourself and others and (c) the micro and the macro—the details and the big picture in life and at work.

You also need to **make organization a top priority.** Take it off the back burner and make time for it *every day*. Get into the organization habit. It will give you a professional edge, not to mention more control and less stress.

Know Your Personal Style

There's no one right way to "get organized." There are many different organization styles as well as a variety of tools and habits you can choose to better complement your organization style.

Your own style and degree of organization at work will depend on a number of factors—your level of activity, whether you're part of a team and/or have any support staff, the image you want to project, if you deal face to face with the public and how you prefer to work. It's up to you just how much organization you need.

Left Brain/Right Brain

Styles often develop because of "brain dominance." Brain research indicates that most of us develop and depend on a dominant right or left hemisphere of the brain. If you are more "left-brained," you will tend to like more order, structure and routine; "right-brained" individuals prefer variety and flexibility. I believe it's possible to modify your natural "style" to a certain degree but it's important to become aware of when you're going against the grain—or rather, against the brain.

For example, a left-brained individual may prefer a clean desk and office where everything is put away. As a consultant I would help that person set up out-of-sight systems. But if a client comes to me stating an aversion to a "neat-as-a-pin" office, I would help design systems that are interesting and flexible as well as within eyesight and easy reach. As you're reading this book, be aware of your current style and perhaps your ideal style, as well as which products and ideas immediately appeal to you and which do not.

Extreme styles

Be wary of *extremes*, however, for which this book will not be helpful. If your natural style (or that of someone with whom you work or live) is extremely rigid, compulsive to a fault and demanding of others, you (or that other person) could be suffering from Obsessive Compulsive Disorder (OCD). While there are many different manifestations of this disorder, one type includes arranging and rearranging rituals that are performed routinely and compulsively. If you think either you, a loved one or a coworker suffers from OCD, contact the OC Foundation at

203/401-2070 (CT) or **www.ocfoundation.org** for information and support.

This book will not be too helpful either for an extreme style that craves too much stimulation and variety. If it's difficult or impossible to stay focused for very short periods of time without getting distracted, Attention Deficit Disorder (ADD) may be a problem and professional counseling by someone specializing in ADD should be sought.

Create Balance in Your Life

"Work has become our religion" according to Benjamin Hunnicutt, a University of Iowa labor historian. For too many of us, when we are not working, we don't know what to do with our time. Over the last decade, Americans have increased their working hours. Too much time with work means less time for family, especially a spouse. Children also may feel the effect of parents working longer hours, including work done at home where the dividing line between work and home is hard to set.

On the other hand, some people are recognizing the value of working less and are tapping into voluntary simplicity, one of the leading lifestyle trends. In fact, the Trends Research Institute reported that many people have voluntarily "downshifted" and are working fewer hours for less pay in order to spend more time with families or pursue other interests.

Creating balance in your life involves two main steps:

1. Identifying your professional and personal goals by determining what really is important and has meaning to you

2. Using your goals to help you consciously decide how to spend your time and balance professional and personal demands

Proactive Stress Management

While we're on the topic of balance, I encourage you to pay attention—lots of attention—to stressors in your life, particularly if you think they are affecting your work performance, mental outlook, energy level, amount of sleep and quality of health. Stressors can keep you way out of balance.

Remember, we all have stressors but look at the severity and duration of them. Don't ignore long-term stressors and stress; the research continually shows that stress can take quite a toll on your health, leading to increased risk for heart disease and a depressed immune system.

When I teach stress management, here are four suggestions that I typically offer:

1. **Take care of your body** by exercising regularly (three or more times a week), eating a good diet with plenty of fresh fruits and vegetables and getting enough sleep.

2. **Take care of your mind** by relaxing it (e.g., through meditation, private reflection, prayer or listening to music); learning something new; practicing recreational skills and activities (such as playing an instrument or participating in a hobby).

3. **Remember to laugh** a lot because laughter is a form of mental and physical exercise that lowers blood pressure, activates the immune system, triggers the release of endorphins (the body's natural painkillers), reduces stress hormones and produces a general sense of well-being.

4. **Be positive and proactive** in your life by building supportive relationships with others, celebrating achievements (even small ones), making decisions, solving problems and *getting organized*.

And an important part of getting organized—Positively Organized!—is setting goals and taking action steps toward your goals.

Target Challenging, Achievable Goals

Good organization starts with clear, meaningful goals, which give you direction because as Yogi Berra once said, "If you don't know where you're going, you'll end up some place else." This is the first secret to being organized. All the organizational tools and techniques in the world and this book are useless if you don't know where you're headed, that is, what you want to accomplish at work and in your life. Keep in mind that it doesn't matter how fast you're running (or how busy you are) if you're going in the wrong direction.

Start with an up-to-date list of goals. Not having this list is like taking a trip without a map. Goals give you focus, purpose and direction. Goals can help you **attain** something you don't yet have or better **maintain** something you already do. Don't underestimate the power of combining these two types of goals. **Maintenance goals** can keep you on track anchored in the present and help instill a sense of gratitude for what you have, while **"attain" goals** let you yearn and strive for an even better future.

Effective goals are simple, clear-cut and direct. They should also reflect both professional and personal values—what's most important and meaningful to you and if possible, your life mission. Chiropractor Dr. Mha Atma Singh Khalsa stated it well in his newsletter: "Discover and clarify your mission in life—your overriding purpose."

Radio talk-show host Dennis Prager suggests his listeners ask themselves the following question after each day of work: "Are you proud of what you did today?"

Write down your goals on paper periodically during the year (this means more than once!). Make appointments with yourself to plan your goals on paper. Twice a year may be sufficient—in January and then again in July. Others prefer quarterly goals.

How to Write Down Your Goals

Use the Goals Work Sheet in Figure 2-1 to identify the "what," "why" and "how" of each goal.

Begin by listing "what" you want to attain or maintain and the extent or degree of accomplishment. In describing your goal, ask yourself what you want to **do, be** or **have**. Be as specific as you can. Write your goal in the present tense for a maintenance goal and in the future if it's not a regular part of your life right now. (Or you may prefer to write all goals in the present tense, making them double as positive affirmations of what you want.) Here are three "do, be, have" examples of personal and professional goals:

Do: I exercise three times a week; I play volleyball on Sunday, tennis on Tuesday and racquetball on Thursday.

Be: I am a peaceful person who greets problems as challenges and opportunities. (Here's an affirmation style goal.)

Have: I will have a job in my chosen field that is financially and personally satisfying by this time next year.

Answer "why" by listing any benefits and results you expect from
accomplishing your goal. The "why" should also state the value this goal
has for you in your life as a whole. If you choose goals that conflict with
your life values, you'll be setting yourself up for sabotage and failure.
Let's suppose, for example, one of your goals is to get a promotion
within the next few years and to do so will require that you put in many
more hours at work. But one of your values is to lead a balanced life that
includes plenty of time spent with your family. You could have a conflict
on your hands—a real values clash.

Your goals need to be in harmony with your most important life
values. Taking the "do" goal listed above, here are some benefits or
results to be derived: feeling fit; increased energy and vitality; getting
those endorphins flowing; decreased stress; feeling more relaxed (exercise
is one of the four natural tranquilizers—laughter, music and sex being
the other three); having more fun; a better social life; and balancing a
hectic lifestyle.

Answer "how" by listing specific ways you plan to achieve your
goals—any strategies, action steps or tasks, in addition to the amount of
time required (per day, week, month or year). Assigning deadlines—or
"lifelines" as one person I know prefers to call them—will make your
"hows" much more specific and helpful. Some specific "hows" for the
"do" goal could include: calling to make reservations; confirming tennis
and racquetball times with a partner; writing down activities and times in
a calendar; and putting out sports clothes the night before by the door.

The power of the pen

Putting your goals in handwriting helps affirm your commitment. Your
chances of achieving your goals are much greater when you write them
down. It makes your goals more real. It also helps plant them into your
subconscious. One professional woman I know writes down her goals
each year in January, seals them in an envelope, opens the envelope at the
end of the year and discovers she has accomplished almost all of them.

Now take five to ten minutes to complete the Goals Work Sheet in
Figure 2-1 to quickly jot down three or more of your goals, including the
"what," the "why" and the "how" for each one (or better yet, make a
photocopy of the page before completing the form).

Aim high

Who says you have to accomplish all your goals? There's a saying that goes like this, "If you accomplish everything you planned, then you haven't planned well enough." You *should* plan a little more than you may actually do; practice aiming high because you'll probably accomplish more than if you lower your expectations and make them "realistic."

Figure 2-1. GOALS WORK SHEET

Date: _____

WHAT is your goal?	WHY do you want this goal?	HOW will you proceed?
1.		
2.		
3.		
4.		

Techniques to Ensure Success

So aim high and use these eight ways to increase your chances of reaching your goals:

1. Put your goals in writing.
2. Read them daily before you do your planning and before you go

to sleep.

3. Take some action on your goals every day or at least every week.
4. Share them with one other person (and listen to theirs). But only share them with other people who also set goals of their own and reach them. Those are the kind of people who will be most supportive.
5. Every week write down and accomplish smaller goals that relate to your long-term goals. List these weekly goals where you will see them every day.
6. Review and revise your goals at least twice a year, always making sure they reflect your deepest values.
7. Let them inspire, not haunt you.
8. Include both professional and *personal* goals to increase the balance of your life. Make sure, too, that your goals harmonize with those of your career, position or company; if they don't, you could experience some conflict(s) in your life.

How Organized Are You at Work?

As a consultant I usually begin working with clients by giving them a quick survey, which helps them determine their own organizational strengths and weaknesses. Here's one for you that ties in with the subject areas covered in this book.

Read and react quickly to each of the items on Figure 2-2 and check off the appropriate letter that describes how effectively you and/or your workgroup handle each item below—O for Outstanding, S for Satisfactory or N for Needs Improvement. If an item is not applicable to you, then write N/A.

How to Select the Most Important Areas to You

Look at the "Ns" you've checked. Decide which three Ns are most important to you right now. Star these three items. See which chapter numbers come up most often. Now go to the table of contents and select the most important chapters for you to read. (Keep in mind, too, that the chapters in Parts 1 and 2 are "required reading" and those in Parts 4 and

Figure 2-2. A QUICK SELF SURVEY

	ORGANIZATION / PERFORMANCE AREA	Your Rating		
		O	S	N
1.	Your system for planning, prioritizing and accomplishing work and achieving your goals [Chapters 2, 3, 4]			
2.	Instant communications (email, instant messages, text messages, voice mail) [Chapter 5, 11, 16]			
3.	Your daily paperwork [Chapters 4, 8, 9, 10, 11]			
4.	Access to needed information [Chapters 4, 5, 8, 9, 11, 12]			
5.	Your phone time (landline and cell) [Chapters 5, 11]			
6.	Managing long-term paper and possessions [Chapters 8, 9, 10]			
7.	Your follow-ups [Chapters 3, 4, 5, 11]			
8.	Your reading load [Chapter 8]			
9.	Your desk and workspace [Chapters 6, 7, 8, 9, 11]			
10.	Organizing computer files, folders and info [Chapters 12, 13, 14]			
11.	Working with others [Chapters 5, 15-17]			
12.	Juggling multiple projects and priorities [Chapters 3, 15]			
13.	Dealing with interruptions [Chapter 3]			
14.	Filing and records management [Chapter 9]			
15.	Your on-the-go, traveling office [Chapter 11]			
16.	Communications and teamwork [Chapters 5, 15-17]			

5 are "highly recommended" no matter which "elective" chapters you choose to read.)

Take a moment now to reflect on what it would mean to you, your business, your career and your life to improve your top three starred items. Think about the benefits that you would experience. Take 60 seconds to jot down as many benefits that come to mind on a sheet of paper or in a notebook or right in this book if it belongs to you. Star the most important benefit to you.

Now look at your goals in Figure 2-1 and note which chapters will best help you reach those goals. And remember, the idea isn't to be organized for the sake of organization. It's being 'positively organized' in order to be your best—that means the best you can be at whatever you do in your life.

Part 2

Positively Organized! Essentials

Managing Your Time, Info
and Communications

3

Time Management: What You Really Need to Know

Quick Scan: Discover the secrets to getting the most important things done in your life. Learn the art of planning and prioritizing and why time management is the foundation for good organization. See how to better balance the "great juggling act." After reading this chapter, see Chapters 4 and 5 to discover the wide variety of quality high-tech and low-tech tools to manage your time as well as your info and communications.

Every problem with organization is in some way a problem with time. If your time isn't well organized, chances are your priorities, projects and papers won't be either and you won't be as productive as you could be.

Time management is the foundation of good organization and the backbone of your personal **Positively Organized! System.** I define a **system** as using the best **tools** and **habits** to get a job done or reach a goal. Your Positively Organized! System is a reliable yet flexible set of tools and habits you select for organizing your time, tasks, priorities, projects, information and communications. Pay special attention to consciously choosing and using good time management habits.

Do the Most Important Things

Many people think the purpose of time management is to get as much done as possible. Not so. **It's getting the most important things done**.

Do you *often* have days when it feels as if you have accomplished nothing? If so, you aren't taking advantage of time management. You're not doing the most important tasks and activities.

Have you considered what "most important" means? Is it something that has an urgent deadline? Is it something your boss wants? Is it something *you* want that relates to one of your goals?

It can mean all of these. But watch out if you're only making *other people's demands* the most important things you do. To be your best, make time every day to accomplish something that *you* consider important.

Activities you deem important flow from the values and goals you identified in Chapter 1. Without clear goals and values, your time management decisions will be made in a vacuum or else will be externally determined by outside circumstances and people; in either case, you won't be in charge. So take charge and start choosing activities that contribute to your goals.

How Time Management Helps

Time management is the great simplifier, putting things into focus and perspective. Time management is an awareness of time coupled with the ability to choose and control purposeful activities related to your goals. It's the basis for decision making.

Time management is making choices about activities that have meaning to you. These choices should balance short-term and long-term, urgent and less urgent, internal and external activities. Time management helps you control what you can, when you can.

Time management is also using the right tools and habits to improve *how* you do something. Effective time management tools and habits can improve the quality and quantity of your work, help you make better decisions and give you a real sense of accomplishment.

How to Plan and Prioritize

Planning and prioritizing are two essential habits that are the bread and butter of time management. Use them to balance long-term and short-term goals and activities.

Why take the time to plan and prioritize? Research indicates that for every hour of planning, you save three or four hours. Effective planning and prioritizing ("P and P" for short) will help you get the most important things done each day, week, month and year. And since your work seems endless but time isn't, remember **Parkinson's Law**: "Work expands so as to fill the time available for its completion."

You've already started with long-term P and P in Chapter 1. Long-term goal setting is a real time-saver because it's a handy yardstick against which you can measure all your day-to-day P and P decisions.

Learn Your ABCs and Numbers

To master P and P, begin by learning to identify your "ABC" priorities. Author Edwin Bliss, in his wonderful book *Getting Things Done*, differentiates between these three priorities. He says A priorities are "important and urgent," as in crisis management. B priorities are "important but not urgent," as in long-term goals. You should try to spend most of your time on As and Bs. C priorities are "urgent but not important." Try to spend as little time on Cs as possible.

You're probably pretty good at handling As, which fall in the "fire-fighting" category, but how many Bs do you work on each day? **Make time every day to work on your important-but-not-urgent B priorities and goals.** A good source for these priorities are the goals you listed on your Goals Work Sheet in the first chapter.

Another way to describe A, B and C priorities is to substitute these three words: "must," "should" and "could." In other words, an A priority is something you *must* do, a B priority is something you *should* do and a C priority is something you *could* do.

And here's a trick using numbers that I learned from colleague Marjorie Hansen Shaevitz when she and I each spoke professionally at the same conference. Using a scale from 1 to 10, ask yourself these two questions if you're indecisive about whether to do an activity:

1. How much do I really want to do this activity (against the backdrop of everything else that is going on)?
2. How important is this activity?

Add D, D and D to your P and P

To get the most important things done each day, add three other ingredients to your planning and prioritizing: **discipline, dedication,** and **desire**.

There is no substitute for a daily dose of **discipline**. Build planning into every work day and give it as much importance as if you were going away on a two-week vacation. (Did you ever notice how good you get at planning and prioritizing the day before you go away?)

Build a specific time slot into your daily schedule to work on top projects or priorities—and stick to it. For example, authors set aside certain hours of the day to write.

No matter what else happens, keeping that commitment to yourself will make you feel good about the day and your accomplishments and give you a sense of control. Nothing beats out single-mindedness of purpose when it comes to getting the most important things done. What we're talking about is real **dedication** to your most important priorities.

The key question to ask yourself

Start out the morning by asking yourself, *"What are the most important items for me to handle today* that would allow me to call this a successful day?" Take time to acknowledge your accomplishments each day. Pat yourself on the back. This is a good way to spark your desire, which in turn will fuel your dedication and discipline. Keep relating your activities to your goals, which should also feed your desire.

Seven Ways to Maximize Your P and P

Now that you've learned the ABCs of planning and prioritizing, you're ready to use them plus these seven ways to improve your short-term P and P:

1. Start with the right planning tools that give you the micro and macro views of your to-dos. Most people need to *see* reminders of their tasks, appointments, projects and commitments—in the short term as well as long term. I don't mean a flood of reminder notes scattered all over your desk. Effective planning tools are visual and versatile, letting you prioritize and categorize info in a variety of ways so you can see the details and the big picture. Tools could include Outlook, a mobile device (such as a BlackBerry), a wall chart, project management software or a paper-based planner. The point is have them accessible whenever you plan; avoid trying to rack your brain to remember your tasks. Also have tools accessible throughout the day so you can type or write down things-to-do as you think of them. (For much more on tools see Chapter 4.)

2. Write down several key goals, activities or projects for the week. Select no more than four and write them some place (or key them into your electronic device or computer) where you'll see them every day as you do your daily planning.

3. Plan tomorrow, today, and put your plan in writing. Take five or ten minutes today to type, key in or write tomorrow's to-do list on your computer, mobile device or organizer so you can start tomorrow fresh. (If you're an early riser, however, you can do your plan the same day by setting aside some quiet time at home or at work to plan before the day really gets going.) Planning and prioritizing lets you actually see what you need to accomplish and when. Also, weed out those tasks that you really don't need to do. It can put a drain on your time and your brain to even think about activities that really won't make a difference in your work results.

4. Consolidate and group similar activities together and avoid long laundry lists. If you're tired of making long lists of unrelated to-do's, then shorten your lists and group like items together. Have one section of your to-do list for scheduled appointments. Try grouping activities by category (such as "calls" and "correspondence"). Use priority groupings where you first list your top A priorities of the day—limit the number to three or four—and then list your B priorities.

5. Make time every day to work on B priorities. These are the priorities that most closely tie in with your goals. But most people tend to put Bs on the back burner, selecting only the more pressing, fire-fighting A priorities.

6. Make at least one, screened-time appointment with yourself each day. Give yourself at least one hour of "screened, prime time" every day to work on top priority work. "Screened time" is quiet, uninterrupted time allowing you to concentrate and "prime time" is the time of the day when you're most effective. You can screen your time by doing any of the following: coming in or starting an hour early, continuing to work an hour later, having your calls screened by an assistant or colleague (and offering to do the same for them), working in another location (at home or a quiet, inaccessible office), closing your door, relying on your voice mail system and putting a one-hour appointment with yourself on your calendar.

7. Revise your plan—stay flexible and know when to reprioritize and renegotiate deadlines. Check your daily plan several times throughout the day and if necessary, rearrange, postpone and yes, even procrastinate on purpose. "Planned procrastination"—consciously choosing to put off—is what prioritizing is all about. Remember daily planning is a guide and most people don't get everything done. Use common sense as you plan out your priorities. If something comes up during the day that bumps another item in importance, so be it; simply move the item to another time or day. Weigh the value of doing an item at a particular point in time. For example, it may be better to call John Smith at 1:00 p.m. today, even though John is only a "B" priority, because you're sure to reach him at 1:00 p.m.; otherwise you'll be playing phone tag with him for the next two weeks—a real time waster.

7 Ways to Juggle Multiple Priorities

Rarely, if ever, do I meet people who have the luxury of working at a leisurely pace. There are always countless deadlines and shifting priorities, which all add up to mounting pressure.

When you handle many different projects, priorities and deadlines, you're very much like a circus juggler who runs around keeping a dozen plates spinning on sticks. Sure, you can try to keep up this act all day, but you will certainly burn out before too long. Unfortunately, this method is used by far too many people. Instead, to prevent burn out, you need to take a good hard look at *how* you work and to see if there are better ways for you to get things done.

The issue is not how much you have to do but rather how much you have to do *that is really important.* You learned how to sort the important from the less important in Chapter 1 and earlier in this chapter. You learned how to organize work into categories and priorities so that you could *see* what you had to do.

Now that you've also learned the ABCs of planning and prioritizing in this chapter, you're ready to put all of this to work to help you juggle multiple priorities and let you get the most important things done each day.

Here are seven ways to help you save time and energy, handle the great juggling act and create more balance and control in your life (they work for me):

1. Get clarity from people making demands on you. Determine the real, not imagined, urgency of each request. Encourage others to indicate both the nature of the request and the specific time frame for its completion. Chapter 15 describes a simple written form delegators can use for this purpose that's attached to paperwork landing on your desk or your email inbox. A written request doesn't usually interrupt you (unless it's an instant message popping up on your screen) and lets you plan and prioritize similar requests and time frames more easily. As for emails and IM (instant messaging), don't assume that these instant mediums always indicate an equally instant deadline; always determine the deadline up front and negotiate it when necessary.

If several people from the same department or office are regularly making conflicting demands on your time, bring it up at a staff meeting for a brainstorming session. Often, people may not be aware of the severity of the problem. Involve them in a cooperative way, not through finger-pointing, but through an exchange of ideas that can solve a problem. (For more on problem solving, communication and teamwork, once again see Chapter 15.)

2. Know how and when to respond. To prevent unnecessary interruptions and to give you more control over when you'd like to communicate, use voice mail (rather than taking every call) and email (rather than instant messaging) for incoming communications. Ask callers to leave you the best time(s) to call them back. If you have a short, nonurgent phone message to leave someone and you don't want to get involved in a lengthy, unnecessary conversation, don't call their cellphone. Instead, call their landline phone at a time when you know their voice mail or answering machine is more likely to be on. Better yet, email a short message.

3. Don't keep too much in your head. Rely on good **planning tools** to help you see, categorize, prioritize and remember everything you have to do. Use reliable **follow-up, reminder and tickler tools** such as Outlook reminders to give you timely notice of upcoming deadlines, meetings and tasks. (See Chapter 4 for more on tools.)

4. Confirm appointments, meetings and deadlines that have a significant lead time. It's always good to make sure those pressing scheduled items are still on schedule and to make sure any particularly busy people with whom you have appointments are running on time.

5. Turn downtime into useful time. Sometimes do two things at once, such as listening to a self-improvement audio program while commuting, reading while waiting in line or deleting unneeded emails while you're on hold for a phone call.

6. Don't rush. There's a saying that the faster you go, the slower you are going to get there. It's the old tortoise and the hare story. If rushing makes you crazy, make a commitment to stop doing it whenever possible. As a famous Simon and Garfunkle song says, "Slow down, you move too fast." Some rushing may be unavoidable. Beware though if it's a regular habit of yours. Advance planning can prevent most cases of rushing.

7. Be realistic about time by becoming more *aware* of time. Be honest with yourself about how long an activity will *really* take. Estimate the minimum amount of time and a maximum and then aim for an amount in the middle. Follow your own time clock but speed it up and slow it down when necessary.

Things usually take longer than we think (the unexpected almost always comes up). And although Parkinson's Law says that work expands to fill the time available, sometimes the opposite is also true: work contracts to fill the time available; it's amazing how much you can get done quickly when you have to.

If you practice setting your own realistic deadlines and sticking to them, as well as eliminating unnecessary or time-wasting activities, you will soon accomplish so much more and with less rushing.

How to Control Interruptions at Work

And as you juggle your way through the work day, you'll probably want some better ways to handle interruptions, a common workplace complaint I hear. The main question to ask yourself is how many of these interruptions can you control, minimize or influence in some way.

In my training programs I often use the chart on the next page to have participants list all their typical interruptions.

First, jot down as many interruptions as you can imagine and be sure to include those from others as well as those you initiate *yourself* (such as checking for email too frequently or answering *every* cellphone call). How many times a day do you interrupt *yourself* to handle something now when it should be handled later, switch to something more pleasurable as an escape from the difficult task at hand or simply decide to do something easier?

Second, check whether each interruption is one you can control or influence "Almost always," "Sometimes" or "Never."

INTERRUPTIONS	I can control them...			How I *could* control or influence them
	Almost Always	Sometimes	Never	

Third, for every interruption that enters your day, ask "Is this interruption *necessary?*" Some interruptions *are* part of your job. If you're a customer service representative or a receptionist, for example, telephone interruptions (and emails) are your business. Even so, as you'll see in Chapter 5, you can learn to maximize your telephone and email time so that you have more control. Write an "N" for Necessary next to each interruption that indeed needs to be handled.

Fourth, using your imagination, jot down anything you could do to control or influence each interruption in some way. It may be an interruption is necessary but could be handled later. Perhaps you could prevent similar interruptions from occurring in the future.

The idea is to start looking for ways to control and prevent interruptions. Analyze interruptions carefully. Don't just assume they are all necessary. Become proactive, not reactive, whenever possible. And always use common sense and good judgment, especially when dealing with interruptions and concerns of other people.

Procrastination and perfectionism

Procrastination and perfectionism can often be examples of self-generated interruptions—although not always. There is a positive place for both. Earlier I described planned procrastination as a form of prioritizing; there are times indeed when you should consciously choose *not* to do certain things.

And certainly perfectionism can have its place, depending on the type of work or project; for example, I'd certainly want a brain surgeon to be a perfectionist! But countering the myth that everything worth doing is worth doing well, speaker Mark Sanborn has said, "Some things are worth doing well, some things are worth doing very well and some things are just worth doing."

When procrastination and/or perfectionism stop you and you feel negative effects such as Newton's Law of Inertia—a body at rest tends to stay at rest—then it's time to try some strategies such as the following:

1. Set a small goal for yourself in a small chunk of time and just do it!
2. Take a break and get some distance and perspective through exercise, rest or a change of scenery.
3. Try some brainstorming techniques such as Mind Mapping (discussed in Chapter 4).
4. Get some other input or coaching from a colleague or friend— share the load whenever possible.
5. Remember it's not brain surgery unless, of course, it is!

How to Finish Your Work and Still Have Time for a Personal Life

If your work hangs over you like a dark cloud and follows you wherever you go, it's time to stand back and gain some perspective.

I'm not concerned about an occasional heavy schedule or major deadline. But if you think about work all the time, take too much work home every night (where your office isn't in your home) or suffer from insomnia over work-related problems, you need a break! Make sure, too, you're not just playing a martyr role by taking on too much work or that you're giving in too much to your perfectionism ("no one else can do this as well as I").

In fact, you need more than a break; you need **balance**. Granted, your need for balance will be different at various times in your life. But the first step is developing some awareness of when you're losing your balance and then to take some realistic steps.

Redefining Work

The term "work" is replacing the term "job," which harkens back to the Industrial Revolution, where work was much more narrowly defined. Also, many of us have 24-7 work unlike the past where we may have had a shorter nine-to-five job.

It's important to be aware of "work creep"—where we inadvertently let the amount and duration of work take over our lives.

In addition, many people today have what author William Bridges terms "portfolio careers," which consist of a mixture of part-time jobs or a full-time position supplemented with freelance work or self-employment.

Partly because of portfolio careers and partly because of our demanding times, people are working harder than ever putting in long work weeks. There are some steps to take initially.

Avoid pointless *face time*—the assumption that you should sit at your desk or be at work for longer hours, sometimes before, as well as, after work. Face time also assumes in some businesses that you would never leave the office before a certain time, say, 7:00 p.m. Face time can be devastating to not only one's personal life but to productivity as well. Remember that you should be paid for the results you produce, not for face time.

Make time for yourself every day ideally but certainly every week at the very least. Plan things you look forward to doing that nourish you. Make time for family and friends. Some alone time every day is also essential to reflect on your life and recharge your batteries.

Remember the core values that shape who you are and strive to live them every day. These values will help you save time by eliminating meaningless activities and will encourage you to use your energy in more meaningful ways for yourself and others. You may actually discover a hidden reservoir of energy as you do activities that align with your core values.

Alternative Work Arrangements

Don't overlook new alternatives to your work life as a solution to your situation. Consider the following: (1) telecommuting and working from home at least part of the time; (2) having flexible hours so you can better balance your professional and personal life, (3) reducing your work hours or (4) changing careers so your workload isn't so demanding.

For some people, it's helpful to add more structure to their schedule. Establish a quitting time each day and stick to it! That's more difficult than it seems for the workaholics among us. One company started a "time management" program in which employees were urged *not* to stay late; they were told it's the results that count, not the hours.

If you must take work home (and who doesn't these days), make an appointment with yourself. Decide to spend thirty minutes and thirty minutes only, for example, reviewing that report for tomorrow's staff meeting. (If necessary, use a timer.)

Make an effort to talk openly with your boss or coworkers about your heavy work load. Don't just assume that there's no solution.

Be creative, open-minded and look for better ways of doing things. Share ideas with your friends and colleagues. Find out how they organize their day and life.

When Too Much Is Just Too Much

It does help to have a cooperative boss or coworker. If you're working, however, with someone who's out to sabotage you or the company or you truly do have too much to do and too little time, it may be best to look for a different working situation altogether. This is a last resort but consider it if you've tried all the time management tools and techniques in this chapter (and book), all to no avail.

At every seminar I give there's at least one person in one of these "impossible situations," with an autocratic boss or a highly bureaucratic structure where no amount of organization could help. Or maybe you're currently involved in a downsizing effort, alternately called "right sizing" or just plain "capsizing," depending upon which boat you're in. If you're in any one of these "impossible" situations, it may be better to cut your losses and bail out. (On the other hand, some of these downsized organizations can provide you with some empowered ways of working where you can develop new skills.)

Don't take job stress lightly. According to the Families & Work Institute in New York, job stress is three times more likely to spill over into the home than family problems are to crop up at work.

But if you put time management to work for you, you'll consciously take steps to align your work with your personal and professional goals and values.

4

Organization Tools
to Manage Time & Info

Quick Scan: Discover high-tech and low-tech tools to use every day and the key features to have.

There is no one best time management or personal organization tool; there are, however, the best tools for *you* at this point in your life and career to help you plan, prioritize and organize your time, info and communications so that you can get the most important things done each day.

What's so great about today's tools is that at least one of them will function the way you like to work. You have more choice and flexibility today when selecting and customizing the features you need. (Remember, though, not to feel guilty if you don't use each and every feature that comes with a tool—use only what you need.)

The key is to identify which tool(s) will most easily adapt to your work style and lifestyle. Here are three rules of thumb to follow:

1. Look for the *essential* features you need, not the total number of features.

2. Remember that the *fewer* the number of tools you have, the better.

3. Consider ease of use including the time required to learn how to use a tool.

One thing is certain: the more complex and demanding your life and career become, the more you need a **Positively Organized! System** every day to help you track the complex demands on your time, manage your info and accomplish your goals.

You may recall a **system** is a combination of the best **tools** *plus* the best **habits**. You can create your own Positively Organized! System by choosing and using the best time management *habits* from Chapter 3 along with the best features and *tools* from this chapter.

We'll be exploring the following three major topics: (1) six basic selection criteria, (2) high-tech vs. low-tech organization tools and (3) seven key features of organization tools.

Before looking at tools and features, keep the following criteria uppermost in your mind.

Six Basic Selection Criteria
for Organization Tools and Features

Here are the basic criteria for selecting the right time and info organization tools and features:

1. **Ease of use**—How easy is it for you to physically use? (For example, if you need to do a lot of typing, a mobile device touchscreen or keypad may not meet your needs).

2. **Learning curve**—Will it take you a long time to learn the features? Are you willing to spend time reading the manual or taking time to play with the tool?

3. **Portability and mobility**—How portable does it have to be?

4. **Accessibility of info**—How easy is it to find and access info?

5. **Compatibility**—How easy is it to use with your other tools? With your work or life style?

6. **Features and adaptability**—How complete is the features set for the way(s) you work and if applicable, how others work with you?

High-Tech or Low-Tech Tools?

The trend is for people to choose high-tech, computer-based organization tools. But because paper is still very much with us, low-tech tools clearly have their place. Use the criteria above as well as your own preferences and work requirements to select your tools, be they high- or low-tech. Let's also look at what they each have to offer.

High-Tech Tools

High-tech tools generally let you organize and easily find information, especially large and complex amounts of info.

You may have to take some time up front, however, to learn how to operate high-tech software and/or hardware, but it may well be worth your time to do so. You may also have to proactively protect your high-tech tools from theft or security breaches or deal with "techno-stress" if your tool gets a bug and doesn't work right. And you could develop health issues from repetitive stress/strain injury (RSI) or other nonergonomic ways of working with equipment. (See Chapters 6 and 14 for ways to protect yourself.) Nevertheless, the positives for most high-tech tools usually far outweigh the negatives for most people.

Laptops vs. desktops

Laptop (notebook) computers now outsell desktops in the U.S. because a properly equipped laptop computer can do almost anything that a desktop computer can and it also offers mobility.

Over the years, I've become a convert to laptop computers used as a desktop substitute. My latest computer is nearly as powerful as any desktop and I can take it with me anywhere.

But you'll want a desktop if you need (a) space to hold multiple and larger hard drives or (b) speed for manipulating complex graphics and video or handling complicated number-crunching.

For computer ergonomic considerations for both laptops and desktops, see Chapter 6.

Mobile devices

If you need a lot of portability in your work, consider a mobile handheld device, which is much smaller and more portable than a laptop but is fast becoming a pocket-sized minicomputer.

For business people looking for serious tools, there are two main categories of mobile devices (often called simply "handhelds"): (1) **PDA** (**personal digital assistant**) and (2) **smartphone**. Both of these categories are undergoing tremendous change with ongoing morphing and converging of features and functions as well as new features being added all the time.

When you see the term "**PDA**," think of an organizing device that can manage your personal information—through such features as an address book, a calendar, a to-do list and a note taker. Instead of a keyboard, PDAs usually have a stylus to tap selections on menus. Sometimes you can use the stylus to tap out letters that appear on a keyboard projected on the device screen. Data can be **synchronized** (**synced**) between a PDA and a desktop or laptop computer so that they have identical versions of files and info. Going one better, some PDAs have a hard drive and can run computer applications. PDAs can also have cellphone capability. The PalmPilot was one of the first PDAs; it's now simply called the Palm.

Smartphones are answering the demand for cellphones that provide email, instant messaging (IM), text messaging and Internet access. An additional benefit is the ability to add applications such as scheduling software, contact management and GPS navigation software, to name a few. You'll also usually see a typical phone keypad or a modified QWERTY keyboard on a smartphone. Popular brand names as of this writing are BlackBerry, Treo, Nokia and Samsung.

Remember that mobile devices keep evolving and you can't go by what they're called to know what they really do. As mobile devices take on more of the power and capability of computers—they're becoming minicomputers (as well as entertainment centers)—see which features you really need and see if you're comfortable working with these features on a small device. Just because you *can* do it doesn't mean you *should*. There are some important ergonomic/health issues involved with handhelds so be sure to read Chapters 6 and 11.

Web-based solutions

The Web also offers many time management/productivity solutions. Having your calendar, contact list and maybe your files on the Web may be a great convenience since you may be able to access them from nearly any location. And you may be able to synchronize this information with your computer or mobile device. A website may also allow you to schedule group meetings, check scheduling conflicts and send out email invitations and reminders.

Some Internet service providers (ISPs) and websites provide online organizers or **PIM** (**p**ersonal **i**nformation **m**anager) services.

However, before you jump in and decide to go with an online approach, consider a few issues. First, your connection to the Web may not be fast enough. Second, sometimes your Internet connection may go down and be unavailable. Third, it may be much more convenient to just have all of this information already on your desktop or laptop computer or mobile device so the information is already at your fingertips. Finally, security and privacy issues are more problematic when you deal with the Web.

Web-based solutions do offer the advantages of accessibility with an Internet connection, including the ability to have company-wide information and software applications easily kept up to date for all users. And if you're with a company that has its own intranet and a sophisticated IT (information technology) department, chances are good your company has built-in software and computer solutions available today—check them out!

Computer software programs

There are many computer software solutions for managing your everyday time and info. Although Microsoft Outlook may contain all the time and information management functionality you need, you may find that PIM or other contact manager-type programs can not only organize your time but also provide many other benefits. These types of programs are available for computers and mobile devices and are also on the Web.

By the way, the term "PIM" was first coined by Lotus Development Corp., who used it in conjunction with their former "Agenda" program. Lotus founder, Mitch Kapor, developed Agenda because he was looking for a better way to organize himself and his personal information.

Just as mobile devices are morphing, converging and adding features, the same is happening with PIMs and contact manager programs. Programs in each category keep expanding their features so don't just rely on the label given a program—look to see if it has the features you need to manage your calendar, to-do's, master list, reminder functions, phone and address database, projects and ideas as well as other time management/productivity features. (See the Resource Guide for names of software programs.)

Many of these programs work on both computers and mobile devices and data can be transferred and synced between them. Whether a software program can work on all of your equipment can be an important factor in deciding which program (or equipment) to buy.

Features in PIMs and contact managers

So what are the main features of PIMs or contact managers?

1. Such programs usually combine most of the time management tools (your calendar and often the schedule of your workgroup, to-do list, master list, tickler system and planner/organizer) in one system. You can schedule calls, emails, meetings and to-do items. Some also provide sales and marketing tools and handle project management as well as other work-related information and correspondence/email.

2. Most of these software programs can work/sync with mobile devices and can often connect you to the Web.

3. They let you quickly input and retrieve information. In some cases, you can not only include complete contact information, emails and history but also presentations, proposals and attachments.

4. With some programs, you have the flexibility to store and arrange random bits of information such as notes, ideas, plans and activities in a free-form style, linked loosely by categories that you create.

5. With some programs, you and coworkers can pool your information and share all of these contacts, notes, histories, opportunities, documents and details on a particular company or contact.

6. You have many ways to view information such as on a daily, weekly or monthly basis.

7. You can often customize how your database information appears on the screen.

8. You can use the program to communicate with customers and colleagues via email or by writing letters with a built-in word processor or your usual word processing program.

9. Because many of these programs allow you to print out information onto paper forms that will fit right into a notebook or maybe your paper-based personal organizer, you can have the best of both computer and paper worlds.

10. It's also easy to make backups for added protection.

Make sure this software is accessible if you're away from your computer much or most of the time. You don't want to make lots of handwritten notes and then tediously input all those notes into the program when you return to your office. A better solution is to use a laptop computer or mobile device away from the office that has the same program with a synchronization feature or a Web-based program.

One especially nice feature of this type of software program is that you can quickly search for information in a variety of ways. Let's suppose you want to find every contact you've had with a particular customer. You could search that customer by name but that may bring up too much info. You could do a narrower search by specifying the *context* for a search such as limiting the search between specific time periods say, January to March of a given year.

Don't confuse this search capability with that of *desktop search programs* as discussed in Chapter 12, which can find every occurrence of a name or word *anywhere* on your computer (or in some cases, multiple computers).

Low-Tech but Tangible Tools

You're not alone if you'd prefer to touch, hold and see all your data on real paper rather than storing it digitally. You may not feel as comfortable using electronic or computerized technology. (Even Nobel Prize winner Jack Kilby, the inventor of the semiconductor chip and the handheld calculator, owned a conventional sweep-hand watch instead of a digital watch and used a slide rule instead of a calculator.)

Although new mobile devices come on the market almost every day, what's best for you may be going with what Cox News Service calls "retro chic," which is why, for example, why many CEOs still use paper day planners.

You may also find it too difficult to get through the technological learning curve to get up to speed. Or, if it ain't broke, why fix it? That's fine.

Or you may be worried about techno stress. Sometimes new "time-saving" technologies can drain a lot of your time, energy and productivity trying to get all the bugs to disappear.

But don't overlook having a **hybrid approach** combining computerized and paper-based approaches. You may want to take advantage of the flexibility and speed of accessing information that's stored electronically in a computer, a mobile device or on the Web *and* also regularly print out that information as a paper backup or to work with as hard copy. Keep in mind that one potential advantage of the electronic solutions is they may provide a complete system with many built-in features that often eliminate the need for other tools and reentering data.

Planners and organizers

If you're trying to cram too much information into your paper-based calendar or appointment book, consider a larger format or a different time management tool, such as a planner or an organizer. A calendar is for mapping out long-range plans; it's not generally the ideal tool for detailed, daily planning. If you're continually using many slips of paper to make notes to yourself because your calendar simply isn't big enough, you're ready for a change.

If you need portability and versatility in a paper-based tool, planners and organizers may be just the ticket. (The trend, however, is for using mobile devices, laptop computers or the Web to handle short and long-term planning, your schedule, the schedules of your workgroup members, your contact list, your to-do list and your master list.)

What to look for in a paper-based planner

If you want to use a paper-based solution and you need more than a calendar or appointment book but less than a full-blown organizer, a planner may be the perfect solution. And in fact, every organizer should include a good planner as its main feature.

A good planner combines both **long- and short-range planning**. For long-range planning, you should be able to see the major events of the year and/or each month of the year. For short-range planning, you should have planning pages that show each day or preferably, the entire week.

Your planner should have enough writing space. If you're adding notes all over the place, you could either be short on space or the format isn't working for you.

Decide whether you want a **dated or undated** planner. With the latter you'll have to spend more time writing in the dates.

If your planner has a loose leaf phone directory, ideally it should have pages for *each* letter of the alphabet rather than two letters combined so you can use the pages not only for phone/address info but also as subject dividers for resource information. For example, on an "R" page, write last names that start with that letter and behind that page keep pages of resource information that start with the letter "R," such as a "Restaurant" page listing your favorite restaurants.

The size of your planner may pose some problems. You may want it to be small and compact enough to carry with you yet large enough to carry standard size papers. A tradeoff may be necessary. Select a planner that has the most important features for you.

Do you really need a paper-based organizer?

Usually housed in plush ring binders, organizers manage both time and information. Organizers incorporate a variety of planning, scheduling and information tools and forms as well as accessories.

A variety of styles and sizes adapt to many different professional needs. Some are small enough to fit in a coat or shirt pocket; others fit in a briefcase or purse; still others are self-contained mini-briefcases or combination organizer/purses that can be carried on the shoulder with a strap. Many come in leather and make for professional accessories that are attractive as well as functional.

Some professional women find the combination organizer/purse with shoulder strap particularly useful. It's portable enough for an organizer and large enough to carry items you would otherwise have to carry separately in a purse.

In the interest of health, keep any shoulder purse or organizer as light as possible and try not to carry it on your shoulder most of the time. Use the shoulder strap for convenience (or safety) when it's not feasible to hold the organizer in your arms like a notebook.

Some people ask, "What would you do if you lost it?" Here are three measures to prevent the dire consequences of such a disaster. First, always photocopy any critical hardcopy material and store it in a safe location. Second, use computerized PIM or contact management software (see the Resource Guide) or a mobile device, print out your hard copies (which you can use in your organizer) and make regular data backups (which can include Web backups). Third, write the following statement on a business card that you laminate and attach to the inside front cover of your organizer "REWARD: $150 for returning this lost organizer." (By the way, you could attach a label with similar wording to your laptop computer or mobile device).

Your Daily Paperwork System (DPS)

Because paper is still very much with us and the paperless office is still a pipe dream, you need some tools (and habits) to handle your everyday paper-based info. We'll look at a few of the basic tools I recommend to clients and audiences as part of creating a **Daily Paperwork System** (DPS).

Start with "third-cut," colored manila folders for your active projects, staff members, reading materials or whatever constitutes your categories of active work papers that need to be accessible. Put these folders in upright organizers such as the vertical wire rack, the desktop file organizer or the magazine file boxes shown in Figures 4-1 and 4-2.

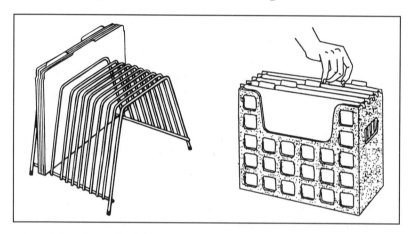

Figure 4-1. Colored manila folders for your Daily Paperwork System (DPS) work great in a vertical wire rack (shown at left). A desktop file organizer that accommodates hanging file folders works well for your DPS, too.

Follow-up desk files, sorters and accordion files

Several tools may be particularly useful in your Daily Paperwork System. I use the **Smead Desk File/Sorter tickler system** (Figure 4-3) to sort what would otherwise be miscellaneous follow-ups into an organized, chronological system. The **desk file** or **sorter** is a paper-based tickler system that opens like a book and has an expandable binding on the spine. Look for the style that has both 1-31 and January to December

Figure 4-2. Besides storing magazines as shown here, magazine files or holders work great for the everyday folders of your DPS—I use them for my DPS.

tabs. You can use the desk file every day for follow-ups and action items that are connected to some paperwork, such as a letter or related notes. (You could also use it for birthday cards to be mailed.) It's important to keep the desk file conveniently located.

The **accordion file** is similar to the desk file except it is enclosed on three sides and usually has a flap that folds over. Some people find it less convenient than the desk file/sorter because it is more enclosed. And if it's less convenient, you'll be less likely to use it. If, however, your paper-based tickler needs to be portable, the accordion file could be a wise choice.

File folder tickler systems

Some people prefer a **file folder tickler system** that has file folders labeled both January to December and 1-31. A file folder tickler system can sit inside a desk drawer or in an upright rack or caddy on a nearby credenza, return or table.

There are many uses for such a system. One consultant I know uses a ruled sheet of paper in the front of each monthly folder to list follow-up

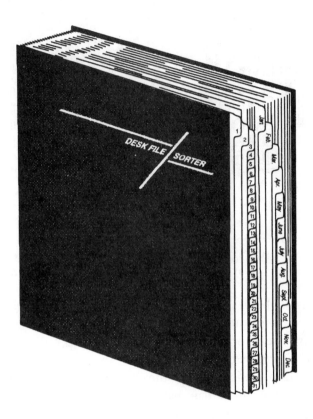

Figure 4-3. Combination 1-31 and January-December Desk File/Sorter by Smead (www.smead.com)

calls for the month. He keeps corresponding notes for the calls inside an alphabetical notebook.

A file folder tickler system can also get reminder papers off your desk and into a chronological system. These are papers that require action on or by specific dates. They may include papers such as conference announcements, letters, memos, notes and even birthday or anniversary cards. If you like visual, tangible reminders instead of a note jotted down in your paper-based calendar or planner, this system could be ideal for you.

Suppose you have some notes you'll need to use at a meeting on the ninth. Get those notes off your desk (or out of a generic, overflowing "pending file") and put them behind the "9" tab.

A file folder tickler system is very similar to the desk file/sorter and accordion file in that it has file folders labeled January to December and/or 1-31 and it, too, is designed to handle paper-triggered actions. You can have more flexibility for tab names; for example, you could use weekly tabs. This system can sit inside a desk drawer or in an upright rack or caddy on a nearby credenza, return or table. Again, it's not quite as convenient as the desk file/sorter and some people are afraid that if it's out of sight in a file drawer that they'll forget all about it. Once it's a habit, however, and part of your daily routine, that shouldn't be a problem.

Seven Key Features of Good Organization Tools

Good organization tools are visual and versatile. They let you see and access info quickly by providing some or all of the following seven features:

1. Calendaring and scheduling
2. Reminding (or tickling)
3. Managing your contacts and communications
4. Categorizing and prioritizing
5. Listing
6. Charting
7. Collaborative computing

These features often overlap with one another (as you'll soon see) and continue to evolve, especially in software, Web-based and mobile device solutions. Here are some ways to currently take advantage of these important features.

1. Calendaring and Scheduling

The most basic organization feature is calendaring/scheduling to track future dates, events, meetings and appointments over a long range of time—at least a year out.

When selecting a calendaring/scheduling feature, decide how you like to view calendared, scheduled items—including future events, meetings and appointments as well as blocks of time (appointments with yourself) that you set aside to do specific tasks or projects. Depending on your calendaring feature or tool, you can see such info by the day, week, month, quarter or year.

Most high-tech tools including Web-based calendars, Microsoft Outlook and other information management software programs give you plenty of options to view your own calendar and also provide group calendaring, scheduling and meeting management to help you see and coordinate other people's schedules.

By contrast, a paper planner may show you only one view (monthly, weekly or daily and perhaps a yearly) view of your calendar but that may be all you need. Many other formats are available, too, such as a detailed daily appointment calendar with quarterly-hour appointments. There is a lot of choice but you won't have the flexibility of changing calendar views that software and many mobile devices provide nor the ability to do group scheduling. (For more on paper planners, see "Low-tech Tools" and the "Resource Guide" later in this chapter.)

Ten questions to ask about a calendar

Don't underestimate the importance of your calendar selection. Since this is an item you use daily, you should give your selection some thought. Don't be afraid to change to a different one, even in mid-year. Ask yourself these 10 questions:

1. Do you have more than one calendar?

2. Is it troublesome to carry it with you or to access it when you're away from the office?

3. Is it difficult to add items to your calendar if you're out of the office?

4. Are you unable to see all your calendar items when you're out of the office?

5. If you're using a calendar with a mobile device or laptop and/or desktop computer, is it hard to sync the calendars on your device and computer(s) so they all have the same data?

6. Is your calendar either too small or too big?

7. Is it easy to miss seeing important dates (because they're hard to spot, there isn't enough room, your calendar is too cluttered or the text or the screen is too small on your electronic device)?

8. Are you afraid of losing your calendar?

9. Is it difficult to back up the information on your calendar?

10. Is it difficult to share your calendar with coworkers and colleagues?

Calendar criteria

If you have one or more "yes" responses, consider reevaluating your calendar choice according to these criteria:

- Your calendar should be accessible to you, both in and out of the office.

- You should not have more than one calendar unless you have a staff person and/or a foolproof routine to maintain the additional one. (Keep personal and professional items on the same calendar; you should be able to hide personal items for online calendars.)

- Select a calendar whose size and style are adequate for your work and appointment load. Don't force yourself to use a calendar you've outgrown even if it is the middle of the year; switch to another one.

- Have a calendar that permits team members needed accessibility.

- Maintain a reliable backup system. What would happen if you lost your calendar? If it's computerized or on a mobile device, do you have backups as well as hard-copy printouts? If it's a paper-based calendar or planner, do you have photocopies of the most important pages?

- Your calendar should have the right look for your profession; more important, it should appeal to you in terms of appearance and ease of use.

Calendar options

Paper-based calendars come in all shapes, sizes and configurations and often by many a name: date books, diaries, appointment books, desk calendars, desk pad calendars and wall calendars. And of course, there are all kinds of high-tech calendar options—let's look at two basic categories.

Web-based calendars

Web-based calendars are increasing in popularity for three reasons. First, you can always have your calendar with you if you have an Internet connection (that's working!). Second, they provide one calendar inside or outside the office to write down all of your items. Finally, for projects and teams, it is often essential for coworkers and colleagues to have access to your calendar to know your availability for meetings and calls as well as what you're working on. Note that you can allow or restrict access to your online calendar (similar to what can usually be done on computer networks). As with anything on the Web, make sure you can still function if your connection is down and check out the security features.

Mobile device/computerized calendars

Virtually all mobile devices have a built-in calendar function. Especially with the smaller screens on these devices, see whether you get enough of the big picture of your calendared items to meet your needs.

In addition, there's plenty of calendaring computer software including PIMs and contact managers that may also work on mobile devices, computers and the Web. With this software, you can create tasks, schedule repeating tasks, organize tasks by date or category, set automatic reminders, manage contacts and communications and share calendars. (See the Resource Guide.)

2. Reminding (or Tickling)

Reminders, alarms and *ticklers* are all terms for features that remind us to do things on a particular day or at a certain time. Almost all of us need to have our memories reminded or "tickled." A "tickler system" is a reminder system that "tickles your memory." (By the way, the term "tickler" originally referred to a special feather that was used to tickle churchgoers who nodded off during a sermon.)

Computer analyst and writer Lawrence Magid jokingly calls software programs with alarms and reminders "nudgeware." Most of my Outlook clients love and use "Outlook reminders." Even most cellphones and other mobile devices have a basic alarms feature even if finding it on your device may be a bit time consuming if you have to scroll through several menus.

And there are paper-based, manual reminder and tickler systems that have been standbys for years; a paper calendar and a to-do list are the most common forms. One of my favorite paper ticklers is the desk file/sorter, which we discussed under "Low-tech Tools."

Here's a tickler tip: use "prereminders" several days *before* your final deadlines so that you're not surprised by an especially important deadline reminder.

3. Managing Contacts and Communications

Whenever possible, store your contact info digitally through an address book function on Outlook, your ISP (Internet Service Provider) and/or your mobile device. Not only can you access info instantly but you can also back it up usually fairly easily so you have another copy. Problems arise, however, when information is (a) scattered on different devices or programs, (b) not synced up and/or (c) not backed up. Let's look at some software solutions.

Contact management programs

Contact management programs or **contact managers** are either standalone software programs or part of programs such as Outlook or PIMs for computers or mobile devices. (See the earlier "High-Tech Tools" section in this chapter, which discusses PIMs.) Such programs let you stay in touch with 50 to thousands of people on a regular basis, schedule and track calls, remind you with alarms when to do follow-up calls and encourage you to keep notes on calls and meetings with contacts.

    Customer relationship management (**CRM**) programs are more "robust" or fully featured and are designed for those in sales or for organizations who want to better manage their customers through systems, processes and procedures.

    (See the Resource Guide for names of popular programs and a more detailed list of features.)

Consolidating your communications

Communications is such a big part of how we work today and managing all of its different forms can be a job in itself. Managing communications is indeed such a big topic that I'll be covering it in several chapters. In the meantime, what I've observed is that many people aren't taking advantage of the organizing features and systems that *are* available—for example, Outlook's folders, flagging and filtering features for email management (we'll cover these in the next chapter). Another approach is **unified messaging.**

Retrieving communications through unified messaging

Due to the complexity of today's communications, the trend is towards simplifying and consolidating whenever possible through unified messaging, a service that consolidates your voice mail, email, text messages, instant messages and faxes in one mailbox. This one **universal in-box** allows you to retrieve all these messages in one place through a variety of methods. With a computer or mobile device with Internet access, you can read and reply to email, text messages and faxes and listen to voice mail—all located on one Web page.

Unified messaging is expanding to mean more than just picking up all your messages and communications in one place. For example, with the right software, you may be able to instantly switch from text messaging to video conferencing by clicking a button. (See the Resource Guide for unified messaging products and services.)

4. Categorizing and prioritizing

The brain loves categories, which help us group similar kinds of information and link them by say, topic, project or person. Prioritizing is a form of categorizing that groups items by different levels of importance. Categorizing and prioritizing are especially important to use with the next two features, listing and charting, as well as with the feature on managing communications.

5. Listing

Lists are great for nonscheduled activities such as to-do's that don't need to be done at a particular time. Let's look in more detail at two essential lists you should probably be using: the **to-do list** and the **master list**.

To-do lists

Most people should use some kind of to-do list for daily or weekly planning at work and/or in their personal life.

If your work is very routine or very physical, it's possible you don't need this tool. But if you're a manager or supervisor with administrative responsibilities besides hands-on work, you need a to-do list. And if you have a busy personal life, a to-do list is essential.

To-do lists can be as simple as a word processing file showing all the items you need to handle where you use the edit and search features to move, keep track of and find items.

If your needs are more complex, software such as Outlook, a PIM or a contact manager program on your computer or mobile device can not only show your to-do's but also eliminate rewriting ones that don't get accomplished that day because incomplete to-do's can be transferred (sometimes automatically) to another day. Also, you have more flexibility in rearranging items on your list.

With a Web-based to-do list, you (or team members, if you want) can access your list as long as they have an Internet connection.

Even with all of our electronic solutions, some people just plain prefer to work with paper when it comes to a to-do list. You can buy forms separately or as part of a time management system or organizer. On paper-based systems, to-do list forms come in dated and undated styles and are available from stationery and office supply websites, stores and catalogs.

Whether you use high- or low-tech to-do lists, here are some important tips.

A to-do list should link two basic types of task info: (1) **scheduled activities** (calendared items) and (2) **nonscheduled activities**.

Scheduled activities include appointments as well as blocks of time that you set aside to do specific types of work, e.g., projects, planning and paperwork.

Nonscheduled activities are items on your to-do list that aren't scheduled to be done at any particular time of day; nevertheless, you should **group (categorize) certain common tasks** together, for example, all your phone calls, emails or top A priorities. It's great if there's additional space, also, to write notes or to show information related to goals and results.

Whatever type of system you use, it's important to see both your scheduled and nonscheduled activities at the same time and have them next to or near one another. Whenever possible or feasible, **turn your nonscheduled tasks into scheduled ones** because they're more likely to get done; when you've set time aside and attached a deadline to accomplish a task, you're more likely to do it than if it's just an unscheduled item on a to-do list. If you've set aside time to do tasks and you have trouble gauging time, use an electronic countdown timer from an electronics store such as Radio Shack to help you stick to your schedule. You'll probably work faster, too, according to Parkinson's Law, which we discussed in Chapter 3.

Master lists

A **master list** is useful for listing activities that will occur over a period of time, from one week to several months. A master list serves three functions. First, it consolidates ideas you've been storing in your head and on your desk into one source. Second, it gives you an overview and some perspective of the "big picture." Third, you can use it to select items to place on your daily list.

To make your master list more effective whether it's on computer, a mobile device or on paper, categorize and prioritize it and keep it short— put it on one page (if possible). Many software and email programs allow you to prioritize and sort tasks by their priority level (low, normal or high or with different colors representing degrees of urgency). Some people with paper-based systems simply flag the most important items with a red star. You may want to combine a red star with a start date or a due date.

Some of my clients create two separate lists, one for personal and another for professional. Some create a separate list for each project or type of work. Usually the fewer lists the better, but the trick is to remember to use them. The more lists you have, the easier it is to forget to use one of them.

To keep it really simple, just use your computer's word processing program to create a master list—completed items can be deleted (or archived by adding "Done" next to the item or transferred to a "Done" file) or reprioritized through the edit feature.

If you handwrite your list, use pencil (to write really small and get more items on a page, use a mechanical lead pencil with 0.5mm lead). Writing in pencil lets you erase and rewrite items when your priorities change. Keeping your master list on computer and/or mobile device affords you that same up-to-date flexibility but without needing to manually rewrite or move items. Remember to include some kind of deadline or time frame because almost nothing gets done without one.

If you work on projects with many detailed steps, use a **project sheet** or **project planner** in addition to or instead of a master list. Make a simple list for each project or buy project planning forms that are commercially prepared. (If your projects are very complex, dedicated software management software such as Microsoft Project may be necessary.)

6. Charting

Especially useful for master lists and for project management, **charts** are information pictures that let you see a lot of info at a glance. They show relationships between different components and are often in the form of graphs or tables.

Charts show relationships visually and graphically. Charts show details and the big picture at the same time. They summarize information at a glance. Sometimes a chart is large enough to go on a wall (as you'll soon see) or small enough to fit on a form or computer screen.

Charts are also good at showing numerical information, which, according to research, helps produce quicker, easier decisions. When information is expressed in numbers rather than words, complex decisions can be made 20 percent faster. It's also easier to evaluate many more factors and options with numbers than with words; there's an added strain when making decisions with words alone.

The **spreadsheet** is an example of a chart; many of my clients use it as a master list to show the status of their projects and work flow. It lets them see right away what needs to be done and when, as well as what already has been done.

Wall charts

If you work with others on joint projects, you may prefer large **wall charts** or **visual control boards** that display activities or specific project tasks for many people to see at one time. Also called **scheduling boards**, wall charts provide visibility to keep you on target. They're not the most attractive things in the world but if you have a workroom or don't have to impress anyone with aesthetics, they are very functional. Different varieties include "write-on-wipe-off" boards and magnetic boards with movable strips and cards. If portability is not a factor, these boards can be just the thing.

Wall charts have an advantage over other tools because they crystallize your ideas, intentions and plans and make them visible to you and others. A wall chart gives you a visible game plan and very little escape; it's staring you straight in the face. Color coding works great for wall charts. You can color code people's names, types of activities, progress and deadlines.

Use wall charts to track one complex project, several simultaneous projects, a production schedule, your master calendar, personnel schedules and marketing or fund-raising campaigns. They come in many different sizes, styles, configurations and materials. **Magnetic wall charts** have different components that you can move around. See Figure 4-4 below.

Figure 4-4. Magna Visual Magnetic Work/Plan Kit

Simple charts

For simple charts, use the table feature in your word processing program or **quadrille** or **graph paper** to make your own paper-and-pencil charts. The "non-repro blue" lines will not photocopy but they will guide you in drawing your own lines. They come in many different styles and are available from your office supply store or catalog as well as a number of personal organizer companies.

Here's a simple but important use: comparison shopping. If you're comparing prices and features for products (such as computers) or services from suppliers (such as print shops) consider developing a simple chart so you can record the information as you go. It's a lot easier than whipping out all those notes later on. Your chart keeps you on track by reminding you to ask the same questions of everyone. Leave some blank spaces for additional questions that come up as you do your research.

Checklist charts

In working with clients who have many ongoing projects where each project has most of the same tasks, I have developed the **checklist chart**. This type of chart can be generated on your computer with a spreadsheet or word processing program and printed out as a hard-copy chart or blown up onto a wall chart. Figure 4-5 shows an example of the checklist chart I helped design for the office of a busy professional speaker. The chart is a preprinted, 8½-by-11-inch form kept in a transparent plastic sleeve that sits conveniently on the desk of the speaker's assistant, who uses it to coordinate all upcoming program details on a daily basis.

Scheduling/Project Charts

Available in Microsoft Project and other project management programs, these charts are a good way to show the relationship between periods of time and people, tasks or projects. Some scheduling charts list the months and weeks of the year.

The **Gantt chart**, also called a "milestone chart," is a common scheduling chart that includes a timeline with task start dates, "milestones" (important deadlines or checkpoints) and responsibilities. A man named Henry Gantt invented this useful chart while working for the government during World War I. (See Figure 4-6 for an example.)

Charts using diagramming software

If your work could benefit from charts that show either a *process* (such as a flowchart that maps out workflow or the steps needed to complete a project) or *structure* (such as an organization chart), consider using **diagramming software**. With single purpose or multipurpose diagramming software packages you can create such diagrams as flowcharts, process charts, organization (org) charts, floor plans and space plans. (See the Chapter 4 Resource Guide.)

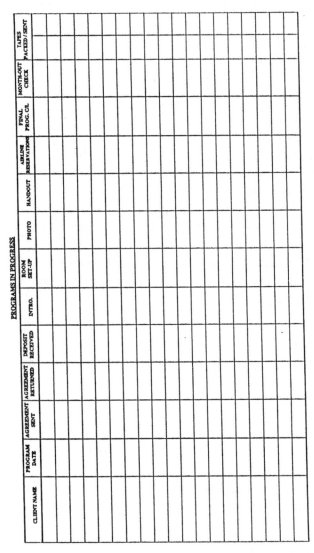

Figure 4-5. A checklist chart for a professional speaker's office

YEARLY PROJECT SCHEDULE

(✓)	#	PROJECT	WK	January					February				March			
				1	2	3	4	5	6	7	8	9	10	11	12	13
	101	Smith Residence							S						R	
		Foundation							S			F				
		Framing & Roughins										S			R	F
		Drywall														S
		Painting & Trim														
	102	Jones Residence										S				
		Foundation										S		F		
		Framing & Roughins											S			
		Drywall														
		Painting & Trim														
	103	Martin Residence														S
		Foundation														S
		Framing & Roughins														
		Drywall														
		Painting & Trim														
	104	Hamilton Residence														
	105	Kite Residence														

Figure 4-6. A portion of a Gantt chart where "S" refers to the Start time, "R" is for Review and "F" is for Finish.

Mind Mapping & other brainstorming charts

There are many exciting ways to capture and harness all those creative ideas you (and others) may have in your head. One way is to chart them out.

Let me share with you one of the greatest and simplest tools I use to chart ideas whenever I begin a project or a writing task. It's called a **Mind Map** and it was originally developed by Tony Buzan. I first heard about it at a professional communications meeting devoted to "writer's block."

The Mind Map is an effective way to free up your mind and let your ideas flow. It's a combination brainstorming and outlining tool where you can see your ideas and thought patterns more graphically. The Mind Map is a great organizing tool for writing, speaking, project planning, meetings, training, negotiating, learning, memorizing and thinking.

I've also used **clusters** or **clustering**, another graphic organization tool, which is similar to Mind Mapping. Clusters are described in Gabriele Rico's book, *Writing the Natural Way*. See also Figure 4-7.

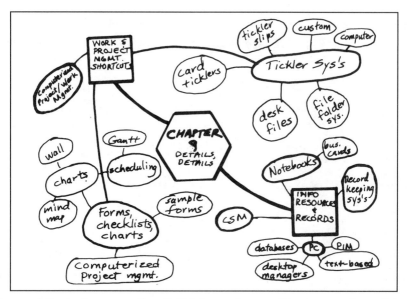

Figure 4-7. A cluster outline I did for a chapter from an earlier edition of this book

7. Collaborative Computing

Your need for collaborative computing features depends on the work you do and/or your type of work group. If you work with others and it is project-based or you communicate extensively with others, you may need such features as group scheduling, meeting management, online meetings and conferencing, online file and document sharing, online project management and online sharing of ideas and thoughts. We'll be exploring these in Part 5.

Resource Guide

Time and info management is an ongoing challenge and adventure. There are no magic wands but hopefully this chapter has opened your eyes to the variety of solutions that are available to transform how you work. (Also see **www.adams-hall.com** for updates and my new book, *Teach Your Computer to Dance.*)

High-Tech Organization Tools
Calendaring, contact management and PIM software

If you have a mobile device and a computer, always check to see whether a software program (personal information manager, customer relationship management or contact management program) will run on both devices.

ACT! by Sage is a powerful, award-winning, easy-to-use contact and customer management program designed for sales professionals, small teams, corporate workgroups and mobile professionals. It offers a tightly integrated contact database, word processor, report generator, an activities scheduler and sales opportunity tracking tools. It's available in two versions: ACT! by Sage is for individuals and small teams of up to 10 networked users and **ACT! by Sage Premium for Workgroups** is for workgroups of up to 50 networked users. These ACT! programs each include **ACT! Link for Palm OS** and **ACT! Link for Pocket PC** to synchronize ACT! data (including contacts, notes, history, appointments, activities, to-do's and custom data fields) with handheld devices. Sage Software, 877/501-4496 [CA] **or www.act.com**

AnyTime Organizer Deluxe is a PIM that's easy to use, inexpensive and has a large selection of printouts. The program has a familiar, notebook-like interface that's intuitive, making the program easy to learn. Individual Software, 800/822-3522 or **www.individualsoftware.com**

GoldMine is a comprehensive contact manager that lets you automate common repetitive office tasks. Features include calendaring, email, mail merge letters, telemarketing, sales forecasting, lead tracking, fax/merge, wireless data synchronization, sophisticated security, "remote transfer synchronization," a report generator, user definable screens and fields and unlimited additional contacts. FrontRange Solutions, Inc., 800/776-7889 ext. 7378 [CA] or **www.goldmine.com**

OneCalendar is a connected Web-based calendar that you can use to bring your work, personal, family and community group calendars together into one easy-to-use online calendar. OneCalendar enables you to share calendars with individuals or groups by posting calendars on the Web or emailing the calendar using built-in tools. You can even organize

your combined multiple calendars in a color-coded list. Trumba Corp.,
www.trumba.com

Charting, diagramming and idea mapping software

FastTrack Schedule lets you create and update presentation-quality
Gantt chart schedules quickly and easily. AEC Software, 800/450-1985
[VA] or **www.aecsoft.com**

Flowcharter enables you to clearly and quickly communicate ideas and
information with ready-to-use diagrams such as flowcharts, timelines and
network diagrams. This is full-featured flow-charting program that allows
for customized application development. iGrafx, 503/404-6050 or
www.igrafx.com

Inspiration award-winning software programs for computers and
handhelds are great for brainstorming, project planning, diagramming,
organizing info, visualizing, flow charting, writing, learning and more.
877/674-7687 [IN] or **www.mindServegroup.com**; 800/877-4292 [OR]
or **www.inspiration.com**.

SmartDraw is an award-winning program that includes nearly 65,000
professionally designed symbols and templates to meet most any drawing
need: flowcharts, floor plans, calendars, org charts, schedules, flyers,
certificates, presentation graphics and most any kind of chart or diagram.
www.SmartDraw.com

MindManager combines the power of Mind Mapping with your PC and
has integrated Internet conferencing. MindManager is a Mind-Mapping
tool to help you not only organize and act on information but also
crystallize your thinking. 877/646-3535 [CA] or **www.mindjet.com**

Visio is an award-winning, multipurpose, enterprise-wide business
drawing and technical diagramming program that lets you easily create
flowcharts, org charts, network diagrams, software and database
diagrams, technical schematics and more. Microsoft Corp.,
www.microsoft.com\office\visio

Low-Tech but Tangible Tools
Paper-based calendars, planners, organizers and accessories

AT-A-GLANCE planners have been around a long time and are widely available in office supply stores (as well as online). The Monthly AT-A-GLANCE #70-120-00 has two yearly calendars for the current and coming years; a traditional monthly calendar for scheduled activities; a name/address page; and 23 blank pages that can be used for planning nonscheduled to-do's (tip: use the front for listing to-do's and use the back for notes related to any particular to-do's). MeadWestvaco Corporation, **www.ataglance.com**

Day-Timers, Inc. has perhaps the largest variety of products for organizing time and info. Their product line includes traditional planners with a wide variety of loose-leaf forms and refills; slim wire-bound or sewn-bound planners; and a wide selection of business cases, totes and accessories. Day-Timers, Inc., 800/457-5702 or **www.daytimer.com**

FranklinCovey has paper planning systems that include kits, forms and binders; tech planning systems that feature handhelds/PDAs and software; accessories that include totes and business cases to accommodate laptops, phones and other handheld devices. Franklin Covey, 800/819-1812 [UT], **www.franklincovey.com**

The **Planner Pad** is a unique time management paper organizer. It works like a funnel to help you organize your week's tasks, daily to-do list and schedule everything in a single, convenient system. Planner Pads Co., 800/315-7526 [NE] or **www.plannerpads.com**

SCAN/PLAN The Creative Organizer Instant Information Scan System uses unique transparent plastic pockets that hold index cards and remarkably let you read and write on both sides of the cards without removing them! These versatile systems are great for managing time, projects and all kinds of information and come in a variety of different sized planners and accessories. SCAN/PLAN Bottom Line software is also available. SCAN/PLAN, Inc., 800/722-6752 [CA] or **www.scanplan.com**

Time/Design planners provide planning, goals, project and reference sections and focus on self-management as well as time management.

Time/Design's Technology Companion is a paper-based solution to bridge the gap between paper and Outlook, Notes or a PDA with sections for current goals and projects, yearly/monthly calendars, next actions list ("to dos"), notes, meeting notes, telephone log, information and contacts. It offers space for brainstorming, meeting notes and other notes when away from a computer or when it's not feasible to use a mobile device. Time/Design 800/637-9942 [MA] or **www.timedesign.com**

Tickler systems

The **Tickler Record** is a three-part, colored NCR (**no c**arbon **r**equired) paper tickler slip system designed for attorneys but good for anyone who wants visual, tangible reminders. This system is especially useful for delegations; the delegator keeps the original, a copy goes to the "delegate" and another copy can go into a master office system. All-State Legal , 800/222-0510 [NJ] or **www.aslegal.com**

Smead makes **Top Tab Indexed Folder Sets**—preprinted alphabetic, daily or monthly file folders you can use in a **file folder tickler system** for monthly or daily follow-up. These manila folders have 1/5-cut tabs with preprinted monthly (Jan.-Dec.) or daily (1-31) headings. Use both sets in combination for a full year follow-up file or use the 1-31 daily folders for the current month. Alphabetic (A-Z) indexed folder sets are handy for maintaining small desk drawer paper files that don't require their own file folders and/or are related to the papers in your file folder tickler system.

Wall charts and boards

Magna Visual magnetic boards and accessories come in a variety of different styles. Magna Visual, Inc., 800/843-3399 [MO] or **www.magnavisual.com**

Magnetic Concepts has a variety of whiteboards and "Rol-a-charts," which have rotating sleeves that allow for continuous scheduling. Customized boards are also available to meet different scheduling needs. Magnetic Concepts Corp., 800/334-4245 [IN] or **www.bigboards.com**

Timewise offers a good selection of wall planning charts and boards. Timewise, 800/246-5250 [MN] or **www.timewiseboards.com**

5

Communications: Managing Email, Instant and Text Messages, Phone Calls and More

---

Quick Scan: Read this chapter if you want to prevent and manage communications overload including emails, spam, instant and text messages, phone calls and voices messages and get a handle on unified messaging. See the chapter Resource Guide for additional resources, products and services.

Communication technology is here to stay. The trick today is to make the most of it and to control the barrage of information that is undoubtedly coming your way. Chances are your greatest need is to get a handle on and take control of the never-ending bombardment of emails, instant messages, text messages and phone calls. You probably received at least one while reading this paragraph.

The types of communication keep evolving and changing in their usage, popularity and form. Phone calls have been supplemented and partly replaced by emails. Over 80% of companies use instant messaging (IM) as the preferred or at least a common mode of communication. *Web conferencing, wikis* (collaborative websites) and other types of real-time collaboration and communication are now common and often preferred methods of collaborative communication to save time and reduce travel costs (for more on these topics, see Chapters 16 and 17).

Because of the need for organizing and simplifying the retrieval of all these forms of communication, the trend is towards **unified messaging**—unifying the way you can receive different modes of communications so that they are routed according to your specific preferences. (See the Resource Guide for names of unified messaging options.)

Dealing with Technology Interruptions

The average business person receives hundreds of messages a day, which include emails, instant messages, text messages, faxes, conventional and cellphone calls, voice mails and that old standard—letters. How many on average do you receive daily? You know technology has taken over your life when your business card has: (a) no white space, (b at least four phone/telecommunications numbers (c) at least two email addresses and (d) addresses for a Web site and/or blog.

Along with all this technology come a sense of urgency and an expectancy of working quickly. Emails and IM in particular convey a false sense of urgency simply due to the instantaneous nature of the medium (and also that the sender may know whether or not you've read the message).

We have instant communications that are leaving many people breathless. One *Wall Street Journal* story was entitled "Pushing the Pace: The Latest Big Thing at Many Companies is Speed, Speed, Speed" and another story outlined the "multitasking" occupational hazards that type A personalities develop in using technology—they're using several different communication tools at the same time. As a consultant, I'm terribly concerned about these aspects of technology that are producing a pressure-cooker workplace. That's why it's so important to select communication tools carefully and to not only use specific guidelines and habits that maximize how and when to use these tools but also be open to trying different tools (e.g., wikis instead of just emails) to work collaboratively.

Unfortunately, technology can present some time management issues. You need to decide how and when to use it. How often is often enough when it comes to checking email, for example? How many times per day? How many times per hour? And how quickly should a reply be sent? How should instant or text messaging be handled? Before you answer these questions, consider the results of a study done by a psychiatrist at King's College, London University.

Emails and IQ

A King's College study of over 1,000 participants found that their intelligence declined as tasks were interrupted by incoming emails and text messages. Email users suffered a 10% drop in IQ scores.

Researchers said the deterioration in mental capacity was the direct result of an addiction to technology. Email addicts were bombarded by context switches and developed an inability to distinguish between trivial and significant messages.

Among the other findings were:

- Almost two-thirds of the participants checked their electronic messages during out-of-office hours and while on vacation

- One-third of all adults responded to an email immediately or within 10 minutes

- Half of all workers responded to an email within 60 minutes of receiving one

- One in five were "happy" to interrupt a business or social meeting to respond to an email or text message

According to Glenn Wilson, the author of the study, "Info-mania, if unchecked, will damage a worker's performance by reducing mental sharpness. Companies should encourage a more balanced and appropriate way of working." The rest of this chapter is about finding that balance for you.

Positively Organized! Email Management

If you're like most of us, you have a love-hate relationship with your email. Billions of email messages are sent *every day* in the U.S. (It only *seems* like you're getting all of them.) On average, workers are spending about one-third more time on email than they did one or two years ago. Emails now dwarf regular mail as well as phone calls in most workplaces and most of that email time is wasted time with an ever-increasing amount of spam.

I attribute the popularity of email to several factors. First, it's easy to use. Second, it's an effective communication tool that can be quicker and/or clearer than other methods. Third, it's versatile and flexible—you can send a message to one or more individuals, with or without a document attached; you can do it whether you're in the office or on the road; and you can easily reply to a message. Fourth, it's usually less expensive to use email to communicate. Fifth, if you're dealing with people in other time zones where it's difficult to reach one another on the phone due to the time differences, email allows you to send much longer messages than would be feasible or workable as a voice mail message. Sixth, there is greater connectivity now than ever before between email users of all types—those on corporate networks, commercial online services, the Internet and via mobile wireless devices.

Because of its popularity, the sheer volume of email is 16 times greater than the volume of just two years ago. Some estimates put the volume of spam at 25-80 percent of all email received. In addition, many people don't know and use the important email organization features built into their software; such features help separate the wheat from the chaff—the important emails from the irrelevant ones. This is a common problem for most of my clients.

Know the "Rules" and Other Key Features

Fortunately, there are solutions to help you get control of email if you take advantage of the features your program has to offer.

For starters create an **"Email Message Management System"** by using your email program's **folders** for storing and organizing messages (just as you can create a "Daily Paperwork System" with paper folders for your everyday paperwork described in Chapter 4 and 8). Your email program may come with several generic folders and also let you create your own.

Remember to work the system at least once a day and be sure to regularly clean out old messages. Ideally, you should also set up **rules** so files are automatically put into the correct folder.

The **rules** feature is like having a bouncer at your email front door deciding who stays out and directing those permitted in to the right place. This feature can help you with your electronic filing of emails by automatically filing different types of messages into separate folders. You could also have an **archival** rule so your program automatically archives old emails say, before a certain date into a designated storage section (Outlook has, for example, .PST or "personal storage" files). Note that as archiving email has become more of a legal concern, companies are getting legal advice on what to keep and for how long.

The rules feature can guide you in setting up **filters** to accept or block messages from certain people or on certain topics. Filters are crucial for preventing information overload. They can alert you to emails marked "urgent" as well as those from key individuals, such as your boss, and can literally sound an alarm. Filters can highlight mail you want to read by sending them to a special high-priority folder.

In Outlook you can use the **flagging** feature, too, to visually show you those filtered emails. In Outlook, there are a variety of different flags you can use—"follow up," "fyi," "forward no response necessary," "read," and "reply"—to name a few.

Outlook also has a variety of visual **priority codes** you can use to help prioritize incoming and outgoing emails. In Outlook you can mark emails with "high," "normal" or "low" priority and you have a host of other options to select for identifying and differentiating emails such as "sensitivity," "delivery receipt," "read receipt," "reply redirection," "do not deliver before" and "expires after."

Use **color coding** for email messages, if possible, particularly if you're lucky enough to have someone else screen your email. One company uses "red" for urgent, "yellow" for moderate urgency and "green" for information only. You can send colored electronic sticky notes, too.

Your email program may allow you to calendar **reminders** to take action on emails or to alert you when emails arrive from certain people.

If you need to find an email, the email software's **search** feature may be good enough. Or you could use a **desktop search program** to help you find an email. The search programs work differently as far as what they search— e.g., some search emails, attachments and instant messages and files at the same time. (See Chapter 12 for more information on desktop search programs.) In general, it's best to have well-organized email folders and use a search program as a supplement, but not as a substitute, for good organization.

Check out the **meeting management and scheduling** features, too, if you get involved with setting up meetings and coordinating different people's calendars.

The bottom line is **learn about your email software.** Discover the shortcuts that are built in and design ways to customize the software for you and/or your workgroup(s). One shortcut could save you time every day.

Six Email Time Management Tips

In many ways, handling, going through and organizing your email is much like what you should be doing with your paperwork. Here's what to do:

1. Check at set times, **not constantly.** It's better to use set blocks of time or appointments with yourself, if possible, throughout the day. You will be more in charge of your day and control interruptions better. And if the results of that King's College study on emails and IQs are correct, you'll also be sharper and better able to separate the important from the unimportant. You will also be training coworkers and other recipients not to expect an immediate response. If you respond immediately to every email, you'll find your email load and stress level will increase even more.

2. Scan. Just like in the paper world, it's a good idea to go through your email inbox quickly. Easier said than done, of course! Begin by scanning **subject lines, message headers** and **sender names** (or set up a filter to do this).

3. Set up a clearly-defined message priority system with coworkers. When you use priority terms on your messages, such as "Urgent," "Regular" or "Special Attention" or Outlook priority codes, make sure you and your email correspondents have determined in advance what these terms mean and/or when they should be used. Another option is to include a deadline date or response needed date. (See the work priority system described in Chapter 15.)

4. Prioritize your messages. Handle your most important messages first as quickly as possible.

5. Delete or file daily. Take time every day to delete as many messages as possible or to file them in an appropriate folder. It's easier to deal with emails while they're fresh so you don't have to go back and reread them to decide what to do with them. A good time for pruning and filing is while you're on hold during phone calls. Prevent email clutter in your inbox and folders.

6. Know how to handle email attachments. There are four potential time management issues with *attachments*—files attached to or sent with emails. First, opening attached files is the main way viruses and worms are spread. Computer malware takes advantage of your trusting a known source such as the sender of an attached file. So, open attachments with great caution only after scanning them for viruses, even an email attachment from someone you know (whether or not you're expecting an attachment from them). Second, postpone opening messages with attachments, unless they're from a key person. They can really eat up your time. Third, the size limitations on sending or receiving attachments may prevent your email from going through or your receiving an email from someone else. This is as a good time as any to find out what the incoming and outgoing size limitations are for attachments with your email system. Finally, if attachments fill up your email storage capacity, this may cause all other incoming emails to be returned to the senders.

Seven Ways to Reduce the Amount of Email

In addition to using your email features and following the preceding email time management tips, here are seven important ways to cut down on the quantity of email you receive:

1. Don't give out your email address to everyone. I know of a city mayor who refused to give out her email address to anyone. A few companies have eliminated email because the downsides outweighed the benefits. While I'm not recommending these extremes, do be careful.

2. Limit the number of mailboxes. If possible, use just one or two. Some people have one for work and another for personal email. Or you could have a public one for posting to newsgroups and then another one for private email.

3. Limit distribution lists. Decide whether recipients will really need or want the information.

4. Use intranets or wikis. If you work for a large organization, post announcements on a central-access area on an intranet, for example, or create your own workgroup-specific wiki website rather than just using email for everything.

5. Establish and publicize company email policies. For your company or at least in your immediate workgroup, set up a policy that strongly advises everyone to exercise the same restraint that they would show when writing memos or letters. The policy should further remind them that anything they put in writing, even in an email, could have legal ramifications and even be used against them or the company in a court of law. "Electronic data detectives" now make their living searching for incriminating email messages on computers and backup media. Another policy should require **resisting the urge to copy or forward** ad nauseam. The forwarding craze has to stop. To save computer and storage facilities space, another policy should **limit the number of email messages that can be saved** and for how long. Such a policy should relate to your organization's overall records and document retention and legal policies. Another policy should warn employees to **exercise caution** before forwarding any message internally or externally, especially if it contains confidential or sensitive material.

6. Try "eom" to cut down on unnecessary, reply emails. Many times you may send an email and there is no real need for someone to respond or even say thank you. If indicating "FYI" (for your information) still causes unnecessary responses, try putting "eom" (end of message) in the subject line of your email (or even in a cellphone text message you send). Since not everyone knows what this means, make sure the recipient is educated about this timesaver or you'll get another email asking you to explain "eom."

7. Use automatic responses if you're going to be out of town and not checking your email. Electronic versions of the form letter, "autoreply" or "autoresponse" mechanisms are also good for replying automatically to common or repetitive types of messages, questions or subjects. Be aware, however, that this can verify for spammers the validity of your email address.

Finally, let's face it—email is not as secure nor as private as some other communication methods. And it's a good idea to reemphasize your email policies at frequent intervals; it's also very easy to fall into a false sense of privacy and end up writing "very personal" notes and sensitive messages.

Reducing the Amount of Spam

Then there's the issue of **spam** (junk email) which can clog mailboxes with junk email.

Spam can rob you not only of the time it takes to separate the wheat from the chaff but also of the time it takes to remove **viruses, worms** and **spyware** you can inadvertently put on your computer by opening an infected email or attachment. (For more on ways to protect against viruses, worms, spyware and other unwanted guests on your computer, see Chapter 14.)

Some companies, as large as General Motors, are moving away from email back to voice mail so that vital messages aren't lost in all the spam.

There are a variety of approaches you can take to deal with spam. First, your ISP (Internet Service Provider) may catch spam before it hits your email inbox and delete it or separate it from your other email so you can decide whether to keep or delete it. Second, your email program may have antispam capabilities. If not, get an **antispam program**. There are ways to filter spam out of your email inbox by having a software program look at not only the email's subject line but also the email's contents.

Third, you may want to institute a **challenge/response system**. If you receive an email from someone not already in your email address book, your computer can send a challenge question or task (e.g., copying random-generated numbers on a screen) to prove that it's a person and not an automatically generated (spam) email. Unless the challenge is met, the email does not go through. Finally, you may decide to go with a **whitelisting** program that only allows email from senders you specify. (See the Resource Guide.)

Eleven antispam tips

1. Safeguard your email address. Make sure only people you want to receive email from have your email address. You may decide to omit your email address from your business card or have two cards—one with and one without your email address. Don't pick an obvious email address such as Mary@mycompany.com.

2. **Use free email accounts.** Free email addresses can be abandoned if spam overwhelms them.

3. **Use a spam filter.** Use a program designed to filter out spam.

4. **Avoid accidentally replying to spammers.** With some email programs, the default setting is to always send a response. This can verify for spammers the validity of your email address. Check the setting on your email program.

5. **Don't answer spam or respond to the "remove me" option.** Similarly, if you respond to spam such as by requesting to have your email address taken off a list, you've just confirmed to the spammer that yours is a valid email address.

6. **Keep your email address off the Net.** Spammers scan the Internet looking for email addresses in places such as chat rooms, newsgroups and online guest books. This is where a disposable email address can come in real handy.

7. **See if you can avoid giving an email address.** If a site really doesn't need your email address, see if you can avoid giving any email address.

8. **Determine whether there are opt-out boxes to check.** Sometimes on the Net, you may sign up with a site or a service and also expose yourself to spam and other unnecessary emails unless you *uncheck* the boxes where you are agreeing to receive email offers and other solicitations.

9. **Read the privacy policy.** Although almost no one actually reads those privacy policies, you might be surprised to what you're agreeing to as far as the site's use of your email address and your personal information if you click the OK button.

10. **Don't advertise email addresses unnecessarily.** If you forward an email, don't include the email addresses of all the other recipients of the email, unless necessary.

11. **Stop unfounded rumors.** One way spammers pick up email addresses is by seeing forwarded emails that contain the email addresses

of five to ten prior forwards of a rumor. Go to **www.snopes.com** to check out hoaxes to avoid forwarding them on to others.

How and When to Use Email

Know when to use email over another communication method. The phone may be faster, but that's assuming the person on the other end is there or regularly picks up and responds to their messages. Email can be too impersonal, removing the human connection and sense of relationship so important for work teams.

Beware of using email inappropriately as a way to avoid face-to-face dealings with coworkers. Don't, for example, send performance reviews and other sensitive documents by email as some managers have done.

If possible, send email messages to those who prefer this method and if you have time to wait for delivery of your message and a response.

On a positive note, writing anything (including email messages) tends to require more thoughtful reflection than say, a phone conversation. Studies indicate that email often produces better use of language and clearer communication.

Use it to streamline your phone messaging system. You may prefer to use email phone messages instead of voice mail or telephone message slips. The big advantage is that such a system lets you sort and search messages in a variety of ways. And with integrated messaging/wireless communications, voicemail messages can be sent as text email messages.

Sometimes emails replace other slower communication channels. But often, emails add an additional layer; some people will send an email, for example, and then send a voicemail message indicating they've sent an email message!

Sixteen Email Writing Tips

In my e-writing courses, I teach how to write effective emails. You'll notice that many of the following tips also apply to business writing in general. Email is doing much to revive the art of writing as well as develop clearer thinking and decision-making—all important professional and personal skills.

1. Determine the recipient(s) of your message in advance. Decide who really needs the message. Knowing your audience will help you better frame the message. Indicate if a message should be restricted. Too many messages are copied and forwarded indiscriminately. You may want to include a confidentiality statement in case your email is mistakenly received by someone else.

2. Write a subject line that gets noticed and isn't rejected as spam. If your subject line looks too much like a sales pitch, it may be automatically rejected by a spam filter. Make your subject relevant to the reader and to the content of your message. It's useful to build in some kind of action and/or deadline that's required for the recipient. For regular correspondents, consider also using all capitalized code words, acronyms or other abbreviations followed by a colon in subject lines that immediately reference a project, client or subject. And change your subject line if the subject of your reply email has changed.

3. Put the most important information right up front including any request for action. If the action item is important, include it up front in the subject line as well as in the email message itself. In the opening paragraph, spell out what's needed, any deadline and why it's important. If, however, your main purpose is reinforcing a relationship, put relationship-building content in the first paragraph(s) and any request for action in a subsequent paragraph.

4. Be brief. Using block style, write brief, concise messages in short paragraphs (with no more than three sentences each) that put your main points right up front so that they show up on the screen before any scrolling. For informal emails as well as instant and text messages, use **Net lingo**—a quick, shorthand way of writing that saves time, reduces keystrokes and speeds up communication (assuming you're using commonly understood terms). Here are two Net lingo sites: www.aim.com/acronyms.adp?aolp= and www.netlingo.com.

5. Use good graphic design elements. In addition to short paragraphs, use the following elements to make it easier to read your emails:

- Bullets or numbers to list key ideas without long, wordy sentences

- Subheads to organize main points and guide your reader(s)

- White space to prevent and break up dense text

- Boldface and color for highlighting key points but don't overdo it

- Appropriate graphics that don't take too long to load
- A **sans serif** type font such as Arial is easier to read onscreen; avoid the use of all upper or lower case letters, which are difficult to read

6. Delete extraneous information such as cluster addresses (distribution lists) whenever possible—This applies to either sending an original message or forwarding one. Not only will it protect the privacy of those other recipients, it may prevent spammers from harvesting those addresses from your post. It also removes the need to scroll past them to get to the body of the message. And it's more professional as well as personal; no one likes to be on everyone's list. On the other hand, you may have certain "group lists" where you want everyone to know that they were each informed of an event, an announcement, etc.

7. Use the bcc (blind carbon copy) function—Chances are your email program will allow you to send out an email to many people but hide the email addresses of the recipients. This helps prevent those addresses from being harvested by spammers.

8. Know when to use "reply" versus "reply to all. You don't want to accidentally broadcast a reply that was meant for only one recipient.

9. When replying to a message, clearly refer to the original message you received, if it's not included in the reply. If it is included, be sure to include only those parts to which you are responding. You may want to boldface your responses or use a larger font size to make your responses clearly stand out. Even if the original message appears below in a reply, I strongly recommend including pertinent parts of the original message *in an alternating fashion*; the first part followed by your response, the second part followed by your response and so forth.

10. Use a signature file (or "sig") at the end of your message—This should include your name, title, and possibly your phone number. Limit it to no more than four or five lines. To make mine friendlier, I generally sign my messages with my first name and then I insert my sig. Omit a sig for very informal messages or for people you know well.

11. Be very careful what you write and pay special attention to tone. Any number of others could see your email(s), without your even knowing it. Expect your work email to be read by your employer—the workplace norm is for companies to have email scanning software to determine whether email uses and content are appropriate. Be careful about conveying negative information through email. Use the appropriate tone, style and emotional content for the intended audience. Avoid jokes and sarcasm. Be careful about conveying negative information through email. Warm up email by using the recipient's name at least once and preferably twice; otherwise, email can be too cold and impersonal. Limit the use of words (except acronyms) or sentences in all upper case letters. Besides being difficult to read, overuse of caps is the online equivalent of screaming at someone. See if your email program has an "Unsend" feature, too.

12. Read carefully—This goes for rereading a message you're about to send as well as reading messages you've received in their entirety.

13. Avoid sending unsolicited attachments (files) without first notifying the recipient by just a text email or phone call. Otherwise, your email may be deleted as spam since the "best" way to catch a computer virus, worm or other unwanted visitor is by opening up infected attachments. Instead first call or send a text (no attachment) email to alert them.

14. Make sure attachments aren't too big to be sent or received— Before you send an attachment, find out the size limit that your email service/ISP allows you to send. (There may be different sending size limits for recipients who use the same service and those who don't.) Sending large files as attachments may cause your email to be returned unopened because the recipient's computer system or email mailbox is too full. And if you send a large file that fills up someone's email inbox so all their other incoming email is rejected, they won't be looking favorably upon you. Similarly, find out the limit on your receiving end. You may want to be diligent about clearing out attachments you've received so you don't run out of room for other email you'll be receiving.

15. Indicate if a message should be restricted—Since it's all too easy these days to copy and forward messages, be sure to indicate any restrictions, confidentiality statement or limited access in case your email is received by someone else by mistake.

16. Add a confirmation of receipt if needed—Try adding the following in all caps at the beginning of your email: *** PLEASE REPLY TO THIS EMAIL TO CONFIRM RECEIPT ***.

Email Security

Encryption may be the best solution to not only protect your messages but also your email address. Powerful encryption can help ensure that only your intended receiver can decipher your message. An encryption program is ideal for anyone with proprietary or sensitive data.

The **electronic** or **digital signature** can be another valuable security tool. The goal of an electronic signature is to tell the recipient with certainty who "signed" the document and to guarantee that nothing was changed. The electronic signature is a typical feature of encryption programs. Note, however, that standardization work in this area is still ongoing. The EESSI was created to coordinate the standardization of electronic signatures (see **http://www.ictsb.org/EESSI_home.htm**).

Don't overlook the power of **passwords** to limit access by others to your email, computer or online service. Security experts suggest your chosen password should contain *at least* **eight characters** (letters, numbers and symbols). Don't share your passwords with anyone and change them at least every two months. Passwords should not contain real words or relate to your name, birth date or anything personal. (For more tips on passwords, see Chapter 14 and my new book, *Teach Your Computer to Dance.*)

Instant Messaging

A more immediate, spontaneous, personal extension of email, instant messaging (IM) helps to reach out and connect people. Computer columnist Lawrence Magid wrote that IM is to email what email is to formal letter writing.

Remember that any IM you write, as with all email, can be saved and/or printed and leaves a cyber paper trail. Exercise caution, good judgment and restraint.

Instant messaging lets you set up a special "buddy" or contact list that can provide immediate access to one another. The software indicates whether a contact is online and if so, you can then send the contact a message, which pops up on their screen in a little box right in the middle of whatever they're doing.

Dealing with IM Interruptions

IM is "interrupt driven" and is analogous to someone knowing that you're at home and barging in unannounced saying, "I'm here," regardless of what you're doing at the moment, asking for some of your time. It's a virtual barging into your office or cubicle.

With more and more devices connected to the Internet all the time, IM can make you all too available. As with all other time management interruptions (see Chapter 3), you need to have some ready responses to take control of IM as well as practice some considerate "netiquette" of your own.

Start by asking (as you should do on a phone call) whether the person is available. You could start your message by asking "Busy?" or "Got a minute?" If your buddy doesn't have time to chat, it easily lets them off the hook. And if you don't have time to chat, let your buddy know that as well. Have short reasons ready: "Sorry, on the phone" or "On a big deadline. Later." When you're ready to sign off, a simple "Bye" or "Gotta go" can do the trick.

Some IM programs also have blocking features to prevent selected (or all) individuals from knowing you're online or sending you messages. You just may want to use this invisibility feature more often than not.

On the other hand, it's also possible to have private group IM chats. For collaborative work or for customer support, IM can be a great channel of communication.

Just because you *can* use IM, doesn't mean you *should*. See if this is the best medium for you or a given project.

And as with email, you can get junk messages. In IM talk, they are known as **spim**. As this increases as a problem, better solutions will evolve to handle it.

Finally, security is always an issue no matter the mode of communication. Be aware that more public modes of IM may be less secure than your company's IM system.

Text Messaging

I am a fan of text messaging. Text messaging respects the privacy of the recipient and is less intrusive than instant messaging or phone calls. It's more similar to emails in that you are not making immediate contact where a person has to take a step to tell you, "Not now."

One downside to text messaging is that without an adequate keyboard on your mobile device, it's difficult to type in and send much of a message. And with our thumbs doing the typing, we risk ergonomic injuries from overusing that appendage.

The typing limitation is more on the sending end. Note that someone may be able to use their cellphone provider's website to type in a lengthier message (within limits) from their computer keyboard to be texted to your mobile device.

There's one other facet of text messaging that's very important. In the event of a disaster, a text message may have a better chance of getting through than a cell call. The reason is that text messages travel on the portion of a cellphone network that is reserved for data. If a cellular network is overloaded, a cell call can just be dropped; however, a text message just waits in turn in a queue. Emails also wait in a queue.

Phone Calls and Voice Mail

Although email, IM and text messages can claim a big portion of your day, it's important to also use the best techniques to control time when dealing with phone calls and messages.

Six Ways to Max Your Phone Time

Many consider the telephone both a drain on time and the single greatest source of disrupting interruptions. Others, however, use it too much as an entertainment tool to escape from the tedium of emails and other work. Actually, the telephone can be your greatest ally if you follow these six essential ingredients to make your telephone time work best for you.

1. Take control through preparation and planning.

The key to mastering the telephone is doing much of your telephone work in advance, making more outgoing calls and taking fewer incoming calls. Whenever possible, set up telephone appointments. Prioritize and consolidate all callbacks. Prepare for each outgoing call or telephone appointment by having all the necessary material in front of you and *writing down* in advance any key questions or areas to cover as well as a projected time limit for each call.

Planning the time you call can be critical in preventing telephone tag. The busiest time for business calls is usually Monday morning, between 9 and 11 a.m. Sometimes calling before 9 a.m. or after 5 p.m. is a good time to catch those hard-to-reach people.

Deciding *when* to use the telephone instead of email, for example, is also an important part of planning your calls. Some things are best communicated by phone—particularly sensitive issues or those requiring back-and-forth discussion. The telephone is usually better for building rapport and problem solving.

2. Do something about being left on hold too long.

Get a telephone headset or use your speaker phone and handle items you've accumulated to do when you're left on hold. If you've been on hold for at least 10 minutes, email the head of the company or the press relations person and simply write, "I've been on hold for <u>10</u> minutes today and thought you'd like to know. I'm a current (prospective or former) customer of yours." (Use the appropriate words.)

3. Remember what you say goes a long way with a PTA.

Do you have a "Positive Telephone Attitude"? A PTA is essential for building rapport and good working relationships.

In particular, there is nothing like the power of praise when you're trying to accomplish your goals through the telephone. Acknowledge good telephone behavior by those who assist you, be they colleagues, contacts, prospects, receptionists or your own staff members.

I make a big point of thanking assistants who have gone out of their way to take down a long message or connect me with someone who's been difficult to reach. I often will tell their boss. A fundraiser sends thank-you notes to assistants and hotel operators as well.

A PTA also includes helpfulness and follow-through. A well-intentioned PTA becomes hollow indeed if what was promised isn't delivered.

4. Use concise communication.

Be specific when you communicate. Corporate communications consultant Dr. Allen Weiner teaches professionals what he calls "bottom line communicating." I advise clients to focus on the result(s) they want before and during each call. Nothing will speed up a call like getting to the point sooner.

Try these two proven techniques: first, set time limits up front (e.g., "I've got five minutes to talk") and second, outline your calls (e.g., "I'd like to discuss these two questions...").

Even your voice mail or telephone answering machine message should be as concise as possible. We get a lot of compliments on our voice mail message: "Thank you for calling Positively Organized! Please leave your name, number *and the best time to call you back.*"

Finally, consider whether the telephone is your most concise and time-saving tool for any given communication and whether it should be used in conjunction with email, IM, fax or another communication channel.

5. Take notes and take action.

Take notes during the call if you think you may need to refer back to the call in the future. Don't rely on a good memory and don't be tempted by the thought, "I'll remember this call."

Whether you take notes on computer or paper, always date the entry and list: (a) who initiated the call, (b) any main points to be covered and (c) the covered comments, which you should number as you go along. Also include the starting and ending time of the call so you'll have a better idea as to a good time to next reach and/or talk to the other party.

Right after the phone call, highlight key points and take any necessary follow-up steps, such as transferring information to your calendar or listing the next action step in your PIM or contact manager software, mobile device or paper-based tickler system.

6. Train your telephone team.

If you're fortunate enough to have someone else in your office handling your telephone, you have an opportunity to boost your effectiveness, provided you *train* that person on how to screen and prioritize calls, take messages and use all of the effective telephone habits listed here.

VoIP

VoIP (Voice over Internet Protocol) lets you route telephone calls through your broadband (e.g., DSL or cable modem) Internet connection or the connection at many Wi-Fi hot spots. The main benefit of VoIP is saving money.

Not only can you get long-distance calling plans at a low rate or no cost, you can also have virtual phone numbers. If your company is based in Texas and has a large number of clients or customers say in Boston and Seattle, you could have a virtual phone number for each area code so calls would be local, not long-distance calls.

With VoIP, you can check your voice mail by phone, receiving an email with a message as a sound file or by logging onto the virtual phone's company website and listening to your messages over your computer.

The potential downsides of VoIP are: (1) problems with your broadband service mean problems with your phone calls, (2) enhanced 911 may not be available to help locate a phone's location in case of an emergency, (3) fax with VoIP may have transmission problems, (4) a loss of power means no phone service unlike traditional landline phones or cellphones which can work if the power is off and, most importantly, (5) security and privacy issues can arise from using the Internet as the mode of transmission.

Value Voice Mail and Phone Time

For the purposes of this section, the term "voice mail" includes multi-user, computer-driven, menu answering systems—called "interactive voice response" or IVR—and also the automated answering systems found in stand-alone answering machines. Voice mail has become a valuable, timesaving telecommunications tool. Its many advantages include: reducing telephone tag (but don't fall into "voice mail tag"!); screening calls during critical work projects; not having to return a call if a caller's message is complete enough and/or requires no response; receiving private, usually more accurate messages; and accessing messages at your convenience.

Telecommunications are important to the bottom line. Poor telephone contact or voice mail can affect customer retention. A Rockefeller Institute study found that of the eight to 15 percent of a company's annual client loss, 68 percent was due to poor telephone treatment.

Be sure your company, organization or workgroup has written telecommunications policies with regard to how calls are picked up (when and by whom/what) as well as when they are returned. Periodically evaluate your entire phone system—the tools, the technology and the personal telephone habits you're using.

Yet, if you value voice mail itself over the needs of your customers, you can quickly lose the advantages this automated system has to offer.

The trick is learning how to make it serve your external as well as your internal customers. I encourage you to evaluate your system and follow these twelve guidelines:

1. Focus first on serving your external customer. Determine if all the options and directions of your voice mail maze encourage or discourage contact. Regularly check out the system yourself (or better yet, ask a friend who hasn't used your system) for any bugs or annoyances and survey your customers' reactions.

2. Always give your caller the option to speak to a real live person. (But make sure that the referral's voice mail isn't also on, though!) Not having this live person option is sometimes called "voice mail jail." (How many times have you been transferred to someone who supposedly can solve your problem but you're connected to their voice mail and you have no idea what that person does and whether you'll ever get a return call?)

3. Limit, if possible, the number of punch-in options to no more than three. Too many choices can be confusing and impersonal. Design your "automated attendant" or "electronic menuing" feature to keep the menu simple and avoid layers of menus and choices.

4. Ideally, have a well-trained receptionist handle your company's main phone number. Because so few companies do this anymore, you'll really stand out. (I almost always tell such receptionists how nice it is to speak with a real person and I'm often told they've heard that from other people as well.)

5. Your outgoing message should be short and inviting. Avoid generic, nonspecific messages, if possible, and give the caller specific information about your availability and other options for more immediate assistance. Give your name, job title, department, division or any pertinent information. Most importantly, **ask callers to indicate the level of urgency and when they need to hear back from you.** You may also want to provide your email address.

6. Be sure to tell the caller how long they have to speak. If you get many voice mails a day, give callers a short time limit on messages they leave. Let them know what the time limit is—for example, 60 seconds.

7. On your outgoing message ask callers to leave their phone number two times and to give the best time(s) to call them back (and to indicate their time zone or location) to prevent telephone tag.

Assure callers that their call is important and will be handled in a timely fashion.

8. If possible, set up an electronic phone directory so that callers can easily get a person's extension number even after business hours.

9. Since your system should **let callers speed up or bypass an outgoing message**, provide the extension number or correct codes to move quickly through the system. It's great, too, if you include the option of dialing "O" for a real-life operator—or at least provide some other option of speaking with a person. I like systems that, after a few minutes, will give the caller an option of remaining on hold or leaving a message.

10. Keep your outgoing message current. It doesn't look professional to have an out-of-date message indicating for example, the dates you'll be out of town and you've been back for a week already. Add a reminder in your planner, mobile device or other time management tool before you leave town to change your message when you return.

11. Use "computer telephony integration" technology to avoid time-wasting aggravation. For example, if your system asks for information from a caller, such as an ID number, and then transfers the caller to an agent, make sure the agent doesn't ask for the same information again.

12. Periodically offer short training sessions on your telephone and voice mail system for your internal staff. Rarely does anyone ever read the manual and people generally need more than an initial orientation. It's time well spent to continue learning about some of the timesaving features your system just may have. Since you may have some turnover, there will probably be some new people who are depending most likely on other employees who received a brief introduction but never read the manual!

More timesaving voice mail tips

As to how often you should check your voice mail, it depends. You want to be able to spend time getting projects and essential tasks done and to have some time for thinking and planning. But you don't want to get repeat messages from the same person either on voice mail, email or another channel or to have them feel you've dropped off the edge of the earth because you've taken too long to respond. If you have a policy of checking voice mail at set times, letting people know can help you take control of your time, energy and schedule.

When making a call to someone else's voice mail, **indicate how** (or even if) as well as **when you'd like the person to communicate back with you and the level of urgency**. Perhaps you prefer email; if so, leave your email address. If you're asking for a favor or you're calling someone you don't know well, **give the person a choice** of how they want to contact you. Depending upon the circumstances, I may leave both my phone number and email address.

When reaching a voice mail system, try to **skip the outgoing message** by pressing the 0 (operator) buttons. (Be aware, however, that some systems will disconnect you when pressing one of these buttons or, even worse, make you listen to the entire menu again.)

If you *prefer* leaving a message rather than reaching someone, try calling a landline rather than a cellphone. Many people don't answer their landlines (always letting calls go through to voice mail) and only pick up cell calls.

When calling someone else's voice mail system, leave your name and number (at the beginning and end of your call) and a brief message indicating your reason for calling and any action you may need and when. Include the best time(s) to reach *you*. Also speak slowly and distinctly, especially when giving your name and number. Be complete and concise, yet friendly, with good etiquette, and somehow convey what's in it for them to return your call (recognize that only one in four calls are indeed returned). Write down an individual's extension or direct dial number for future reference so you can bypass the company-wide system.

Resource Guide

For more products, check www.adams-hall.com for updates as well as my new book *Teach Your Computer to Dance*.

Email and Antispam Programs

Eudora is an alternative email program that has received rave reviews for quite some time. Qualcomm, Inc., 800/238-3672 [CA] or **www.eudora.com**

Mailshell provides ways to control spam. Mailshell.com, Inc., **www.mailshell.com**

Email Converter

Aid4Mail helps you convert your old emails if you switch to another email service. The programs supports many popular email client programs. Fookes Software, **www.aid4mail.com**

Encryption

HushMail is a Web-based encrypted email service designed to let you encrypt messages and store and share files from almost any Web-capable PC. Hush Communications Corp., **www.hushmail.com**

PGP Desktop Home and **Professional** programs (PGP stands for "Pretty Good Privacy") are designed to be easy-to-use desktop security solutions that protect confidential communications and digitally stored information with encryption technology. PGP Corporation, 800/650-319-9000 [CA] or **www.pgp.com**

Unified Messaging

Office Communicator 2005 is designed to: (a) manage, in a single view, instant messages, email, voice and other business communications and (b) allow switching from text messaging to a video chat or conference call with the click of a button. At the time of the writing of this book, it is being beta-tested. Microsoft Corp., **www.microsoft.com**

Onebox is for fax, email, voice and conferencing services. J2 Global Communications, 888/ 588-4600 [CA] or **www.onebox.com**

Part 3

Positively Organized! Workspaces

Working Productively and Ergonomically with Equipment, Files, Paper, and Other "Collectibles" in an Office and on the Go

6

Ergonomics:
Increasing Productivity and Avoiding Computer-Related Injuries

---

Quick Scan: To avoid aches and pains and serious injuries, learn how to position and use your computer, monitor, keyboard, mouse, desk and other furniture in ergonomically sound ways. Read this chapter to put yourself in the right position to get the most done with the least amount of strain.

Ergonomics is a vital subject today when most people are working longer hours and spending more of it interacting with technology. Ergonomics is the science of making the work environment compatible with people so they can work more comfortably and productively.

Ergonomics looks at the dimensions, placement and use of a laptop or desktop computer, keyboard, mouse, monitor, work tables, desks and chairs and matches them to the wide range of body sizes and shapes according to certain recommended standards in order to prevent fatigue, eyestrain, blurred vision, headaches, stiff muscles, wrist pain, sore back, irritability and loss of feeling in fingers and wrists. The longer you work at a desk or computer, the more you need to consider the importance of correct angles of eyes, arms, hands, legs and feet.

There can be positive benefits even beyond avoiding health problems. For example, some research indicates that the proper chair can add up to 40 productive minutes each work day.

If your work setup doesn't seem correct or you are uncertain what's right for you, get professional advice because you may be spending half or more of your waking hours in a given work environment.

One good general tip is **avoid long periods of any repetitive activity** whether it's keyboard use or making phone calls. So start being aware of any repetitive, daily activities that could take a toll on your body. For example, if your job requires you to open many envelopes each day, a battery-powered letter opener may save wear and tear on your body. Similarly, an automatic stapler may be of great help to you.

It's important to note that ergonomic standards can change over time as studies or additional studies are done and also as technology (such as mobile devices) is introduced. One example of the latter concerns the widespread use of mobile devices such as smartphones and PDAs where we're changing how we use our fingers. Thumbs are taking over some of the old jobs of index fingers. Overuse of thumbs can lead to **RSI** (**r**epetitive **s**tress **i**njury or sometimes called **r**epetitive **s**train **i**njury) especially if you do a lot of emailing or text messaging with your mobile device. To raise awareness of this problem, the British Chiropractic Association started a campaign called "How to Practice Safe Text."

Below are a number of steps to consider in setting up an ergonomic environment with your computer, monitor, accessories and furniture.

Give Yourself a Break

Because you can do almost everything today at a computer, you may find, like many people, you are sitting there for more hours every day than ever before. But this single type of repetitive activity can be dangerous physically and mentally and lead to RSI. If your work simply demands you spend long hours at a computer, then the suggestions you're about to read are especially critical.

For starters, become a clock watcher and pause every 20 minutes or so to look away from the screen and to change your close-up focus by looking at distant objects in order to **prevent eyestrain**. Try to blink more often. Blinking moistens your eyes and reduces eyestrain. We blink one-third as often while looking at text on a computer monitor. Consider purchasing prescription glasses designed for reducing the strain of viewing computer screens. (See the Resource Guide.)

Also take a short one- to two-minute break and stretch at least every 20 to 30 minutes. Every hour, take a "micro break" from typing for at least five minutes and stretch, stand up, walk around or make a phone call. An exercise break is useful every one to two hours. In fact, there are even computer programs that you can preset that will pop up and remind you you've worked 30 minutes and it's time for a break or even help you go through a variety of such exercises. (See the Resource Guide.)

One study has shown that sitting still for long periods in cars, planes or trains can cause blood clots, even for people in good health. Hopefully, this wouldn't apply to sitting in the same position too long in front of a computer but why take a chance?

The bottom line is you need to do a variety of different activities throughout the day and breaks ensure that will happen.

Choosing and Using Your Computer, Peripherals and Office Equipment

Try it on for size is an important principle when shopping for workspace and computer equipment as well as for clothes. Never buy a chair from a catalog; you should "test sit" any chair you buy. When it comes to keyboards, mice and trackballs, you should play with them first. If a mouse or keyboard is standard issue with your computer and you're less than pleased, then go out and test drive some others and don't be afraid to switch.

I personally think that posture and positioning are critical factors in preventing RSI, carpal tunnel syndrome, tendinitis and "mouse shoulder." (The latter often results from reaching for a mouse and using it too much.) But good design of keyboards, mice, trackballs or electronic touch pads may be just as important and may also build in some positioning features.

The Importance of Positioning

Consider how you like to turn your body in relation to equipment. Do you prefer a computer directly in front of you, behind you or off to one side? Where do you want to place the copy stand and materials—on the left or right side of your computer? (I have my copy stand on the left, which seems ergonomically to make sense since we read from left to right). Most people just don't stop and think about the things that they use every day. Modular furniture systems, which are discussed in Chapter 7, help apply **ergonomics** to office furniture design.

Positioning and **placement** of equipment is an ergonomic factor that also relates to left- or right-handedness. At my Positively Organized! seminars I'll often ask participants whether their desk phone should go on the right or left side of the desk if they are right-handed. Answers are usually evenly divided between "left" and "right." The correct answer is "left." If you're right-handed you'll be writing with your right hand. So place the phone on the left so that the phone doesn't get in the way. You'll want to hold the phone with your left hand to your left ear, leaving your right hand free to write. (If you're using a telephone headset, placement may not be as critical.)

The accessibility principle

Since whatever you use the most often should be the most accessible, the accessibility principle should influence your decisions about equipment placement as well as supplies. Angle your computer, for example, off to the side for occasional use; place it right in front of you for frequent or constant use. As for supplies, even a work surface has areas that are more convenient than others; any supplies you use daily should be kept quite close without any reaching whatsoever.

Special Considerations for Laptops

Whatever type of computer you use, position it correctly, especially if you're using a laptop as a desktop substitute. Positioning becomes trickier with a laptop computer because the screen and keyboard are in one unit. With this fixed design, laptop users often have to hunch over their computers in uncomfortable positions. So what can you do, especially if you use your laptop quite a bit?

First, make sure you can see the screen without twisting your neck (more on this in the "Computer Displays" section coming up soon). Also consider using separate, *external* devices for the keyboard and mouse for better positioning as well as greater comfort.

Make sure your laptop isn't heating up too much for its own good or your lap's by using a protective pad or a laptop desk. Better yet, get a **cooling pad** with a fan that helps reduce your computer's temperature.

A final issue that's present just with laptops is the strain from carrying your computer. Since many of us carry along other devices and accessories (e.g., an extra battery and external backup drives), the computer plus all the extras can be too heavy to carry safely on your shoulder or at your side when traveling. That's where a computer bag on wheels can help lessen your load.

Desks and Other Work Surfaces

If you use one flat surface for both writing *and* keyboarding (typing), be aware that most people prefer a writing surface that's higher than their ideal typing surface height. Generally, people prefer their keyboard sitting on a surface that's 26 inches from the floor but a writing work surface that's 29 inches high. If you just use a flat work surface for both functions, that means you can't be at the best height at the same time for writing and keyboarding. That's why split-surface work designs, adjustable designs and keyboard/mouse tray systems can be helpful not only for different tasks but also for different-sized individuals who may share a work station.

An Ergonomic Phone Area

Set up a separate, clear phone area where you can handle calls without the distraction of other work. When you don't have to shuffle through other tasks and projects, you can really focus on each call. Your area should have enough writing surface and be close to your computer, paper files and other phone information you may need.

Phone equipment should ideally include: a clock (or if necessary, several clocks for different time zones); a timer (if you have trouble keeping track of time and length of calls or your phone doesn't have a call-length readout feature); a voice-mail system or an answering machine; a speaker phone with on-hook dialing, automatic onhook redialing and automatic memory dialing; and a **telephone headset** if you're on the phone at least two hours every day and/or you need your hands free for writing or keyboarding while on the phone. (See the Resource Guide.)

I've used a headset for years. The small price tag for a headset is certainly well worth it for convenience as well as for your health, too. A telephone headset can help prevent neck and back aches and trips to the chiropractor.

Use the speaker phone when you're on hold so you can do other work while waiting. You can also use it for a conference call in your office, provided that confidentiality or disturbing coworkers isn't a problem and the speaker phone sound quality doesn't bother the person(s) on the other end.

With today's cubicles, it can be difficult to have private conversations. Products are being developed to make phone conversations unintelligible to passersby. (See the Privacy section in Chapter 7.)

Chairs

Use a good **ergonomic chair** whose back and seat are adjustable. A good chair is more than a piece of furniture; it's a necessity for long hours of computer work. A bad one is literally a pain in the back. It is generally recommended that the back of the chair be at a reclined angle of 110 degrees and that you have support for both your upper and lower back. Experts differ on whether armrests help you or create problems. If your chair has armrests, they should be adjustable, allow your shoulders to be relaxed and support your arms in a natural position.

And if you're looking for an ergonomic chair that's ecological, too, check out the Steelcase **Think chair**—the multi-award-winning chair with a brain and a conscience. It's intelligent enough to understand how a person sits and is able to adjust itself intuitively. It's thoughtful enough to measure and minimize its lifelong impact on the environment. What's unique about this chair is that it uses parts that can be recycled many times and is manufactured in ways that are the least harmful to the environment; in doing so, Steelcase (**www.steelcase.com**) has taken a "cradle to cradle" approach.

Computer Displays (Monitors/Screens)

In general, you want your display to be as far away as possible and yet still be able to read screen text clearly. For most people, that means placing the display at least an arm's length away. Also make sure you get a display that can tilt the screen to adjust to the proper angle for your eyes.

Proper positioning

The first goal with displays is **keeping your neck relaxed** by not putting pressure or strain on it. That means you'll want the center of your display right in front of you so you're looking at it straight on without turning your back or neck. Generally, your eyes should be about two to three inches *below* the top of the display's case (not from the top of the screen itself) so you're not straining to hold your head up or down while you're typing. The screen should be at or slightly below eye level. The center of the display should generally be around 18 degrees below the horizontal level to let you see more of the screen at one time and see it comfortably. You may need to adjust the screen angle and height to get the right fit for you.

If you wear bifocals or blended glasses while using your computer, you may want to lower the display even more to your reading level to again avoid having to lift your head to do your typing. A better solution may be to get dedicated computer glasses that are optimized for use with a computer display.

If the height and angle of your LCD screen are hard to adjust, you may want to get an adjustable stand (see the Resource Guide).

Reducing glare, brightness and contrast

The second goal with displays is to **avoid eyestrain**. You can reduce glare by using an LCD screen and correctly positioning the screen to minimize glare from sources of light. Glare can be direct or reflected. You can reduce the glare from windows, overhead lights and task lights by putting the display at right angles to windows, adjusting the blinds or curtains, changing the screen angle and controls and using antiglare filters (if your display screen already doesn't have one). Depending on how they're angled and directed, task lights can increase or decrease glare.

You may need to **adjust the contrast and brightness** of your display. Be aware that eyestrain can also come from too much contrast. Laptops that feature very bright screens with a high contrast may produce too much glare for you. There are also ways to calibrate your display (see the Resource Guide).

Advantages of LCD screens

Smaller footprint LCD screens are becoming more popular than traditional, large CRT monitors. LCD screens offer ergonomic advantages in two main ways. First, LCD screens are easier on the eyes because they generally have less glare, are flicker free, are more adjustable and improve visual work performance by reducing visual search and reading times. Second, LCD screens do not emit electromagnetic radiation.

Do note, however, if your work includes displaying high-end graphics and videos, CRTs currently still do a better job in these areas.

Higher screen resolution and smaller font sizes

The trend is for screens to have a higher resolution. A higher resolution can increase your productivity by letting you put up more windows on a screen. The bad news is that as LCDs get larger in screen size (e.g., above 17 inches) with the same high resolution, text on the screen may shrink in size. If the text is too small, this could lead to eyestrain and also less productivity.

One easy approach to increase font size is through the zoom feature in your word processing program; start with a percentage of 100% and adjust it upward to a higher percentage.

There are other solutions, too, such as changing the setting for a lower screen resolution on the control panel, changing the font setting to a larger font or using the built-in *font smoothing* feature of the computer's operating system. Or use one of the software programs described in the Resource Guide to produce larger fonts.

Document stand

Ideally, place documents you're working with on a copy stand at the same angle as your screen and as close to it as possible. You want to avoid twisting your neck. Document stands come in a variety of styles and have special space-saving and design features (see the Resource Guide for some examples.)

Second displays and multidisplay software

Generally, your operating system software will allow you to run two displays off one computer (however, you may need to add a graphics card to do this). Some people run multiple applications to increase productivity, e.g., email on one display and a word processing program or an Internet browser on the other one. (See the Resource Guide for multidisplay software.)

Keyboards

Don't underestimate the importance of ergonomics in relation to your computer keyboard. In fact, your keyboard is one of the most important factors that determines just how happy you are with your computer as a whole.

Increased use of a computer keyboard can lead to RSI. Because no one keyboard or keyboard accessory is the right fit for everyone, listen to your body as you're using a keyboard to determine if it's right for you. And remember that an "ergonomic" keyboard may not necessarily be a good match and may, in fact, turn out to be worse for you than a regular keyboard.

Here's a "key" question to ask yourself: Do you like the touch and feel of the keys, the sound they make and the design of the keyboard? I like the touch and feel of the keys on my keyboard as well as the raised dashes on the "F" and "J" keys, which keep my fingers in correct alignment.

Remember, you can easily and inexpensively buy a replacement keyboard for your computer if you're not happy with the standard issue.

Positioning your keyboard and your wrists

Just as you need to line up your display correctly, the same holds true for your keyboard.

Position the most frequently used part of the keyboard with your display (for example, if you rarely use the numeric keypad portion off on the right side, you may want to center the rest of your keyboard so the "H" key lines up with the center of your body).

The keyboard height should allow your shoulders to be relaxed. An adjustable keyboard tray can help here. The tilt of your keyboard depends on how you are sitting. With keyboard trays that don't have enough room for a mouse, make sure you don't have to reach too far to get to your mouse.

When you're typing, your wrists ideally should be straight and level and not rest on anything. Avoid awkward angles. Your wrists should not be bent down, up or to the side. Avoid pounding the keys since that causes wear and tear on you.

Adapt a work surface that's too shallow with a **keyboard extender** or a **keyboard drawer** that mounts under the desktop and conveniently pulls out. Another type of keyboard drawer is a stand, sometimes made of steel, upon which you can place your display; underneath is a keyboard drawer that pulls out when in use. A keyboard drawer is a space saver and depending on the type, can be a good accessory to lower a keyboard that's too high for comfortable typing.

Articulating keyboard arms are similar to underdesk keyboard drawers but they usually have different adjustable positions.

Reducing keyboard stress

How you use your keyboard, especially if you use it many hours every day, can have an adverse physiological effect on your hands. There are several ergonomic measures you can take to prevent hand disorders such as tenosynovitis and carpal tunnel syndrome:

1. Take a five-minute break every hour to relax your hands.
2. Use a keyboard with programmable keys or macros. A **macro** allows you to use as few as two keystrokes to replace many keystrokes or mouse clicks. Macros are often part of your computer programs.
3. If you're using a laptop computer, see whether an external keyboard puts less pressure on your hands and wrists.
4. Try **voice recognition** to control computer commands and text dictation. Just be sure you don't overuse your voice and strain it (or have inadvertent comments typed into your text). A good way to proceed may be to combine voice recognition software (e.g., for a first draft) with your keyboard and a mouse (e.g., for edits). See the Resource Guide.

Word on wrist rests

Be careful if you select a wrist rest because it may not help you and may actually cause extra pressure on your wrist.

Mouse Tips

Here are some important ergonomic tips for a mouse.

Reduce the number of mouse clicks

Looking for an easy way to eliminate maybe 100 mouse-clicks per day? See if your operating system lets you substitute single-clicking for double clicking. Check out your control panel options.

Perhaps the best way to minimize mouse use is by using **keyboard shortcuts** (sometimes called "keyboard equivalents") for such tasks as bolding, italicizing, deleting or saving text instead of using your mouse for these tasks. To delete a word in Windows, for example, you can move the cursor by holding down the Control key and hitting an appropriate arrow key to get to the beginning of the word to be deleted. Then hold down the Control key and tap the Delete key.

Get the right fit

Get a mouse whose design fits your hand. Look for shapes and configurations that fit the size of your hands and fingers and for any features that reduce the amount of work your fingers, hands and arms need to do.

Try to get a mouse that is as flat as possible to reduce wrist extension. See whether a larger mouse helps you make arm movements rather than wrist movements. Ergonomic mice may help your wrist/hand posture. If you're left-handed, make sure you find a mouse that works for you. You may want a kid-sized mouse for your children to use. But remember that it doesn't matter how ergonomically designed a product is; the final selection boils down to personal preference because one size or style, no matter how ergonomic, does not fit all.

You may prefer a mouse with a wheel in the middle that makes scrolling down pages easier. (I love this feature on my mouse.)

No matter which mouse you select, don't hold your mouse too firmly or squeeze it. Use a light touch with a mouse, just as you should do with a keyboard.

Position your mouse correctly

Place your mouse close to your keyboard so you don't have to reach too far or upward to use it. (Too much reaching, you may recall, can cause "mouse shoulder.") Ideally, position a mouse on an angled platform just to the side of your keyboard or use a keyboard/mouse tray.

Look for accessories that will position your mouse as close to the keyboard as possible so that if you're using a keyboard tray, drawer or arm, you're not reaching for your mouse on the desktop. (See the Resource Guide.)

An external mouse may be more comfortable to use than using the built-in touch pad on a laptop computer—that's my preference anyway.

Resource Guide

Additional info on ergonomics

If you're looking for more information on ergonomics, visit these sites:
www.hfes.org
www.me.berkeley.edu/ergo
www.tifaq.com
To see the ergonomic guidelines of The Business and Institutional Furniture Manufacturers' Association, go to
www.bifma.org/standards/ergoguideline.html

Back support products

Relax the Back is a great store located nationwide and in Canada and has an online catalog of products to help you sit and sleep more comfortably. I've used their products at home and in my car.
www.relaxtheback.com

Computer equipment accessories

Ergotron provides flexible stands and other mounting solutions for digital displays and other computer peripherals to improve the human interface, enhance the viewing experience, reduce stress and improve productivity. Ergotron's portfolio of digital display mounting solutions includes wall and desk mount arms, desk stands, mobile carts, floor stands, pivots and vertical lifts. Ergotron, Inc. 800/888-8458 [MN] or **www.ergotron.com**

Fox Bay makes a number of keyboard, mouse, display and laptop accessories that may work for you. Fox Bay Industries, Inc., 800/874-8527 [WA] or **www.foxbay.com**

Kensington's **ClipNGlow Task Light and Copyholder** lets you clip a document to a holder attached to a CRT monitor or a laptop screen and provides task lighting, too—all in a fold-up device that's light for traveling. The Kensington **In-line Copyholder Underdesk Keyboard Drawer** maximizes valuable desk space and has a mouse platform. Take a look at these and other well-designed accessories at Kensington Computer Products Group, 800/535-4242 [CA] or **www.kensington.com**

Computer exercise and reminder software and printed materials

Don't be glued to your chair and desk. Take a short one- to two-minute stretch break every 20 to 30 minutes. Every hour, take a "micro break" from typing for at least five minutes and stretch, stand up, walk around, make a phone call or just relax.

Computer programs can be preset to pop up and remind you when it's time for a break or can even guide you through a variety of exercises. The following programs alert you once you've reached a certain time limit while working on the computer and provide stretching exercises.

Break Reminder, Chequers Software, Ltd, **www.cheqsoft.com**

ErgoEnterprise, Magnitude Information Systems, Inc., 888/786-7774 [NJ] or **www.magnitude.com**

ExerciseBreak, Hopkins Technology, LLC, 800/397-9211 [MN] or **www.hoptechno.com**

RSIGuard, Remedy Interactive, 831/421-0139 [CA] or **www.rsiguard.com**

Stretchware is the software program complementing a variety of practical printed exercise materials, including "Computer and Desk Stretches," which I use for breaks in my training programs. Stretching Inc., 800-333-1307 [CO] or **www.stretching.com**

Computer prescription glasses

PRIO eyeglasses are prescription glasses specifically designed to reduce or eliminate computer-related vision problems including eyestrain, blurred/double vision and fatigue while viewing a computer screen. PRIO Corp., 800/621-1098 [OR] or **www.prio.com**

Display software

DisplayMate is top-rated monitor diagnostic and calibration software that lets you adjust, set up, calibrate, tune up, test, evaluate and improve image and picture quality. Displaymate Technologies Corp., 800/932-6323, **www.displaymate.com**

nView is multidisplay software that lets you specify which applications appear on each monitor. nVidia, **www.nvidia.com**

Font and icon enlarging software

Liquid View increases the legibility of the Microsoft Windows interface regardless of your display's native resolution. The software lets you increase the size of items that are hard to read on your display. Desktop icons and fonts, your desktop toolbar, and Microsoft application toolbars can be resized with the touch of a button. **Liquid Surf** customizes the appearance of Web content by allowing you to increase or decrease the size of text and graphics within Internet Explorer. Portrait Display, **www.portrait.com**

Web Eyes can instantly change the text size and font of any website you visit. It's an Intenet Explorer plug-in that allows you to adjust type size instantly. ION Systems, Inc., **www.ionwebeyes.com**

Telephone headsets

Where do you buy a headset? Radio Shack has headsets, as do many stores that sell telephones and other electronic equipment. Look for headsets, telephone equipment and accessories in catalogs, too, such as the **Hello Direct** catalog (800/435-5634 [CA] or www.hellodirect.com). Office supply stores have them, also. I can't emphasize enough the importance of compatibility. Very often sales people will not be aware of compatibility problems, so either bring your phone to the store to check it out or if you order a headset, make sure it is completely refundable without any restocking or shipping/handling fee.

Voice recognition software

Dragon NaturallySpeaking has been the best voice recognition and dictation product for years. Nuance Communications, Inc., **www.nuance.com**

7

Workspace Essentials: Enhancing Your Physical Working Environment

Quick Scan: Before you start working on getting your desk and files in order in the upcoming chapters, make sure your overall workspace is optimized. Whether you're planning a move or you just have a sneaking suspicion your office design is missing the mark, this chapter will reveal the physical features your office should have for a more productive, comfortable environment. Many of these features are inexpensive and easy to implement. You'll be amazed to see how the little things can make a big difference in your office or home office.

D o you feel like everything in your workspace has been put in its place with Krazy Glue?

Once you get used to an office or work area, it usually feels pretty permanent. Everything seems as if it's always been there (and always will be). But when you become too used to your environment, you don't see the possibilities. Or if you do, you figure you can't do anything about them anyway.

I love the story that stockbroker Alan Harding shared at one of my seminars many years ago. Harding had wanted a window office. As he saw it though, he didn't need to change offices—he just needed to install a window in a wall that faced the outside. So Harding asked his boss to have a window installed but his boss refused. For most people that would have been the end of it.

Not for Harding. You see, he spent a good part of every day in that enclosed office. He had been with the company awhile and was planning on staying a good while longer. Since he really wanted that window, he decided to spend his own money to have one installed—to which his boss agreed.

But that's not the end of the story. After seeing how serious Harding was about the window, his boss then decided to chip in and split the cost. What's more, when Harding came in on a Saturday to physically do the installation, his boss ended up helping. Harding says, "The whole thing wound up as a cooperative effort." It's amazing what can happen when you keep open the "windows of your mind."

There are three types of physical factors related to your office over which you have some control: your physical space, your furnishings and your total environment.

How to Organize and Maximize Your Workspace

Look at where and how your workspace is organized. Two space factors come into play: location and layout.

Location, Location, Location

Where is your main work area located? It sounds like a simple enough question. But you probably could provide many answers.

For example, any of the following could be truthful responses: in my den, near the freeway, 40 miles from home, next to the water cooler, on the fifth floor, far away from clients or close to the marketing department.

The last time you probably thought about your location was when you changed jobs or moved to a different office or to a home office. But so often we just forget about location factors. We may even experience some irritation and not realize that the irritation is directly related to the location of our work area.

So just take a moment to think about the location of your work area, to see if there are some aspects that really bother you. Take this little survey. Next to each item, write "O" for Outstanding, "S" for

Satisfactory, "N" for Needs Improvement or "NA" for Not Applicable (or not important):

1. Commuting distance
2. Proximity to your market—clients, customers or patients
3. Proximity to vendors or suppliers
4. Proximity to colleagues
5. Traffic flow in or near your office
6. Privacy
7. Noise
8. Lighting
9. Proximity to equipment and supplies
10. Proximity to personal or professional services—e.g., restaurants, shops, attorney, accountant

Take a look at any "Ns" you've marked. Are there any ways you could change or modify undesirable locations? Don't just accept things the way they are, especially if your performance and productivity are really suffering. Be creative—like Alan Harding.

Latitude in Your Layout

Workspaces are shrinking and changing in their design. Spurred by a need to reduce rental costs and create a more egalitarian, team approach, large, open rooms with cubicles for everyone are replacing window offices for managers and windowless offices for the rest of the employees.

Keeping in mind the size limitations of your workspace, take a look at your **layout**—the location and arrangement of the furniture and equipment within your own workspace. There are two essentials of every good office layout: adequate **workspace** and **storage space**. Sometimes it's hard to tell, however, if work and storage spaces are adequate, especially if a desktop hasn't been seen in years, filing is less than routine and a move hasn't occurred in more than a decade.

Work vs. storage space

Differentiate between work and storage space. Unfortunately, in far too many offices, the distinction is nonexistent. Work and storage spaces are all lumped (and I do mean lumped) together. You'll be making great headway if you can separate these two basic spaces.

The biggest problem comes when your desktop becomes more a storage space than a workspace. Too often the desk becomes a place where things are waiting to happen; instead, make it a place for action. Think of your desk as an airport runway. If you were a pilot, you wouldn't find spare parts in the middle of the runway. They would be in the hangar. So, remove the obstacles from your work surface and **clear your desk for action!** Get out of the habit of keeping everything at your fingertips.

How do you break the keep-the-clutter-close habit? First, **set up appropriate systems for paperwork and projects** (see Chapter 8 on desktop management, Chapter 9 on paper files and Chapter 10 on managing "collectibles").

Second, **put only those items you use most frequently**—be they accessories, supplies, furniture or equipment—**closest to you**.

Third, make sure you have enough workspace! I generally recommend at least **two surfaces plus adequate, accessible storage space** for most people. The surface right in front of you should be your primary work surface and ideally should contain only things you use every day. This is the area where you are doing your most common work activities such as using your computer. A secondary surface off to the side or behind you could be used as a work area for a particular activity, such as telephoning (unless that's a primary work activity). This secondary area could also provide storage for items you use frequently such as your Daily Paperwork System and stapler.

Five layouts

Figure 7-1 shows four typical layouts.

An **L-shape** layout uses two surfaces—a primary one such as a desk and another one off to the left or right side at a right angle, which may be attached or free standing. It's easy to create an L-shape layout by putting a table alongside your desk. Or if you don't like using a desk at all, try two work tables at right angles.

A **U-shape** layout gives you more work surface and usually more accessible storage.

A **triangular** layout takes advantage of a corner, makes good use of angles and plays up the importance of the desk as a focal point.

A **parallel** layout places the main work surface, such as a desk, parallel to and in front of a storage unit (a credenza or lateral file cabinet, for example) or another work surface, such as a table.

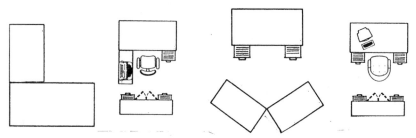

Figure 7-1. L-shape, U-shape, triangular and parallel layouts

I use a modified U-shape in my office—I call it a **J-shape**. I use modular computer furniture with work tables. I also use two two-drawer filing cabinets and a small bookcase that provide additional work surfaces and storage space. Figure 7-2 shows my office furniture in two, mirror-image layouts.

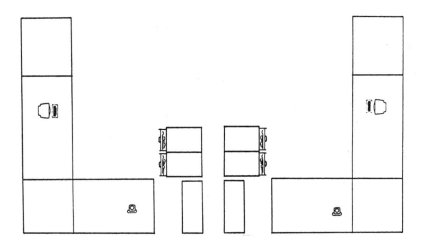

Figure 7-2. Because I have modular furniture, I've been able to use my J-shape layout and easily reverse it to better accommodate different offices.

Design your own layout

Get objective about an existing or proposed office layout. As with many other tasks, you can use a manual or a computerized approach.

Some business drawing and technical **diagramming software** programs such as **Microsoft Visio** have a space planning feature (see www.microsoft.com/office/visio).

Or if you're a paper-and-pencil kind of person, make a quick, little sketch of your layout. Or better yet, particularly if you're planning a move, buy some graph or engineering paper (quadrille pads work well), draw an outline of your office to scale and make **paper cutouts** of your furniture to scale. Cutouts work great if you have a small office space and your furniture is going to be a tight fit. Also, it's a lot easier moving cutouts around on paper than moving the real things. I've yet to see anyone throw out their back moving cutouts around.

Experiment—don't design yourself into a corner

Even if you're not moving, remember you're allowed to move things around. I consulted with a public relations executive who had one of the most beautifully designed and equipped offices I had ever seen. But she had been designed into a corner.

She had a huge pedestal desk, with a large, cumbersome chair. Behind her was a custom-built, corner credenza with all kinds of shelves and drawers, which she never used. Instead the surfaces of her desk and credenza were piled high with papers.

Why didn't she use the credenza? Simple—she didn't have enough space to easily move the chair and access the credenza. My solution: move the desk farther out from the credenza! Why hadn't she thought of moving the desk? Probably because the designer had indicated where the furniture was to go and there it remained. Also, the desk top was a heavy piece of glass. These factors suggested real permanence.

Alexis Kyprianou, a colleague of mine, related how she once had a boss who spent a lot of money on a design that wasn't functional. The boss insisted, "We'll make it work!" What he didn't realize was that it becomes *real* work when the design doesn't work.

Essential layout questions to ask yourself

Once people are in their offices or have been designed into a corner, the thought of changing a layout simply doesn't occur. Here's a chance to check out your layout. Quickly sketch out the main elements of your office space—furniture, equipment, walls, windows, light sources and plants. Don't worry about scale at this point. Ask yourself these questions:

- Do you have enough workspace including space for your equipment, especially your computer equipment?
- Do you have enough storage space?
- Is your layout convenient?
- Are the things you use most often close at hand?
- Do you like the way your office is configured to meet with others—coworkers, clients or customers?
- Does your layout invite irritating distractions? (For example, do you always catch someone's eye as he or she walks by?)
- Do you have different areas in your office for different types of work or activity, e.g., telephoning, computer work, meeting with clients? How and where do you like to do various kinds of work?

All of these factors may enter into the kind of office layout you can live with. Some of these factors are very subtle but their subtlety shouldn't diminish their importance.

Proxemics

One subtle layout factor concerns **proxemics**—the study of spatial configurations and interpersonal relations. Do you know that the seating arrangements in your office influence the relationships you have with your colleagues as well as your clients? Your seating arrangements make subtle statements. If, in the first example in Figure 7-3, you are "A," sitting behind your desk, and you're meeting with "B," you are in a distinctly authoritarian, powerful position. This configuration may be totally appropriate when meeting with a client but if you're meeting with a colleague, perhaps the side-by-side configuration in the next example would be more effective.

If you have meetings in your office and you tend to run meetings in which you assert your authority, you would select a rectangular table, as shown in the third example, and sit at the head. If, however, you tend to meet informally and you're trying to foster that "good ol' team spirit," select a round table. Of course space considerations as well as purpose will affect your final layout decisions.

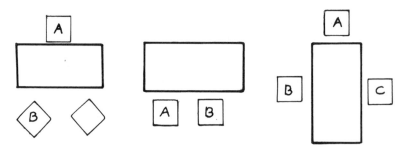

Figure 7-3. These three seating arrangements make three statements.

The doorway

Decide, too, where to place your desk in relation to the doorway. If you're facing the doorway (or the opening of your cubicle) and you're in a heavy foot-traffic zone, you may find interruption is your constant companion. Turning your back to the doorway may appear too severe or even antisocial. You may prefer instead to angle your desk so as not to catch everyone's eye but to remain responsive.

When Kim Villeneuve was a divisional vice president for a major department store in Southern California, she changed her position toward the doorway, depending on the type of work she was doing. Since she needed to remain open to staff most of the day, she generally sat facing the door. But when she used the telephone and didn't want interruptions, she would swing her chair around to the credenza behind her. Her telephone sat on the credenza, where she did her phone work without inviting interruption. The credenza became an area designated for important telephone work, without interruptions of people as well as any distracting paperwork on her desk.

The closed door and other signals for your home office

It's hard to work at home if you're continually interrupted by children or a spouse. Here are a few tips to help you complete your work. First, close your office door when you're working. Let that be a signal that it's work time. Second, have regular office hours or use a sign on the outside of the door that says when you'll be available for nonwork matters. And consider having a clock there, too, to help children know when you'll be finished working.

Your evolving work style

Finally, when you design your layout, consider how you like to work and remain flexible. As your work style needs change, so should your design.

Dr. David Snyder, a physician in Fresno, California, had a desk in his private office with a credenza behind him. Then he eliminated the credenza. He used his desk to process patient files and other paperwork quickly and efficiently. He said, "I will never have a credenza again—that's where I put stuff I didn't have time to do."

Today he has added a two-drawer lateral filing cabinet behind him. The close proximity of the cabinet gives him access to reference files. He uses the top of the cabinet for his Daily Paperwork System, which includes a vertical rack that holds active project files.

Furnishings That Fit Your Needs

Walk into your office as if you were walking into it for the first time. Pretend you've just arrived from Mars. (Some days don't we all feel that way!) Look at your office with fresh eyes and notice all your furnishings—your furniture, equipment, accessories and supplies.

Are they all well-organized, in good repair and well placed? Are they as functional as they should be? Do you have enough storage space? Do you have a good ergonomic arrangement? (For more on the latter, see Chapter 6).

Furniture and Equipment

With today's changing technology, workforce and workplace location, *flexibility* is a key word to apply to your choice of furniture and equipment. **Modular** furniture (often called "systems furniture") with interchangeable components works great, particularly in today's smaller offices, because it's flexible, can save floor space and yet can increase the amount of work surface.

The flexibility and functionality of modular furniture is particularly important if you'll ever be moving your office. Since buying modular furniture for my office, I have moved five times. Each of my offices required a different configuration. Figure 7-2 shows how I was able to take my original configuration from one office and simply reverse the components to fit another office space.

Figure 7-4 shows an illustration of modular furniture. Notice how the combination of a single compact pencil drawer and notched side panels provide for completely unobstructed leg-room, protecting knees when swiveling to different areas. If you have a mini-tower computer CPU (central processing unit—the main box containing your computer) on the floor, place it where it won't obstruct your leg room, such as under a connector, which is shown in the figure.

If you need more drawers, consider getting a portable drawer unit or file cabinet on casters which is also shown in Figure 7-4. Sometimes such portable units are called **pedestals** and come in different styles. Some consist of two file drawers and function as a two-drawer file cabinet on casters. Other models, especially underdesk units, may come with one utility drawer and one file drawer.

Some modular work tables come with recessed, half-depth shelves underneath for storage that don't obstruct your movement.

As for equipment, a laptop computer or a desktop computer with a smaller footprint can free up valuable desk space. Also, if you're short on space, it may be time to look at an all-in-one **multifunctional device (MFD)**—a multipurpose machine that combines a computer printer, a copier, a scanner and sometimes a fax machine. (If you have heavy copying, faxing or printing needs, check to see whether having separate, standalone pieces of equipment designed for higher volumes may be better.)

Figure 7-4. Modular computer work station components and accessories

Modular systems we've been discussing are a fine example of applying **ergonomics** to office furniture design. For more on ergonomics, the science of making the work environment compatible with people so they can work more comfortably and productively, see Chapter 6.

Accessories and Supplies

In my consulting work I notice that clients either have too few or too many accessories for their paperwork, telephone and computer. Those who have too few generally lump their work all together on the desk, on tables, on shelves, in drawers and on the floor. Those with too many (if one pencil holder is good, six are better) collect accessories along with good intentions. They buy a new accessory every time they're inspired to "get organized." Soon the accessory becomes just another catchall rather than a clearly defined tool. The original purpose is too soon forgotten.

Remember, to keep it simple; sometimes the simplest, least expensive accessories can save you a lot of money. You might even avoid the "$12,000 paper clip." It's the little things that count as one man found out after losing two $12,000 copiers because of paper clips that somehow became lodged inside. This man now uses a $3 magnet attached to a piece of Velcro tape on his copier to hold paper clips. (By the way, we use Velcro tape to attach a writing instrument to each of our office phones or any place where a pen or pencil has a way of just walking off by itself.)

Any time you add a new accessory to your environment, define its purpose and *get in the habit of using it*. And from time to time, check to see if it's doing its job. If it has outlived its usefulness, get rid of it!

Let's look at some of the most useful workspace accessories (see also chapters 4, 6, 8, 9 and 10 as well as this chapter's Resource Guide).

Computer accessories

Straighten up your computer cables and wires—for aesthetics as well as safety—with cable management accessories.

To guard against the possibility of electrical power disturbances wiping out data, use a **surge protector**, also called a **surge suppressor**. Typically, you use a surge protector for computers and printers but it's also useful for copy machines, faxes and other equipment. Service calls fell by 51 percent at Arizona State University after surge protectors were installed on copy machines.

Surge protectors help prevent hardware damage and data loss. Some models add phone protection that prevents spikes and surges from reaching your modem, fax, answering machine and other telecommunications equipment via phone lines. Surge protectors that allow your computer to power up even after a voltage spike make your computer susceptible to a second spike. That's why you want to look for a surge protector that has a warning indicator that is UL 1449 safety certified.

Uninterruptible power supplies keep the power going to your computer even when the electricity fails because of a blackout or a power failure. This can prevent the loss of data by allowing you to save your work.

While we're on the topic of managing energy and computers, many people mistakenly believe that computers and other equipment will last longer if they are left on all the time. They not only will not last longer but they will also use up more energy. So, if you don't plan to use a computer for at least an hour, turn it off (or use an **energy-saving option** such as "standby" or "hibernate") to save energy and to prolong the life of the equipment. By the way, screen saver programs do not save energy.

Paperwork accessories

One of the most versatile paperwork accessories is the **expanding collator** (see Figure 8-1 in Chapter 8 for an illustration). It comes in plastic or aluminum with 12, 18 or 24 slots. If you're a CPA or an attorney, use it for large, bulky active client files that you're referring to daily or several times a week. (While it's always safer to put client files away each night in filing cabinets, using the collator is a good intermediate step for anyone who is still piling files on couches and floors.)

In addition, use the collator near your copier or printer to store different types of paper. You can always use the collator for its original purpose, too—collating! It's great for assembling or sorting literature and handouts.

The **stationery holder** is a wonderful accessory to hold letterhead, envelopes, forms and note paper. Some stationery holders are designed to fit inside a desk drawer; others sit on top of furniture or on a shelf. Place a stationery holder where you'll be using it.

Magazine files or **holders** are indispensable boxes for storing magazines, catalogs and directories as well as current project files. They're usually made out of plastic, acrylic or corrugated fiberboard. (See Figure 4-2 in Chapter 4 for an illustration.)

When you type, use a **copyholder**. Get one that can be placed at the same focal distance as the screen; otherwise, it's hard on the eyes to keep refocusing to accommodate different focal lengths. Some copyholders are free standing; others can mount to either side of a computer display screen. Look for copyholders made by Fellowes, Kensington and 3M and also see Chapter 6.

If you have wall partitions, consider installing a **wall unit paper management system**. As office space decreases into more flexible, partitioned "cubicles," using vertical wall space for accessories makes sense. Wall systems help you get paper off your desk and yet make it accessible and organized.

If you do a lot of hole punching, stapling, folding or trimming, consider getting accessories to help you automate these processes. **Electric hole punchers** and **staplers** and **letter folding machines** can save you a lot of time and reduce the stress on your body.

Don't forget about **color coding**. Simple, small **colored adhesive dots** on locks and matching keys will help you save time, too.

Keeping supplies in order

Deciding what supplies to buy isn't as much a challenge as keeping your supplies organized and stocked. The following will help:

- Organize your supplies for easy access, keeping the most frequently used most accessible.

- Group supplies by type as well as by frequency of use.

- Label supply shelves, drawers or cabinets and/or use color coding.

- Replenish supplies regularly and systematically and have one person per work group in charge of the ordering process; you may want to use a special office supply order form (paper-based or online) that includes typical supplies to check off and pertinent time frames, e.g., when supplies are ordered and when they're needed.

- Place a reorder chart near supplies for people to indicate special requests or whenever a supply is getting low.

- Place reorder slips strategically close to the bottom of supply boxes: whoever gets a slip turns it in to the person who orders supplies.

- Prepare a "frequently ordered items" form for each vendor you use, listing items and stock or catalog numbers; refer to these forms to speed up the reordering process.

- If you use forms in your office, consider putting the master on an overhead transparency sheet and placing it on the bottom; that way no one will use the last form and the master is always within easy reach to make more copies.

With regard to printer paper and toner cartridge supplies, I'd like to recommend that you use recycled products but you should check with your printer manufacturer. Your printer warranty may not cover damage from a remanufactured cartridge or from using recycled paper. Major printer manufacturers and office supply stores have instituted model programs for recycling used cartridges so those cartridges don't end up in the trash; often there's an incentive involved, too, such as coupons or free reams of paper.

As for paper, there is a definite move to switch to recycled paper. The entire California court system for one has mandated "the use of recycled paper for all original documents filed with California courts." Knowing that 50 percent recycled paper is less likely to jam than 100 percent may help but you should still ask your manufacturer(s) what is best for your printer as well as your copier.

Making Your Total Work Environment Work for You

How do you feel about your workspace? Do you feel comfortable there? Is it you? Is there something about it that rubs you the wrong way (or the right way)?

Aesthetics, air, comfort, safety, lighting and privacy—these are some of the important environmental factors that affect how you feel about your workspace. See how much you're aware of these and other factors and whether there are any you should modify.

Aesthetics

If you spend at least one third of every week day in your workspace—
that's at least eight hours a day—you deserve to have a working
environment that's aesthetically pleasing.

Color

Many studies have revealed the "psychology of color," showing the effect
of color on our emotions and state of mind. They have found, for
example, that red excites us; in fact, when red is used in restaurants it is
supposed to make us salivate! But used in moderation, red can be a great
accent color, particularly for a sales or marketing office where you want
an upbeat atmosphere.

Blue is perhaps the most universally pleasing color and is generally a
calm color, depending on the shade, of course. Grays, browns and other
neutrals are even more subdued. All three can work well in professional
offices.

Burgundy and deep forest green are rich colors that can work well
together or separately in professional offices, too. They can be used as
main or accent colors.

Use of "trendy colors" can give a more contemporary feeling, which
may be important for your type of office. You do run the risk, however,
of having those colors go out of style more quickly. Use of more
traditional colors and color schemes avoids this problem and may convey
a more permanent, solid business environment. Base color decisions on
the nature of your business, who comes into your office and your own
particular preferences.

Choose light and dark colors to enhance your space. Lighter colors
tend to open up space and work well in smaller offices. Darker colors
make rooms feel smaller, cozier and more intimate. They work well in
large office spaces that could otherwise appear too intimidating or sterile.

Don't ignore the impact of color. The question to ask is: What are
the right colors for you and your office?

Personalization

Color alone is not enough. Your office is not just a place to work. It
should be a reflection of you. It needs to be personalized with objects

you love, such as art, photos or plants. Just remember, they should complement, not clutter, your workspace.

If you've become bored with your office, consider moving personalized objects to different places. We all need variety; just moving things around or changing objects from time to time can make a big difference.

And remember what Tom Henschel of Essential Communications says, "Every object you put in your workplace, beyond standard issue furniture, tells a story about you...You're designing a non-verbal portrait of yourself that will speak as loudly as any of your actions."

Air

What can you do about the air you breathe? First of all, be aware of it. Second, see if you can change any unpleasant atmospheric conditions or adapt to them.

Airborne toxins

The most obvious toxin in the air is cigarette smoke. Some studies have shown that cigarette smoke is more harmful to someone nearby inhaling "secondary" smoke than the smoke inhaled by the actual smoker. If smoke is a problem for you, stay away from it!

Many cities and companies now specify that smokers must go outside or to other specially designated areas to smoke. If your city or company doesn't have such requirements, consider working toward establishing them. Sure it'll take some of your precious time, but isn't your health precious enough? At the very least, make sure that office workers who smoke have an air cleaner or purifier unit on their desk to remove at least some of the smoke.

As far as other toxic substances, such as asbestos, read your newspaper to stay current on new discoveries and legislation. Notice, too, whether you experience certain symptoms such as nausea and dizziness only in your office environment. Invisible toxic substances pose a real problem in detection and in identification but we're bound to see more research on this in the future.

One estimate put nearly a third of all new office buildings at risk of indoor air quality problems. Consider putting in some plants. A study by NASA found that plants can remove up to 87 percent of toxic indoor air within 24 hours.

Plants can absorb common office pollutants such as formaldehyde and trichloroethylene. According to the book *50 Simple Things Your Business Can Do to Save the Earth*, use at least one four-to-five-foot plant per 100 square feet. Good plants to use with fluorescent lighting include: philodendrons, golden pothos, English Ivy, peace lily and mother-in-law's tongue. Spider plants and flowering plants such as azaleas and chrysanthemums work well with more light. Before purchasing plants, ask whether they are poisonous (small children may be in your office occasionally or more frequently).

If you're planning to move your office to a new location, consider the air quality there, too.

And here are a couple of reliable resources on toxins: (1) Agency for Toxic Substances and Disease Registry, **www.atsdr.cdc.gov** and (2) EPA Toxic Substance Control Act assistance line, 202/554-1404.

Temperature

Here's one of those factors that is far easier to adapt to than to change. I can't tell you how often I have complained to facilities managers about the temperature, which for me is almost always too cold in modern buildings, where you are at the mercy of a thermostat that either isn't working or is adjusted to somebody else's body!

I used to work for an aerospace company. Our department was on the same thermostat as the computer room. It was always "freeeezing" in the office. I kept a little portable heater on under my desk. (Fire regulations where you work may prohibit this solution.)

I've had offices where I've had to keep an extra sweater in the office at all times, particularly during the summer when the air conditioning tends toward the cool side. Another option is to close off most of the vents in your office in the summertime when the air conditioning is running fast and furiously. If your office is too hot, your only option may be to keep complaining or work at home if possible. But recognize that temperature is a factor in your productivity and your attitude toward your workplace.

Comfort and Safety

Fifty percent of disabling office accidents are the result of slips or falls—most of which could have been prevented.

Keep floors clear of cords, cables and other objects. Even a rubber band on the floor can be a hazard. One office worker slipped on a rubber band, breaking his arm in two places and crushing his elbow. He lost six weeks of work.

Our discussion of ergonomics in this chapter certainly relates to comfort and safety. Check out your chair and your equipment according to the ergonomics criteria discussed in Chapter 6.

I recommend that whether you work for yourself or someone else you should become more responsible for your own safety. Learn what you can to protect yourself. If an employer doesn't provide what you need, you may wish to provide it for yourself or look for another more ergonomic workplace.

Lighting

Lighting is related to comfort and safety, as well as aesthetics. Select the right **amount**, the right **kinds** and the right **direction** to make lighting work best for you.

Make sure you have enough light. Some offices are too dark and depressing. Interior offices usually need additional lighting. That one panel in the ceiling just won't do it.

Make sure you don't have too much of the wrong kind of lighting in the wrong places. If you're using a computer terminal, all those overhead fluorescent lights could be causing irritating glare. Better to use a lower level of overhead lighting combined with **task lighting**, localized sources of lighting for specific tasks or areas. An example of task lighting is a desk lamp that sheds light on desktop paperwork only and stays off the computer screen. Another possibility is to use filter tubes that fit over fluorescent bulbs.

Balance fluorescent lighting with either a natural light source (a window) or incandescent lighting. Fluorescent lighting by itself is very hard on the eyes.

In addition, some research studies indicate fluorescent lighting may be emitting harmful ultraviolet rays that cause such symptoms as fatigue and dizziness. Some retail stores are putting **ultraviolet shields** on their fluorescent lights.

You may also consider replacing your fluorescent lighting with **full spectrum lights**. Full spectrum lighting is defined as a light source that replicates natural sunlight. Such lighting can reduce glare, increase productivity, operate cooler and increase feelings of well being due to the simulation of natural sunlight.

Noise

It's becoming more common for offices to have open plan layouts that don't have separate, walled offices. While this openness can save on rent and create an environment that encourages teamwork, it can also create a noisy environment. Here are a few tips to reduce the noise factor.

Position telephones so coworkers don't face each other. Use ceiling tiles and acoustic materials that are noise reduction efficient or use cubicle panels with additional fabric. Have taller partitions (at least four to six feet high) or add sound-absorbing bunting to ceilings to create barriers.

Have sound-masking systems with **white noise**, which produce a sound similar to moving air. And if you work with a laptop computer, you may be able to move, at least temporarily, to a quieter location.

Privacy

The last environmental factor concerns the need for privacy in your office. Privacy usually comes from some sense of enclosure, which can include visual as well as sound barriers. Having some barriers, be they walls, movable panels, plants, bookcases or file cabinets, is important for most people.

For one thing, effective communication needs privacy. Studies have shown that employees who sit in an open, "bullpen" environment tend to communicate less freely. On the other hand, employees who have some measure of enclosure and privacy tend to communicate more freely and openly.

Privacy also can improve productivity. Most people need to have their own space to focus, concentrate and shut out some of the distractions. A smaller, more controlled environment is also less stressful for most people.

Privacy can also come from knowing conversations are protected and private. One product, **Babble**, can make the content of your phone conversations unintelligible to passersby. Babble changes how other people hear your voice. It is designed to make your voice sound like a small crowd in a restaurant where no one outside your workspace can pick out specific words or understand your actual spoken words. The manufacturer is Sonare Technologies, (**www.sonaretechnologies.com**), a Herman Miller Company (**www.hermanmiller.com**)

Resource Guide

Furniture and Equipment

Whenever possible, see furniture and equipment "in person." At the very least, get fabric samples or color chips of the finish. Never buy a chair without sitting in it first.

Steelcase (**www.steelcase.com**) makes a wide range of high quality office furniture and equipment products.

Wright Line, LLC (800/225-7348 [MA] or **www.wrightline.com** is a good resource for its modular office, multimedia and IT (information technology) furniture and equipment.

Accessories and Supplies

Allsop Inc. manufactures a line of computer and office equipment accessories and supplies that include disk storage and computer cleaning kits. 800/426-4303 (WA) or **www.allsop.com**

CDW's catalog offers computers, supplies, accessories and data communications products. 800/750-4239 [NJ] or **www.cdw.com**

DYMO makes RhinoPRO handheld industrial printers that are great for printing labels for your computer and peripheral cables and many other items. **www.dymo.com**

Hello Direct is an excellent catalog of telephone productivity tools that I have used and recommend. 800/435-5634 [CA] or **www.hellodirect.com**

Secure-It, Inc. makes a variety of anti-theft locks and cables to help you prevent the theft of valuable computers and peripherals. 800/451-7592 [MA] or **www.secure-it.com**

8

Mastering Your Desk and the Paper Jungle

Quick Scan: If you're inundated with the "pile system" on your desk, if your work area is steadily shrinking into nonexistence and if desktop clutter has got you down and under, this chapter is for you. Learn why your desk represents the single most important part of your office, how to make it work for you and what to do about paperwork. Be sure to also check out the Resource Guide for additional resources, products and services.

D o you know where your desk is? This question is usually good for some chuckles at my seminars. The problem is most people can't even find their desk. It's under here somewhere....

You're not alone. You and 60 million other people in the U.S. have a desk of some kind. When I refer to a desk, I mean any piece of furniture that is used as your primary working surface. It may be a large executive model in a traditional office setting, a computer work station or a spare table in a bedroom corner.

Chances are good you spend many hours every day at your desk. Why not have it be the best functioning desk around? And when you're doing your New Year's Resolutions keep in mind that the second Monday of each January is National Clean Off Your Desk Day.

The Myth of the Messy Desk

No matter what you've seen on coffee cups, **a clean desk is the not the sign of an empty mind!** I know those coffee cup clichés will try to tell you otherwise. But don't be fooled. Most people think and act more clearly at a clean, well organized desk.

Don't fall prey to the false notion that a messy desk means you're busy because you look busy. The reasoning is that if you look busy, you're productive. Take the advice of B. W. Luscher, Jr., from the U.S. Postal Service, who warned: "Don't confuse activity with productivity."

What a Messy Desk Communicates

Far from indicating productivity, a messy desk signals a lack of dependability, control and focus, not to mention incomplete work, missed deadlines and lost information.

One manager told me about an employee who had a ton of stuff on her desk. As the manager put it, "All those piles of paper told me she was in trouble."

While the woman was on vacation, the manager went in and saw a six-month-old check lying there with a bunch of invoices. He also discovered an important letter to 20 people that had never gone out. The letter was to announce a meeting the manager had planned. The manager found the 20 letters stuck in a drawer together with papers to be filed. All the letters had been typed and the envelopes addressed. All the employee had had to do was mail the letters! When the employee returned from vacation, she was devastated to learn of her mistake—she could have sworn she had mailed the letters.

What was her problem? The manager says it was a combination of many things. She was very social, always wanting to know what was going on with other people and didn't take care of her own business. The manager observed, "You've got to worry first about what's on your own desk." He also said, "You've got to be a team player and let someone know if you're falling behind." In a nutshell, what she didn't have were the right organizational systems—the right tools and habits that signify a pro who is organized to be her best.

The fact is you are not more productive when you're working out of a cluttered desk. Besides feeling stress, you're continually distracted by all the different papers, piles and objects that keep pulling at you. It's easy to go into sensory overload as your eyes keep flitting from thing to thing and your mind keeps worrying whether you're working on the right task. No wonder you're exhausted at the end of each day!

Here's a general rule of thumb: don't have more than one open paper file on your desk at any given time. You'll be more productive and also prevent papers from slipping into the wrong file. When it comes to desks, a variation of Parkinson's Law seems applicable: your stuff expands to fill the available space.

Think of a clean desk as a little gift you give yourself.

Not a Storage Locker

Do not use your desktop for storage. It's a work surface, not a storage locker. Keep it clear, ready for action. Your desktop is prime workspace and should contain only those items you use every day such as your computer, phone(s), mobile device, planner and possibly a clock. Keep your desk as clean as possible.

But how clean is clean? That depends on a number of factors. First, consider who sees your desk. Colleagues? Clients? Customers? Patients? What kind of image do you want to present to these people? It's quite possible your desk should be spotless before the public but can be more of a workhorse before other staff members.

Incidentally, if you're concerned with image, consider this: research reveals that the cleanest desks belong to those individuals higher up in the organization. If you're on an upwardly mobile career path, have your desk look the part.

Second, consider what your level of aesthetics and function dictates. Start to become conscious of what your ideal level of order is and work toward it.

Some people really are more comfortable with clutter and claim they would dry up in an orderly, "sterile" environment. Neatness counts but neat isn't always organized or necessary. If you're one of those people who prefer "organized clutter," more power to you.

Most people, though, have simply never tried working in a clutter-free setting for more than a day or so. The expression "try it, you'll like it" certainly applies here.

The Paper Explosion

Like most people, you're probably suffering from a paper explosion that never seems to let up. Despite computers, or rather because of them, we have more paper than ever before.

Here are some interesting statistics: (a) 700 pounds of paper are consumed by the average American each year, (b) Washington, D.C., the world's paper capital, consumes so much copier paper that if laid end to end it would reach to the moon and back nine times over, (c) 115 billion sheets of paper are used annually for personal computers and (d) a 50 percent increase in worldwide paper consumption is expected by 2010.

The amount of paper is even affecting office layouts. Rows of taller file cabinets are sometimes being used as space dividers.

The problem with paper is three-fold: first, we produce paper documents faster and more easily now; second, there is a greater amount of easily available information from the Internet; and third, many of us still crave hard copies because we like the look and feel of paper documents.

The Pluses of Paper

Having taught memory as well as organization skills for years, I believe that paper can assist both organization and memory especially for those who rely more on visual memory. Paper provides more visual cues. If, for example, you have a photographic-style memory you may remember such things as the color of a paper, design of a logo or presence of a handwritten, attached note; these are some of the distinctive visual cues that can make a document stand out and be "memorable."

And don't discount the tangible factor of paper—the touch and feel of it—especially for "kinesthetic learners" who need to actually perform a physical activity (such as handling paper) to help with learning and memory.

Computerize More of Your Paperwork

Despite the pluses of paper, you may still want to reduce paperwork by using computers more extensively and at the same time resisting the temptation to make all those hard copies. Instead, when the urge to print out hard copy seizes you, back up your work on an external hard drive or other backup medium more religiously instead. Also, when you see an interesting article online, save it to your disk (in an articles folder on that subject) instead of printing it out. Having articles on a disk may make them faster to find and will save paper, too.

Many years ago I read an article in *PC World* magazine entitled "The Less-Paper Office" *not* the paperless office. Although we are still a ways from the paperless office, the article encouraged readers to embrace computerized work solutions. I have included computerized solutions throughout this book that can help you reduce or eliminate paper. You can put your calendar and contacts on computer or a mobile device (Chapter 4); use email or instant messaging (Chapter 5); use scanners as discussed in this chapter along with document management (Chapter 9); and do document sharing and editing where two or more people work off the same document on computers (Chapter 17).

Scanners and Software

A great solution to getting those papers off your desk is scanning them directly into your computer. The scanner market has really grown and with good reason. The prices have come way down and the quality has gone up.

Make sure the software that comes bundled with the scanner can handle your text and graphic needs. You may also separately purchase document management software that helps you organize, file and retrieve scanned documents.

Scanners can scan paper into editable word processing documents or spreadsheets without tedious retyping. Scanners can recognize photocopies, faxes, small and large text, color and black-and-white images, multi-column documents, tables and spreadsheets.

Some scanner software allows you to manage scanned files and images for many applications by putting them in organized folders similar to the system of your operating system's file management software. The software can also index words in document files to allow speedy searches to locate the right file. You can also use another approach, desktop search programs (see Chapter 12) to index an entire hard disk and find files anywhere on the disk.

Business card scanners have come a long way, too.

How to Turn Your Desk Into a Self-Cleaning Oven

Clients chuckle knowingly whenever I tell them, "Your desk is not a self-cleaning oven." They realize that they need to do something. Even with a self-cleaning oven, there are steps you need to take for it to work effectively: wipe up major spills, remove cookware and set the controls. So, too, there are steps to take with your desk to make it more automatic.

Clear a Path

The first step is "clearing a path," as one of my clients described the process of thinning out the paper jungle and cleaning out the deadwood from her desktop and work area.

Think of yourself as an air traffic controller and your desktop as the runway. You're in charge. You determine which papers, piles, and projects can land on your desk—and stay there.

Use the accessibility principle

I once had a client who sent me a snapshot of his terribly cluttered desk and office before we began working together. The caption read, "My office...where everything in the whole world is at my fingertips!"

Don't use your desk as one giant tickler system. You needn't be afraid that if papers and projects are out of sight, they'll be out of mind provided you use a Positively Organized! system every day (including a Daily Paperwork System first described in Chapter 4 and also in this chapter) to manage your time, info and communications.

Beware of the feeling that everything has to be so accessible. How many of those things on your desktop do you actually use every day? Every week? Every month? Every year? Make a list of the things you use every day. Of those things, which need to be sitting on your desktop? See if there isn't a better place, one that's accessible, but not on top of you.

Accessibility is the key word. It's the frequency of use that should determine accessibility. How often are you using all of your items? Maybe you started out using an item every day in the past and at some point you stopped. But there the item remains. As a general rule, **the more often you use an item, the more accessible it should be.** Give your desk an Accessibility Survey. Sort the items on your desk into the following categories of usage: daily, several times a week, once a week, once a month, a few times a year and rarely or never.

Remember, the frequency of use determines the proximity and accessibility an item should have. Keep close at hand only those things you're using every day or several times a week.

Begin to sort

The Accessibility Principle lets you see the big picture on your desk. Now you're ready to start sorting and grouping papers and other items on your desk, such as supplies and mementos, using another principle: **things that you use together or that require similar action, go together**.

As you sort through papers and other items, start grouping them into broad categories by asking yourself questions such as the following:

1. Do you see active paperwork or files you're using daily or several times a week? Put them on one area of your desk for now. Attach a self-adhesive, removable sticker to label this and the other temporary piles you will sort.

2. Do you see "reminder" papers with information that should be recorded elsewhere, such as your calendar, planner, phone book, mobile device or computer? If you can do it quickly, transfer this information; if not, stack these papers together.

3. Are there any items of indecision that are sitting on your desk because you haven't decided when to handle them or what to do with them? These items make up what attorney Robert Span calls the "problem pile." Pull them together.

4. Do you see reference or resource items that somehow landed on your desk and remained? File them now if you can do it quickly or put them in an area or box for filing later.

5. Is there material to read—maybe magazines, books or reports? Separate personal from professional reading. When possible, tear out articles you wish to read and recycle the rest of the publication.

6. Are there personal items related to a hobby or an interest that belong elsewhere?

7. Are there any supplies and equipment on your desk? Separate them by function and by frequency of use.

The trick is to start categorizing and prioritizing everything on your desk, focusing most of your attention on your active, action paperwork and projects and clearing away the clutter. See how many things you can remove from your desktop and store in other places. Even for items you use every day, don't clutter your primary work surface by putting them all on your desktop. They could still be very accessible in a drawer, on a credenza or on a table to the side. Remove any items you don't use at all.

Set Up a Daily Paperwork System

Now that you've cleared away some items and have begun to sort your desktop paperwork, you may be wondering, "Now where I am going to put this stuff?" When you don't know where to put papers, they inevitably end up staying on your desk or in the in-box on your desk. You may also be making extensive use of the "pile system," which has a way of spreading to every available horizontal surface in your work area. Piles add to confusion and create a sense of work overload.

Let's face it: most of us were never "paper trained." Setting up appropriate categories and containers in a Daily Paperwork System (DPS) can help. The DPS doesn't take the place of your filing system, which is discussed in detail in Chapter 9. The DPS is for active paperwork that you process on a daily basis. It is a set of tools and habits to help you manage your paperwork, projects and desk.

Categorize papers

Begin by categorizing types of papers that come your way most often. Typical categories might include: "Action" (this week), "Financial," "Correspondence," "Calls," "Staff," "Reading," "Filing" and "Pending." You might also include specific project names for active projects you're working on every day. Using the initial groupings you've already created as a guide, make a list of basic category names you could use for your everyday paperwork.

If you're having trouble thinking of ones that fit your needs, try this simple exercise. Next time you process your paperwork, have some 3-by-5-inch index cards handy. Go through your paperwork, making decisions about what to keep and what to toss. (For many people this is the most difficult part. Be willing to get in the habit of freely tossing—more on this in Chapter 9). On an index card, jot down the major category for each type of paper you're keeping (e.g., "Reports," "Must do today"). A broad category name will often describe the general type of activity or level of urgency. Do this for one day or a few days if you have a lot of paperwork.

Go through the cards and **select the broadest, the most general categories you'll use every day.** See if some of them can be combined. A category is a good one if you'll use it just about every day. Remember the purpose of these categories is for general sorting, not filing of paperwork.

Set up a trial paperwork system

After you've decided on your basic categories, set up the tools of your DPS using existing file folders, boxes, caddies or organizers. Label these containers with your categories. Ideally, get as much off your desk as possible. Containers should be accessible but they shouldn't crowd your space.

Set up a trial paperwork system. Buy a package of assorted colored, "third-cut," manila folders at your local stationery store. (The cut refers to the width of the tab in relation to the folder; third-cut folders have large tabs that are cut one-third the width of the folders.) See what you already have on hand in terms of boxes, trays and caddies. Even a simple corrugated cardboard magazine file or holder works great to hold active files.

Don't invest in a lot of equipment; remember this is just a trial system. Some people, after getting all inspired about organization, rush out and buy too many accessories without first thinking through the system. I've walked into offices of some new clients only to find five address books or rotary files, ten letter trays and dozens of file folders— all of which had had "good intentions" but have since been abandoned. The supplies are not the system. They are part of the system. They are only the tools.

First, **start with a simple system.** Select the smallest number of tools and label them with your category names. Arrange them in an easy-to-use, accessible location. A couple of pointers may be helpful. First, use vertical systems whenever possible, as horizontal ones tend to promote the "pile system" of stacked papers. (See Chapter 4 for examples of vertical, desktop active file organizers.)

Second, **try the system out for two to three weeks**, make refinements and then purchase any additional supplies you need.

Your DPS doesn't have to be visible; some of the best ones are "invisible." Use prime filing space in your desk or within an arm's-reach of your filing cabinet or credenza. If out of sight means out of mind, then perhaps a more visible system is indeed a good idea for you. But if you're the type of person who gets anxious just looking at paperwork, then design a more hidden, yet accessible, system and start using your time/info management tools to jot down things to do and remember.

Several tools may be particularly useful in your DPS. I use the **Desk File/Sorter tickler system** shown in Chapter 4 to sort what would otherwise be miscellaneous follow-ups into an organized, chronological system.

There are also the **hanging expanding file** and the **expandable file**, which fit inside a file drawer and provide up to 12 expandable filing sections. Handy tools for your DPS, you can use these files for your hot projects or as a monthly tickler system.

With regard to in/out boxes, consider a number of possibilities. First, consider whether you need them at all. If you're the type of person who either doesn't get much mail or paperwork or who's very decisive and organized and immediately takes action on papers that cross your desk, you might not need them at all. Or perhaps you could get by with just an out-box.

But most people are inundated with paper that doesn't require immediate action. You might consider having more than one box, tray or folder designated for different types of work or priorities and training any coworkers who give you work to presort it into the appropriate accessory. It would be great if each person were to also use a work priority form (as described in Chapter 15) indicating the level of urgency.

Ideally, you would not let the paper cycle through more than once. And of course, try to handle as many papers as possible the first time through the system. But we all have those "C" priority papers that would be nice to handle but simply aren't urgent enough right now.

Survey Your Work Surface

Now that you've cleared a path and set up a DPS, look at your desktop. **Do you have enough work surface?** Many people put up with a desk that is too small to begin with and becomes smaller and smaller as the paper jungle takes over. Now that you've cleared a path, try out your desktop for several days. See if you now have enough space to work.

Most people need at least two work surfaces in their office (not counting a surface for a computer or printer). The second surface should be accessible and placed within an easy swivel of your chair—behind you or at your side.

Don't use the extra work surface as a storage depot or junk table, however. This surface should only hold things that you use daily or several times a week. This surface is great for holding active, working file folders that sit vertically in upright caddies. You might use this surface for your stapler, tape and other supplies as well as reference materials, in/out boxes and mementos. Part or all of this second surface could be designated as a phone area. A nearby table top, a credenza or even a two-drawer filing cabinet can work great as secondary work surfaces. If you prefer that spotless, executive, clean desk look, put items inside furniture storage compartments.

Make Appointments with Yourself

Setting up the tools of a DPS is only half the story; setting up regular routines and habits is the other half. Any organizational system, by the way, consists of two components—tools and habits. I often use this simple equation in my seminars: **a system = tools + habits**. ·

The trick to making your Daily Paperwork System work is simply, to work the system! Here are six habits and routines that can help you work the system—circle any that you could use:

1. **Schedule appointments with yourself to process paperwork**. One training manager I coached schedules "personal administrative time" every week to work in her office. This time has become a "safety net" that allows her to stay in control of paperwork and priorities. She meets with her assistant every Monday to block out her self-appointments on their respective calendars. They both try to protect these appointments.

2. **Open and sort your mail every day you're in the office** and if possible, have someone else open and sort your mail.

3. **Make a decision about each paper that crosses your desk** the first time it crosses your desk. For the papers you're keeping, decide if they can be handled now or later. If a paper will take only a minute or two, do it now. If you're deferring papers for a later time, resist sticking them back in the pile or the in-box.

Decide when you'll be handling each one and where each should go in terms of its function and meaning to you—i.e., where's the first place you're likely to look for the item and retrieve it for action?

4. **Keep it clean!** At the very least, clear your desk and work area before you go home or stop work for the day. Or try the CAYGO habit—Clean As You GO—to prevent paper buildup during the day. And if filing is a real chore use FAYGO—File As You GO— or try cleaning out one file a day.

5. **Use time/info management tools** such as your calendar, master list, planner/organizer, mobile device or a PIM program on your computer to record key information from papers that you can then toss (be sure to back up that key info.)

6. **Consolidate information.** Use notebooks, charts, forms, tickler systems, a good desk side filing system and digital solutions whenever possible.

Catch Up With Reading

Make separate reading appointments with yourself during the week to keep up with professional reading. If your day is just too hectic, make a reading appointment with yourself in the evening. One professional working parent I coached made Wednesday night "Reading Night" where she, her husband and their eight-year-old son curled up and read instead of watching television. With more information available on the Internet, see whether reading online is more productive for you than reading printed hard copy—you may also be able to squeeze in some online reading while you're on hold for phone calls.

Whatever you're reading and wherever you're reading it—try these tips:

1. **Separate** professional from personal interest **reading**.

2. **Make clear decisions** whether what you're reading is really worth your time.

3. To read more quickly, **read selectively**—check out headlines, subheads and first and last paragraphs.

4. Try using a **timer** and/or give yourself reading **goals**, e.g., two journals in twenty minutes.

5. To increase your motivation, tell yourself **positive messages** about reading, e.g., how reading helps you control your paperwork, saves you time, helps you learn more about your field and makes you feel more professional.

Highlight anything you read that you plan to save so that you won't have to reread it the next time. If you're saving online information in word processing files, you may want to use the highlighting feature to mark the most important items.

Here's one paper-based time-saving highlighting technique to use instead of underlining or highlighting whole sentences: draw a **vertical line** (using any writing tool you prefer) alongside a sentence or paragraph rather than underlining each line horizontally. Also, **check or star** any points or paragraphs that are particularly pertinent. You'll be surprised at how fast you can highlight this way as you read.

After highlighting a hard copy document you wish to save and file, jot down the **subject** or **file name** in the top right corner; this will save you time if the paper isn't filed right away so that you or an assistant don't have to reread it before filing. Also, if the info will be out of date by a certain time frame, indicate a **discard date** in the top left corner; this will help you easily toss old papers without having to reread them.

As an experiment, keep track of papers or hard copy files to which you actually refer. Jot down an **R date**—the date you refer back to a paper or file. At the top write "R" followed by the date. The presence of R dates (or the lack of them) will help you decide which hard copy documents to keep and how accessible they should be.

Other Ways to Put Paper in Its Place!

Are you suffering from a paper mill logjam? If so, you may have a tremendous amount of paperwork to process in your job and/or you probably have some difficulty making decisions.

Start making decisions. If you're always drowning in paperwork, chances are you tend to avoid decisions. See if one or more of the following six symptoms apply to you:

1. You're insatiably curious and love to learn to the point of distraction.

2. Perfectionism tends to rule in your life.

3. Everything always takes longer than you thought it would.

4. You're creative.

5. You dislike structure.

6. Your personal and professional goals are unclear.

All of these can contribute to decision-making difficulties concerning paper. But remember, number six is the most important. Making decisions about paper shouldn't be arbitrary. They need to relate specifically to your values and goals in life.

Without goals as a guideline, as a yardstick, it is very difficult to make decisions, including decisions about those papers on your desk.

Difficult decisions about paper often signal ambivalence or conflict about what you want to do now and in the future. "I might need this someday" is such a haunting thought, especially when goals are fuzzy at best. Remind yourself frequently about your goals—every time, in fact, you pick up a paper, a piece of mail, a file folder, whatever. Remind yourself whenever you put down a paper without making a decision. And remember, almost always the worst decision you can make is not to make a decision because this equation is almost always true: **No Paperwork Decision = Greater Paperwork Buildup**. (See also Chapter 2 on goals and Chapter 10 on collecting.)

Preventing and Conquering Long-Term Paper Buildup

Certainly, decision making will be a contributing factor to preventing paper buildup.

Controlling your mail, including junk mail, will also be a factor. Americans receive almost 4 million tons of junk mail every year. Here are some tips to gain more control over the mail monster:

- Cut subscriptions to magazines, share your subscriptions with others or read magazines online so your name doesn't go on additional lists.

- Whenever you order anything by phone, fax, mail or email, ask that your name not be sold, rented or traded.

- To find out info about removing your name from many phone, fax, mail and email national lists, visit the Direct Marketing Association at **www.dmaconsumers.org**.

- Remove your name from company emails or report distribution lists if you're receiving emails or reports you don't need to see.

- Reduce memberships in associations that no longer meet your needs.

- The Privacy Rights Clearinghouse has information on preventing identity theft, reducing junk mail and telemarketing calls and other issues in which technology affects privacy. Log on to **www.privacyrights.org**.

For existing long-term paper buildup, you have these four options available:

1. Recycle it.
2. Quickly box and store it now and plan to sort it later as a long-term project after reading Chapters 9 and 10.
3. Read Chapters 9 and 10 to do something about it now.
4. Create a workable filing system that accommodates resource and reference information you want to keep.

Choose an option based on how important these papers are to you. **Are they worth your time?**

Recycling, Reducing and Reusing

If after all of the above, you end up with a lot of paper that best belongs in the trash can, please reuse or recycle as much of it as you can. And look for ways you can reduce the amount of paper you use.

We accumulate a lot of scratch paper in our office. I always try to reuse paper that has printing on only one side. I use the clean side for taking notes, for printing out drafts and for brainstorming ideas.

Remember to use both sides of a new sheet of paper when photocopying or printing whenever possible (but always first check with the manufacturer to see whether this could harm your copier or printer). An **autoduplexing printer** makes this kind of printing easier.

Sometimes I get graphically interesting junk mail that I give to friends with young children to use in art projects.

I mail **old greeting cards** to a nonprofit organization called Love Letters, which refashions them into new cards for seriously ill children and teens. I've also put together Love Letters parties where I have brought together groups of people (including children) who refashion and personalize our own old and blank cards, which I then mail to Love Letters. (Email me c/o Adams-Hall Publishing at info@adams-hall.com for current contact info for Love Letters, which does not have a website.)

I reuse mailers, boxes and manila envelopes and folders. I put large corrugated boxes that I'd be unlikely to use in our city's curbside recycling bins. It feels great to make these contributions to our planet!

Shredders

You may have papers with private or sensitive information that should be shredded before they are reused, recycled or thrown out. Shredders vary in their capabilities including the sheet capacity, the way papers are cut up (cross-cut small strips are more private than straight-cut strips), the speed and their workload (e.g., light, medium or heavy duty). Also, to prolong the life of your shredder, oil the shredder regularly according to the manufacturer's suggestions.

Resource Guide

Note: As you read about these items, try using online or printed office supply catalogs or visit the listed websites so you can see pictures and learn more about available features.

Paper Management Supplies and Accessories

The selected office products here are handy items you may wish to add to your work area. Most are available in online or hard copy catalogs from office supply stores.

Binders and accessories

Besides file folders (which are discussed in detail in Chapter 9), there are many other options to store and organize paperwork that isn't saved on your computer or online.

The **notebook** or **binder** in all its different sizes is still one of the best paper-based organizational storage devices around for paper resources and records referred to frequently. Sure, it's easier to throw something in a file, but when you go to find it, the notebook wins hands down. Use binders to store articles and clippings, updates, product literature, samples, ideas, active client summary sheets and the latest professional or trade information—the list is endless. (More and more, information such as product literature is readily available online on a company website.)

You say you hate hole punching? Then buy the three-hole pre-punched plastic sheet protectors with a margin that allow you to store 8½-by-11-inch papers without additional punching. They're called **top loading sheet protectors**, **page protectors** or **plastic sleeves** and are enclosed on three sides and "load" through the open end on top. They should be widely available or contact New Century Direct, 800/767-0777 or **www. centurybusinesssolutions.com**. C-LINE (888/323-6084 [IL] or **www.c-lineproducts.com**) makes them in several styles: clear, colored or clear with a colored edge. C-LINE also makes a combination sheet protector with tabs for indexing.

If you prefer, you can use **Avery Extra Wide Dividers** specially designed for binders containing oversized sheet protectors. The point is if you're using sheet protectors and index divider tabs together, make sure the tabs are not hidden from view. **www.avery.com**

Pocket dividers, also called **pocket folders** or **slash pockets**, are handy for items that you don't want to hole punch and are smaller than the standard page size.

If you need to organize duplicate sets of binders with tabs but you don't want to bother with typing and inserting labels repeatedly into plastic binder tabs, consider one of the **multi-colored index systems** on the market that lets you simplify the job considerably. The process is simple: you prepare a master contents page that aligns with plain or preprinted (e.g., numbered) tabs and then you either use a photocopier or a laser printer. Look for "**Ready Index**" products by Avery Dennison (**www.avery.com**) and **Wilson Jones** brand indexes.

Wilson Jones MultiDex features a slide-out Quick Reference Table of Contents that allows you to see titles without having to flip back to the contents page in the front of the binder. It's available in five different numerical sets—5, 8, 10, 12 and 15.

If you are tired of three-ring binders that never close properly and snag important documents, look for binders with a locking mechanism, such as the **Wilson Jones** brand. You'll find the strongest mechanism in **Bindertek's** great two-ring binder, which lets you access, insert and remove documents easily. Bindertek, 800/456-3453 [CA] or **www.bindertek.com**

For a whole variety of preprinted tabs for nearly every area of law, consider those by Legal Tabs Co. You can use them in binders or in file folders to organize your legal documents. Legal Tabs Co., **www.legaltabs.cc**

To easily make your own custom tabs for notebook dividers, look for the **Avery Dennison Index Maker** products, which come with tabbed, reinforced dividers and clear labels, ready for laser printing or photocopying. You apply the self-adhesive labels directly onto the divider tabs.

Business card accessories

If you attend meetings where you collect many business cards and you prefer to physically store them (rather than scan or input them into your computer as described earlier in this chapter or input the information from them into your mobile handheld device), there are a few options. You could start a **business card notebook** with plastic business card sleeves that are tabbed. Label the tabs with either letters of the alphabet or names of organizations and associations. Before you go to a meeting, skim the cards and any notes you made on them.

Rolodex (**http://eldonoffice.com/rolodex**) makes a variety of different business card files as well as some useful accessories. Some Rolodex cards are large enough to hold stapled or glued business cards (without having to recopy the information). There's also room for brief notes. To turn your file into more of a resource database, insert special Rolodex divider tabs with your own category names to divide up your Rolodex. Use an alphabetical system within those categories, not the entire Rolodex. With several different subject categories, it's often easier to look up listings, rather than trying to remember exact names. You can organize your file with Rolodex colored cards and/or colored plastic card protectors. If your system is used all the time, get the Rolodex plastic sleeve card protectors, which are available in clear as well as colors.

While the most common brand name, Rolodex is not the only brand of card file. There are other brands, as well as styles, from which to choose. Compare card files available in office supply stores, catalogs and websites.

Clips

To temporarily group and secure papers, nothing beats the paper clip. What you may not realize, however, is the variety of clips now available.

Rectangular clips hold papers securely and will not catch on other adjacent papers.

Binder clip is the generic name for what is probably the most secure, slip-proof clip you can buy. Use binder clips for loose, bulky papers that need to be held securely.

Plastic paper clips should always be used around computers because metal clips can become magnetized and can destroy computer data. They come in a variety of colors and can be used for color coding different papers.

The **banker's clasp** has a strong grip and is useful for holding bulky papers. The raised short end allows you to easily and quickly slip the clip onto papers.

A **magnetic clip** attaches to the sides of metal file cabinets and is handy for attaching notes or information.

Color coding

For color coding and drawing attention, here are additional products that can help:

Redi-Tags are removable, reusable color-coded tags that have a reusable adhesive on half the tag. They come in 16 different colors and three sizes and many have preprinted phrases. Many come in refillable dispensers. There is a "general office" series with such tags as "FILE," "FYI," and "RUSH!" There's also a medical series that includes "SIGN ORDERS" and "DICTATION NEEDED." If your local office supply store or catalog doesn't have this item, call Redi-Tag Corp. at 800/421-7585 [CA] or visit **www.redi-tag.com** to find a store location near you.

Post-it Flags by **3M** are versatile. Half of the flag is colored and may have a preprinted message such as "Note" or "Sign Here"; the other half is a transparent surface upon which you can write with a pencil or pen. Available in many colors, easy-to-use Post-it Brand Flags keep your paperwork organized. Use them for quick reference, easy retrieval and handy reminders. They are ideal for color coding, organizing and indexing.

Avery See Through Round Color Coding Labels are useful dots for highlighting directly on items such as maps, blueprints and graphs, where it's important the information not be obscured. Available in four colors, these dots are removable. One manager uses them on her voice mail log where red dots are for "immediate call backs," blue for "action items" to do now, green for "correspondence" where she needs to send something and yellow indicates "for information only" with no response needed on her part.

To help you keep tabs on your paperwork, try **Avery SwifTabs** or **Tabbies index tabs**. Both of these products are self-adhesive, durable and come in a variety of colors and styles. Both are also available with preprinted months, numbers or letters. You can write or type on them. Use them on such items as computer printouts, reports or on spiral bound books. For TABBIES self-adhesive index tabs contact Tabbies, a division of Xertrex International, Inc., **www.tabbies.com**.

Desk accessories

In the office supply world, the desk accessory category includes everything from basic desk or letter trays to designer desk sets with matching components. As a general guideline, I advise clients to use the minimum number of accessories and those with the smallest capacity. It's just too easy to start stockpiling stuff.

I also urge clients to lean toward vertical rather than horizontal accessories and whenever possible, to put papers in files rather than piles. Of course, the type of paperwork will often determine which format you should use. A horizontal container often works best for frequently used forms, which often flop over in a vertical accessory. But you'll generally want a vertical accessory for active files.

Desktop file holders come in a variety of styles. Some are designed to hold active file folders; others handle active hanging folders. When not in use, some can be folded flat for easy storage.

Your **in/out box** or basket system will most likely be horizontal because you're probably processing different sized papers. But remember these tips: keep the depth of containers to a minimum, maintain high access and visibility and clean them out regularly.

Look for basic **letter trays** that can stack. Some people prefer wire letter trays because you can easily see what's in them; others prefer plastic or wood trays that keep paperwork less visible. Consider getting shallow trays to prevent paper buildup unless you need deep ones for thick folders or reports.

Balance good function with good design. If aesthetics are important, select a line that has coordinated desk accessories. Upon getting organized, some clients reward themselves with attractive desk accessories. Check out well-designed products in office supply stores and catalogs. Also look at the **Hold Everything** (Williams-Sonoma, Inc.) stores and catalog (**888/922-4117** [NV] or **www.holdeverything.com**). The **Reliable Home Office** catalog is an excellent choice, too, at 800/359-5000 [IL] or **www.reliable.com**.

Special organizers and sorters

An **aluminum collator** (Figure 8-1) is designed to manually collate (organize) documents but I recommend it for holding large, bulky, active client or project files in your Daily Paperwork System that you want to be accessible. It's great for CPA or legal files and comes in 12, 18 or 24 expanding sections. Since aluminum collators aren't as widely available as in the past, try searching for "aluminum collators" on the Web. As of this writing, the Lee Flexifile Expandable Collator/Organizer is available at **www.mypencil.com.**

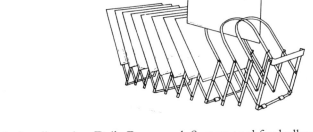

Figure 8-1. A collator is a Daily Paperwork System tool for bulky project files and documents.

Desk File/Sorters by **Smead** are great to use as paper tickler systems. The style I use is the one with 43 dividers—daily (1-31) and monthly (Jan.-Dec.). See Figure 4-3 in Chapter 4. **www.smead.com**

If you have lots of literature or inserts you're pulling together to put into kits or notebooks, consider **literature organizers** and **sorters**. Your selection will depend on a number of factors: the number of separate inserts you need, the quantity of each insert you need to have on hand, the space you have available, the frequency of use and your budget. (See Chapter 9 for an illustration of a literature organizer.)

The **Pendaflex Hanging Expandable File** fits inside your file drawer and has nine expandable filing sections. It comes with blank, self-adhesive labels so you can make custom headings for your paperwork categories. **www.pendaflex.com**

The **Pendaflex SortPal Paper Sorter** is an expanding sorter file that organizes papers requiring specific routine actions, such as faxing, photocopying or signatures. It comes with six preprinted tabbed sections

and includes blank labels to customize your own headings.
www.pendaflex.com

The **Smead Hanging Expanding File** has 12 filing sections with tabs.
www.smead.com

Stationery holders are great for letterhead, forms and envelopes and
come in many different styles and formats. Some sit out in the open and
others fit inside standard desk drawers.

Step files give great visibility to your working files. Some are free
standing; others can hang on partitions.

Supply drawer organizers from Ultimate Office are versatile drawers
that can be stacked. Each drawer can accommodate one or two partitions
enabling you to section off each drawer into two or three compartments
to eliminate wasted dead space. Different style drawers (all with
insertable label areas) let you store a variety of materials—literature,
forms, binders, supplies, stationery, magazines, reports, disks and multimedia. **800/631-2233** [NJ] or **www.ultoffice.com**

If you're short on work surfaces, try using **wall mount files**. Sometimes
these files are referred to as **pockets** and they can be used on walls as
well as on the sides of desks. Some come with magnets and attach to
metal surfaces such as filing cabinets. They don't take up much space and
they can hit the spot when you need a holder for paperwork at the
location where they will be used.

Ultimate Office carries hundreds of organization products including
many styles of versatile paper organizers that provide fast, organized
access to information that's frequently referred to. Examples include a
desk-side **Wall Organizer** model that displays 20 sheets and **Desktop
Organizers** with 10-60 pockets. The **StationMate** project organizer
keeps up to 25 projects in easy view. The cascading design holds 25
translucent pocket files in five colors. Each pocket file is sealed on two
sides, holds up to 50 sheets of paper and includes a fifth-cut tab with an
adhesive label. **800/631-2233** [NJ] or **www.ultoffice.com**

Scanners and Software

OmniPage is award-winning OCR (optical character recognition) software that scans paper into editable Word documents, Excel spreadsheets or live websites without tedious retyping. It recognizes photocopies, faxes, small and large text, color and black-and-white images, multi-column documents, tables and spreadsheets. Nuance Communications, Inc. (formerly called ScanSoft) or **www.nuance.com**

Visioneer makes scanners for all different-sized documents, from business cards to newspaper articles. They also have scanners for mobile use. **www.visioneer.com**

If you're looking for a business card scanner, check out the CardScan, which keeps getting rave reviews. CardScan, Inc., 800/640-6944 [MA] or **www.cardscan.com**

9

Up–to–Date Paper Files and Beyond

Quick Scan: They're out of sight, out of mind—or so you'd like to think until one fateful day when you can't find that all important document. Or until your paper files and filing cabinets are so full that it's physically dangerous to pry open files to slip in just one more paper. In this chapter discover how to organize your paper files so that they become an ally, not an enemy. Find out which filing supplies can make a world of difference. While the main emphasis is on your own personal filing system, this chapter also includes information useful for larger or special office filing systems.

For most people, paper files are like skeletons in the closet—bad secrets that no one likes to talk about. Who wants to admit that files are bulging with out-of-date papers, that they are difficult to handle and retrieve and that very often files are misplaced or even lost?

Then there are the *piles*—the papers that never make it into the files. They sit on desktops, in bookcases, on tables, on file cabinets and yes, even on the floor.

Besides the fact that almost no one *likes* to file, there are three fears people often have when it comes to files and piles. I call these **filing phobias** the "3-Ds" because they each start with the letter "D."

First, people are afraid of **decisions**. If you don't know what to call papers, you'll end up calling them nothing. Papers then collect in unnamed stacks and piles, as well as drawers and in-boxes.

Second, people are afraid of **discards.** Heaven forbid you should throw anything out—you might need it someday.

Third, the fear of **disappearance** haunts many. "Filing a paper in my system is like filing it in a black hole—never to be seen or heard from again," one new client told me.

Let's see how your files stack up.

How Do Your Files Stack Up?

Here's a quick quiz to rate the state of your filing system. Check "yes" or "no" after each question.

	YES	NO
1. Is filing a real chore?		
2. Would it take a long while to catch up on your filing?		
3. Do you often have trouble finding and retrieving papers?		
4. Do you keep many papers or documents *in case* you'll need them?		
5. Are your filing cabinets/drawers jam packed?		
6. Is your filing system more random instead of carefully planned?		
7. Are many of your important files inconveniently located?		
8. Is it difficult to tell what's in each file drawer without opening it?		
9. Are you printer or copier crazy, making unnecessary hard copies or duplicates of papers?		
10. Do you sometimes have trouble naming files?		
11. Would you hesitate to try finding documents while someone's waiting?		

If you have at least three "yes" responses, keep reading! Below are some typical reasons I hear from people who explain why their files aren't as functional as they should be. See if you relate to any of the following:

- I don't have time/I'm too busy putting out fires.
- Setting up a system is menial, clerical work.
- It's not my job.

- I don't know what to call things.
- I'm creative and my work style is "organized chaos."
- I don't have an assistant.

Let's look at some valid reasons for *making the time* to set up or revamp your files. Check any that apply to you:

- It will be easier to get work done.
- I'll feel better when I know where everything is. I'll have more control over my work.
- I'll save time looking for things.
- Accessible, fingertip information (hard copy and digital) is a key resource for my productivity, professional image and peace of mind.
- I'll look and feel more professional and competent when my hard-copy info is organized.

Add some reasons of your own, making them relate specifically to your goals. What will a good filing system help you achieve or accomplish?

Five Easy Steps to an Organized Paper Filing System

Most people in the workplace are foggy when it comes to paper filing systems. They haven't been "office trained," a term coined by one of my seminar participants. They don't realize that the clerical work of filing is only a part of an organized paper filing system. The *mental*, conceptual work is the most important aspect of a good system.

Most people also don't know where to start. What follows is a blueprint to guide you in designing or revamping your system. Here are the five main steps I use with clients:

1. Categorize any existing files as "active" or "inactive" and pull inactive files from your existing filing system.

2. Write out your filing system categories and subcategories *on paper* (or on computer). Get input from any others who'll be using the system.

3. Physically set up the system. Have all supplies on hand as you prepare file labels and purge, consolidate and arrange file folders.

4. Put the finishing touches on your system. Label drawers and prepare a file index or chart for yourself and any others who have access to the system. If others are involved, introduce the system at a special training meeting.

5. Maintain your system by sticking to a routine.

We'll go into more detail about these five steps after becoming more familiar with the thought process behind every good paper filing system.

But first, there are **three essential questions** to answer about each paper or file:

1. **When** is it used? How many times a day, a week, a month or a year do you handle it?

2. **What** is it? Under what category(ies) does it belong?

3. **Where** should it go? Near your desk? In storage? In a filing cabinet? Which drawer? A binder or notebook? Scanned into a computer file? The trash?

Steps One through Three will deal with these questions.

Step One: Active and Inactive

Files should be categorized on the basis of *frequency*, that is, when or how often they are used. There are two basic types: **active** and **inactive**, sometimes also called **open** and **closed**.

Active files

Active (or open files) belong in your office because you will refer to each of them at least several times a year and probably at least every month. You will either add to these files or retrieve something from them. Examples include your financial records for this year and active client or customer files.

Working files are active files that are used the most often—daily or several times a week. They should be the most accessible to you at your desk or work station. They can go on a credenza, a side table next to your desk or inside your most accessible file drawer. The most active working files can be part of your Daily Paperwork System as described in Chapters 4 and 8.

Inactive files

Inactive, closed or storage files are used infrequently, if at all, and should usually be kept out of your office. If you opt to keep these files in your office, put them in the least accessible locations—in the rear of a file drawer, on a top shelf, in an area separate from your main work area or in a storage closet. Whenever possible, remove inactive files to someone else's office or to a designated storage area on- or off-site.

Separating active and inactive files

As you begin to sort through any existing files, be thinking of these two basic categories: active and inactive. Go through your existing files and weed out all the inactive ones and either discard or store them. By the way, this file sorting process should be done quickly by looking at file names only. *Do not sort through papers in files at this time.*

Now that you've sorted through your files, you're ready to tackle any piles of paper you may have accumulated. Go through these piles quickly, pulling active and/or important papers. Don't spend hours and hours going through piles or you'll never create your filing system. These four steps will help you streamline the process:

1. Get yourself a countdown timer. (An egg timer is fine or you may prefer an LCD countdown timer available at an electronics store such as Radio Shack.)

2. Quickly sort through piles using the timer. This is not the time for a thorough analysis of each and every paper. As my friend and colleague Maxine Ordesky says, "Separate the treasures from the trash." For our purposes here, "treasures" are any papers that will go into active files or any important documents that you *must* save and file. Set aside for now "semi-precious" papers that may go into storage.

As far as what "trash" to toss, shred or recycle at this time, apply my two **Discard Dilemmas** rules:

- **When in doubt, *save* legal, tax information** such as records and contracts (also check with your CPA or lawyer regarding suggested *records retention schedules*).

- **When in doubt, *toss* resource information** such as reference, background, industry-specific or professional materials that you "might need someday," you could easily get again and/or you're unlikely to use.

3. Clear the decks. Put your "semi-precious" papers temporarily in records storage boxes with lids. Label the outside of the box "Inactive Papers" and add any specific description of the contents, unless they're just miscellaneous. Try to keep the filing area as clear as possible—that way you'll be able to think and work more clearly.

4. For your "treasured" papers, think about category and file names and jot a name on each paper in pencil. If any of these papers could go in existing file folders, file them now. If they need folders of their own, quickly put these papers in folders and jot a name on the file folder tab in pencil. Or use removable file folder labels for temporary labels. If you have no extra file folders on hand or there are too few papers for their own folder, then paper clip related papers together and jot a future file name down on the top paper or use a removable, colored label for each grouping.

The bottom line is spend most of your time on *important* papers.

Step Two: The Name Game

Once you have the two most basic groupings of active and inactive, you are well on your way.

Naming active file categories

Now you're ready to identify the major areas or divisions of your work and/or your work-related information. Start thinking in terms of the largest, *broadest* categories for your active files.

Naming categories and then files is the most critical element to setting up an organized system because it will aid in the *retrieval of information*. As human beings we are much better at *storing* information than *retrieving* it—whether it goes into our brains, our computers or our file cabinets. Just as our memory works best by connecting to related information, so, too, will a file naming system work better when we create connected, logical categories ahead of time.

One estate planning attorney who is a sole practitioner has designated three main areas of information: Clients, Estate Planning Resource

Information and Business Operations. A management consultant has these three categories: Business Administration (which includes client files), Resource Information (for seminars and articles) and Marketing/Business Development. A computer systems engineer has files for Communications, Software Applications and Hardware.

Here is a listing of general categories. Circle any that might apply to your work. Add your own at the end. Remember to select the *broadest subject areas* (not necessarily specific file names) that apply to you: Accounts; Background/History; Business Administration; Clients or Patients; Communications (in company or organization); Contacts; Customers, Legislation; Management; Marketing; Products; Projects; Reference; Research; Resources; Samples; Staff; Support; and Volunteers.

To start breaking down these broad categories into subcategories and specific file names and to help you visualize their relationship to one another, do the following. Use **colored index cards** with one color for each of your major file categories. Put each file name on the appropriately colored card and put it with the other cards. Spread out the cards and arrange them alphabetically or by subject. You can use the cards later to make up your filing system labels and also right now as you design your system on paper.

Designing a system on paper

A filing system on paper serves as a blueprint that charts out all category, subcategory and file names and shows how they all fit together.

Using your word processing program would be helpful at this step. Besides being able to easily move words around, your word processing program should let you sort (arrange) words alphabetically.

Start with one of your major category areas. Use the file chart shown in Figure 9-1 as a guide to help you easily list your own file categories and names and show how they are related. A file chart is an outline of your filing system.

Look at your existing file folders as well as the paper-clipped groupings and new folders you created in Step One. See if file names suggest themselves to you. Look for patterns, groupings and combinations that go together. Be creative but don't create file names that you won't remember later. Don't try to think of every file name right now; this is not your final system—it's only the beginning.

Using a pencil (or your computer), write down a major work category from your filing system. Now complete what you think will be the main headings. Leave plenty of space between headings. Select names for headings that make sense to *you* (and anyone else using the system). Stick with nouns for headings, if possible. Next add some subheadings. Figure 9-1 shows an example for Resource Information with three headings and two levels of subheads.

Figure 9-1. SAMPLE FILE CHART

MAJOR CATEGORY (or drawer name): **RESOURCE INFO**

HEADING	Subhead	Subhead
Contacts	Consultants Service Stores	Answers on Computers
Manuals	Hardware	
Products	Software	

As you chart out headings and subheads you'll start to see which names belong together and which ones need additional subheads. You're creating your own file design. Don't get too carried away with elaborate headings and subheads. Often one heading and one level of subheads is plenty. Keep your design simple!

Now complete your File Chart for one *major category only*. (You may want to use an outlining feature on your word processing program.) Then, when you're ready, do a chart for each of your other major categories in your filing system. Remember, nothing is etched in stone; your file chart is only a guide. If your file charts are on computer, you may now wish to alphabetize any headings or subheads that are actual names of clients, companies, vendors, etc., or you can wait to do it in Step Three.

Step Three: Putting It All Together

Where files will go in your system is a combination of *what types* of files they are, *who* uses them, *when* they are used and *how much room* you have. You should now know approximately how much room you have after having completed Steps One and Two because you've determined how often files will be used, purged your system of unnecessary inactive files and identified all your active file names.

Location of files

One of the most important aspects of your filing system is location. Here are some guidelines to consider when deciding where to put your files:

- The more files are used, the closer they should be to your desk or main work area.

- Keep like files together. Group files by subject, type or frequency of use.

- Choose appropriate media to store your information—perhaps you want to use notebooks or boxes rather than file folders. Maybe you have large, bulky or odd-sized items that require special filing solutions.

- Security may be a factor; take any necessary precautions to secure confidential information.

- Select the appropriate cabinets or equipment.

File cabinets

With regard to cabinets, start with what you have on hand. If you're starting from scratch, estimate the number of filing inches you now have and project, if you can, how much you'll need over the next several years. Look at your available floor space and your current or projected office layout to determine what will physically fit in your space (allowing space also for drawers to be pulled out).

Vertical cabinets will generally give you a few more filing inches per floor space than **lateral cabinets** but verticals need extra space for opening up drawers. Some people prefer the look of lateral cabinets along with being able to use the drawers either side-by-side or front-to-back. Whether you choose vertical or lateral, look for cabinets with high quality rolling or gliding mechanisms, built-in glides to accommodate hanging files and tilt-proof or nontip safety features.

You can almost triple the number of files in the same floor space if you choose **open shelf file cabinets**. Besides holding a large number of files, these cabinets give you easy access to files. I would recommend getting flip-front doors so you can close and lock the cabinets.

Now you're ready to physically set up your system—a time-consuming task that's nice to share with someone else, if you have such luxury.

Color coding

Decide if you want to use **color coding** in your system. A simple color-coding scheme by drawer or by major category can be helpful, especially when you go to refile a folder. We use blue hanging folder tabs and file folder labels for our business and administrative files, for example, and yellow ones for our resource information files. You're less likely to misfile a folder in the wrong drawer with color coding. You can also see at a glance the type(s) of folders in a particular drawer. (For more elaborate color coding, see "Special Office Filing and Information Management Systems" in the Resource Guide.)

The right supplies

Make sure you have the right supplies available (also see the chapter Resource Guide). Here's a typical "shopping list" I suggest to clients, followed by comments describing why these items are important:

- One box of **hanging file folders** (generally 25 to a box); they come with or without tabs; get them without tabs if you're going to use color coding

- Hanging **box bottom file folders**, one-inch capacity, one box of 25, no tabs included

- Hanging box bottom file folders, two-inch capacity, one box of 25, no tabs

- Plastic tabs for any hanging folders that don't come with tabs; tabs come in two-inch or 3½-inch lengths—I prefer the 3½-inch size; if you're going to color code your files (which I highly recommend), get colored plastic tabs or buy colored plastic windows (to use with any clear plastic tabs you may already have on hand)

- Self-adhesive, colored file folder labels

- **Third-cut interior folders** (100 per box); interior folders are cut lower than ordinary manila folders so that the folders sit inside the hanging folders without sticking up; they come in a variety of colors; third-cut folders work with the standard file folder labels you'll be getting

Folders generally come *fifth-cut* or *third-cut*. The "cut" refers to the width of the folder's tab in relation to the folder. A third-cut folder, for example, has a tab that's cut one-third the width of the folder, allowing the tabs of three folders filed behind each other to be seen at one time. Since the tab is used for labeling, select the size that will best do the job. Use third-cut if you need a larger label surface.

To make full use of your headings and subheads, use *hanging file folders*, especially the one- and two-inch *box bottom folders*, which work great as your major headings. Three and four-inch box bottom folders are available, too, if needed. (See Figure 9-2 in the Resource Guide for an illustration of hanging folders.)

Inside each box bottom folder, place several *interior folders*, specially cut manila folders that can serve as subheads. If possible, avoid using only one interior folder per hanging folder; too many hanging folders will take up too much space and won't take advantage of your heading/subhead classification system, which provides greater retrievability. (Check the Resource Guide for descriptions and pictures of these different folders.)

Use your file chart

Pull out your File Chart (or your index cards, if you used them). Go through each heading and subhead and indicate which of the headings and subheads will take regular, one-inch or two-inch hanging folders. Put a "1" by any that you think will be up to one-inch thick and a "2" by any that will be up to two inches thick. Those with 1s will take one-inch box bottoms and those with 2s, two-inch box bottoms. Write "H" for any of the remaining headings or subheads that would take regular hanging folders; otherwise they would automatically get interior folders. (Most of your subheads will probably take interior folders.)

Folder labels

With your File Chart or index cards as a guide, type and print out your
hanging folder insert labels with a large, *sans serif* font such as Arial—
using the 24-point size for headings and the 18-point size for
subheadings. You can print directly on the label inserts or better yet, get
laser or inkjet file folder labels or even small address labels that you can
print, peel and attach to the inserts.

You might also try printing or photocopying onto "65 lb. card
stock," a heavier grade of paper that you could use instead of the
furnished white label inserts. (Check compatibility of card stock with
your printer or copier.)

Insert the labels into the hanging folder plastic tabs. Put the hanging
folders in the order you listed them on your File Chart. Insert the plastic
tab on the inside front cover at the far left for headings. For hanging
folders with subheads, you may wish to place the plastic tab a little over
towards the right. Also note that you should stagger any tabs that would
block other tabs. If your box bottom folders require you to insert
cardboard reinforcement strips on the bottom, add them now. Set up
your new hanging folders in a file drawer. Place existing file folders inside
the new hanging folders.

Now type and print labels for new interior folders. I use Word's
"Envelopes and Labels" feature (found by clicking "Tools" and then
"Letters and Mailings"). There are many label templates to choose from
that can be used with commercially available label products on laser or
ink jet printers.

And here are two simple tips to prevent label sheets from curling in
your laser printer, which can cause faded and broken type on labels.
Before printing, first pull each sheet firmly over the edge of a table, label
side up, to create a curl in the opposite direction. Second, feed and print
one sheet at a time.

Before you affix labels on the interior folders, place the three types of
folders in front of you: left-cut, center-cut and then right-cut (assuming
you are using third-cut folders). Pull folders in order of left-cut, center-
cut, and right-cut. Don't always start at the left every time you come to a
new hanging folder; keep going where you left off. That way you won't
end up with a lot of extra right- or center-cut folders when you're done.
In addition, you will maintain good visibility in your system by staggering
folders in this way. Now affix the labels.

For even greater visibility and versatility, consider hanging files with a built-in magnifier and/or a large labeling area to increase label readability (see the Resource Guide).

For interior folders that will be handled frequently and will risk dog-earing, cover the label area with either self-adhesive plastic that you'll have to cut to size or, better yet, use pre-cut label protectors (see the Resource Guide).

Best ways to arrange folders

You can arrange your file folders in a number of ways: alphabetically, numerically or by frequency of use. You might even arrange your folders in a combination of ways. For example, you might use a basically alphabetical setup but group frequently used folders in a special, accessible location, for example, in the front of your file drawer.

Certain kinds of information work better alphabetically. For example, client or customer name files work best in an alphabetical system.

On the other hand, subject files do not always have to be in strict alphabetical order. It may be more convenient to place files you use more often in a more accessible location, irrespective of alphabetical sequence. Frequently used subhead files, too, may be placed out of alphabetical order within their hanging folders.

Numerical filing is a better method if you need to arrange files by date (e.g., purchase orders) or by number (legislative bills). Numerical filing is also useful when you want to keep files more confidential (it's more difficult to tell what's in a numerical file). A file index may be needed, however, to readily locate material. The index should be kept in a different location from the files to ensure their security.

Whichever method(s) you select, place all your interior folders into their respective hanging folders. Put any remaining, unfiled papers left over from Step One into appropriate folders.

Fine tuning

You may have noticed that your existing files haven't yet undergone a complete and thorough purge. There's a good reason for this. It's better to set up a *functional* system first and fine tune later. Do your fine tuning now.

Go carefully through each of your existing, *active* folders in your system. Do you really need this information? How accessible does it have to be? Could a folder be consolidated with another folder or would it be preferable to scan the contents into your computer? Use a timer and allot a specified period of time, from 15 minutes to an hour and a half on a given day. Or try giving yourself a goal, say, five folders in fifteen minutes.

You may find you need to add new labels (or delete others). Add or delete them to your File Chart in a different color or highlight them so you'll spot the new ones to add. Don't take time out to make the labels right now; jot down file names in pencil on new folders.

When you've completed the purge for one complete subject area, type or print any remaining labels and attach them to the new folders.

Step Four: Finishing Touches

Now that you've physically set up your system, make sure you can tell the types of files you have in each drawer without having to open them up. You'll need a summary of your file drawer contents. Such a summary could be as simple as labeling each drawer with main headings.

Colleague Beverly Clower makes a "key to the files," which is a map or diagram of file cabinets and drawers plus their contents.

A simple list on paper, such as your File Chart or a "file index," could suffice. Keep a list on your computer so it can be easily updated. Be sure to print out at least one "hard copy" on paper. It's important to have computer listings for both active as well as inactive files in storage boxes. I have a computer document file called "storage" that lists all my inactive paper files by Box A, Box B, etc.

Train anyone who will be using your filing system. Have a special meeting or training session to introduce the system. Distribute a file index, file chart, key to the files or other listing. If appropriate, show how to borrow files by leaving a folder-size **out guide** in the place of the missing file.

Step Five: Maintenance

The trick to a productive filing system is a regular maintenance program by you or someone you designate. Your program should be fairly routine and involve only a minimal amount of time—famous last words! But let's see how it can be done.

Start by making some decisions in advance about your file maintenance program. Answer the following questions:

1. Who's going to do your filing?
2. Will you file some or all papers "as you go"? Which ones?
3. If you plan to file papers in batches, how often and when specifically will filing occur?
4. How many times a year will you purge files and transfer formerly active files into storage? During which months or quarters?

Too many professionals and offices have *no* filing maintenance guidelines. Don't wait until an emergency, crammed file cabinets or a move forces you to take stock. It may be too late or you may be in the middle of a top priority project that prevents you from devoting what will now require a large chunk of time.

Set up your own maintenance system. Decide how many minutes a day or a week you (or someone you designate) will spend on it. Which day(s) will you choose and which time(s)? Be specific. Until your system becomes routine, include your maintenance tasks on your daily to-do list or in your calendar.

The longer you wait to either set up or implement your maintenance system the easier it is for paper to accumulate once again. Get tough on paper!

The hardest part of maintaining your filing system is maintaining enough incentive. You have to believe this is a top priority or you'll keep putting it off. Filing systems often get put on the proverbial back burner until you've run out of filing space or a crisis occurs. Don't let that happen to you.

Three Filing Tips for Every Manager

If you're a manager or you work for one, you need to help implement three key ideas relating to your coworkers and your office filing system.

Filing is Serious Business

First, **take your office filing system seriously**. Filing is not just clerical busy work. It's a vital database for your business, office or department.

Evaluate your current systems, including the central filing system as well as individual filing systems. Begin by using the five steps we've just discussed. See if there's any duplication of effort, e.g., is everyone keeping a copy of certain documents that could be (a) filed in one central location or (b) scanned and kept online?

When she was a manager, CEO Kathryn Johnson created the "vanguard system" in which each of her staff became a specialist in a particular subject area and maintained files on that subject. Because each staff member was "in the vanguard," filing became easier, reading loads were lighter and department morale was boosted. As a CEO, Johnson continued to use the system with her staff.

Reduce What You're Keeping

Second, reduce paper to be filed and stored through **systematic records management/purging, paper reduction and recycling.**

One company has records management guidelines with retention schedules that culminate in an annual event called "Pack Rat Day." This event encourages all departments to review their records for storage or disposal according to the company guidelines. Each department tracks all "pack rat material" on a log sheet, which, along with records for storage or shredding, are turned in to the Records Systems department, the sponsor of the event. There is a Pack Rat Day celebration with refreshments, live music and departmental "Reformed Pack Rat Awards."

One aerospace company has had "Operation Roundfile" every year in which employees clean out their files and offices, tossing as much paper as possible. The company also has paper reduction programs throughout its divisions. One division came up with a motto, "Paper doesn't grow on trees—it *is* trees." This division set a goal of reducing photocopies by 20 percent, lines of computer print by 50 percent and mailing lists by 25 percent.

Adopt a **purge prevention policy** by limiting the number of file cabinets. Look for ways to communicate using less paper, e.g., through email, an intranet, wiki, voice mail or routing one memo (instead of making copies of the memo). Set up a policy to reduce and recyle paper in your office or organization.

Teach Your Filing System

The third filing tip is **value the importance of training**. Smooth functioning office filing systems don't happen by accident. They take careful planning and training.

Whenever more than one person is using an office filing system, you need to set up at least one training session and preferably two. The first session introduces the logistics of the system—how files are named and arranged and how and when they are filed and by whom. This is a good time to introduce the file out guide and distribute a file index.

If you are at all concerned that there will be some resistance to the system, especially if it is a new system, suggest that everyone "try it out" for the next couple of weeks and then meet again at a second meeting to discuss and evaluate the system. The more people are a part of any system, the more likely they are to accept it. You must, however, be open to their ideas.

Resource Guide

Be sure to look for the recycled logo as well as the category "recycled products" for your favorite office supply catalog, site or retailer whenever you shop.

Books and Booklets on Filing and Records Retention

Establishing Alphabetical, Numeric and Subject Matter Filing Systems published by the Association of Records Managers and Administrators (ARMA) is a PDF download. The ARMA site has many other publications. ARMA, 800/422-2762 [KS] or **www.arma.org**

Guide to Record Retention Requirements tells businesses and individuals doing business with federal government agencies exactly which records must be kept, by whom and for how long. CCH, 800/248-3248 or **www.cch.com**

Filing Supplies

Besides checking your favorite online or hard-copy office supply catalog(s), be sure to visit **www.pendaflex.com** and **www.smead.com** to see the wide variety of filing supplies that are available. Below are just some of the options you have.

Folders

Hanging folders are the mainstay of frequently used paper filing systems. They provide easy access to paperwork, good visibility and an organized way to group files.

They are typically made of durable, two-tone green paper stock but many hanging folders also come in other colors and are made of other materials such as plastic or more environmentally sound recycled fibers.

Special scoring in the middle of the flaps and on the bottom makes Pendaflex hanging folders more useful (see Figure 9-2). Scoring in the middle allows you to bend back the flaps so that the folder can be propped open in the file drawer until contents are reinserted. Scoring and folding at the bottom let you square off the v-shape bottom to increase the folder's storage capacity.

To really increase the capacity so that you can more easily use the hanging folder as a container for several file folders (or for catalogs), use a **box bottom folder**, which, depending on the manufacturer, comes in one- to four-inch capacity. Box bottoms come in a variety of colors. Some have special cardboard strips that reinforce the "bottom" edge; others have pre-installed strips. See Figure 9-2.

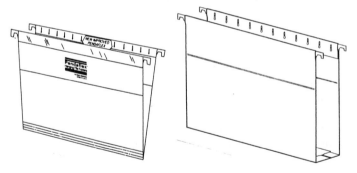

Figure 9-2. The classic Pendaflex hanging file folder (left) is reinforced along the top and bottom with a durable poly-laminate. The Smead box bottom folder comes with a sturdy reinforcement strip, which makes it an ideal folder for holding heavy materials such as manuals or catalogs as well as thick folders.

The Pendaflex Hanging Box File is a blue box bottom with sides that prevent important papers and other materials from slipping out. It is extra durable with tear-resistant sides and pressboard reinforcing inserts to support heavy items.

Interior folders are special file folders cut shorter to fit inside hanging folders without obscuring hanging folder tabs. The Pendaflex line features colors to match Pendaflex hanging folders.

You'll need **hanging file frames** to support your hanging folders, unless your filing equipment already has them or glide rails built in. Traditionally such file frames come notched at half-inch intervals that you can break off to fit your drawer; but since most never break off easily, I recommend having your supplier cut them to size for you.

For manila folders that are handled frequently and are used more outside the filing cabinet than inside, consider getting those with **reinforced** tabs or consider getting plastic file folders that are made in different colors and styles.

If you want papers you file to be more secure, less likely to fall out and easier to locate, consider two-hole punching papers in **fastener folders**. They're essential for important papers that have legal or tax implications where you just can't take a chance of losing any paper. Generally, you'll put papers in reverse chronological order—i.e., the most recent papers are on top. Hole-punched papers take up less space, which is particularly important in businesses where bulky files are the order of the day. You can buy folders with the fasteners already attached or buy the folders and fasteners separately, which is more economical.

Wherever you'd use several fastener folders for one client or project, the **partition folder** is great. The partition folder, also called a **classification folder**, is made of heavy duty pressboard, and lets you group related papers together in different sections of the folder by either attaching two-hole-punched papers to fasteners on either side of each partition and/or by placing unpunched papers in between the partitions. Different styles are available that offer from one to three partitions, some of which are pocket dividers (see Figure 9-3 for an example).

Figure 9-3. This Smead Classification Folder comes with pocket style dividers.

Easy-to-read folder labeling systems

MAGNIfiles are V-bottom or box-bottom hanging files that come with special 11-inch long transparent (colored or clear), durable, magnified plastic indexes that run the full length of the file. Besides greater file name visibility, these file indexes give you plenty of room for file titles—five times the space of conventional tabs. Index strips come in white, full color or color tip styles. MAGNIfiles are available from Ultimate Office Systems, **800/631-2233** [NJ] or **www.ultoffice.com**.

Smead Viewables Color Labeling System for hanging or top-tab folders, classification folders, jackets, or pockets creates a very visual, color-coded system to enhance the filing and retrieval process. The starter kit comes with PC-based software to use with your color printer to generate unique, wrap-around color-coded labels. Go to **www. smead.com** to learn more and see a Flash demonstration of Color Viewables in action.

Other filing supplies

If you frequently pull files out of the filing cabinet and take them to different locations, you may want to use folders that have sides to protect the contents. The **file jacket** comes in two styles—flat or expansion (see Figure 9-4) and in "manila vanilla" as well as many colors. File jackets can be used within your filing system or as part of the Daily Paperwork System discussed in Chapters 4 and 8.

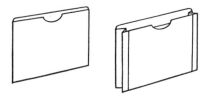

Figure 9-4. Flat file jacket (left) and expandable file jacket (right)

Much sturdier than the file jacket, the **file pocket** in Figure 9-5 has accordion style sides called "gussets" that allow for more expansion and use. The file pocket can fit inside a file cabinet, on a shelf or in a metal collator. The file pocket will hold several related file folders together or other bulky materials, including catalogs and books. You can get file pockets in a rainbow of different colors.

The **expanding wallet** (also in Figure 9-5) is similar to the file pocket except it usually has a flap with a clasp, tie or an elastic cord. It is useful for carrying, transporting or storing records. Wallets come with or without internal dividers or "pockets." I use wallets with pockets to store my annual tax and business records.

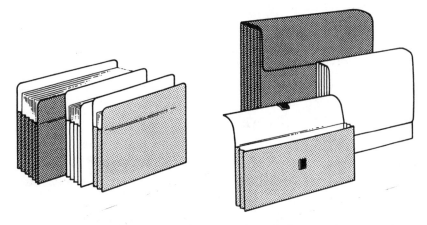

Figure 9-5. Wilson Jones ColorLife File Pockets (left) come in great colors. Wilson Jones ColorLife Expanding Wallets with single pocket and multiple pocket styles include easy-to-use Velcro "Gripper" closures.

The **expanding file** or **accordion file** is similar to the wallet in terms of construction, except it's larger and you can get it without a flap. The expanding file is a box-like, multi-pocket file with preprinted headings such as A-Z, 1-31 and Jan.-Dec.

Self-adhesive vinyl pockets, such as those by Smead, come in different sizes that you can attach to the inside of file folders. These pockets can hold such items as business cards, computer disks, CD-ROMs, DVDs, photos, or any loose items that need to be kept with the file.

Label protectors will help you keep file folder labels and tabs clean and resistant to wear and tear. If you only need a few and don't mind cutting them yourself, look under "Laminating Supplies" in an office supply catalog or website and then look for clear, self-adhesive, plastic sheets that you can cut to size.

Special Office Filing and Information Management Systems

If you're planning to design a filing system for a large office or an office with special information management needs, the products in this section could be helpful. Another place to look for local assistance with your filing or information needs is in the Yellow Pages under "Filing Equipment, Systems and Supplies," "Microfilming Service, Equipment and Supplies," "Bar Code Scanning Equipment" and "Data Processing Equipment."

More on color coding

If your office is a medical office, for example, and has many, many files you'll probably select a more elaborate color-coded system that uses different combinations of colored, self-adhesive letters or numbers to quickly identify folders and prevent misfiles.

If you file patient files by their last name, for example, you would probably take the *first two letters* of their last name and put corresponding self-adhesive colored letters on the folders. Each letter of the alphabet in such a system has a color. For example all the "S's" are orange, the "I's" green and the "M's" purple. Take my last name, "Silver." My folder would have an "SI" on it where the "S" is orange and the "I" is green. When you file or retrieve the "Silver" folder, it's much faster to go directly to "SI" than to check through all the last names that begin with "S." If the next folder is "Smith," you'd see an orange "S" and a purple "M." Color coding file folders lets you file and find them more quickly.

There are other codes you can attach as well to folders, such as yearly codes or colors that signify a type of patient.

The following companies make a whole line of special color-coded tabs: Jeter Systems (800/321-8261 [OH] or **www.jetersystems.com**); Smead (651/437-4111 or **www.smead.com**); and TAB Products Co. (888/822-9777 [WI] or **www.tab.com**). Ask if there are local representatives to help you design your system.

Special filing equipment

High-density mobile filing systems equipment, consisting of heavy lateral filing units that usually run on mechanical floor tracks and all but eliminate wasted aisle space, are useful for large, centralized filing systems. Two manufacturers of these systems are: Kardex Systems, Inc. (800/234-3654 [OH] or **www.kardex.com**) and Spacesaver Corporation (800/492-3434 [WI] or **www.spacesaver.com**). Also see Jeter Systems and Tab Products Co. (previous paragraph).

Document management and other automated filing solutions

Because information continues to proliferate both in paper form and in computerized files, your office may need a **document management system** that includes software and possibly hardware components.

The term "document management" can refer to different types of systems and software, all of which involve use of a scanner. One type is focused more on scanning and storing *images* of documents, which you index with words of your choice. With a stored image of a document you do not have editable text that you can word process.

Another type of system goes a few steps further. It takes the image and turns it into a text file (that you can edit) and also automatically indexes every word in the file. You can search these files for any words or phrases they contain (not just a few keywords). You can also turn the file back into the original image and print it out on paper. This way you don't have to store the original paper because it's stored in the computer either as a graphic image or as text (which may contain graphics). Make sure you have good backup copies.

If you're serious about document management, you're going to need more than one a low-priced, slow scanner, which is fine for occasional use or for desktop publishing needs but isn't designed for heavy duty document management needs. Another caveat is make sure you have enough disk storage space for document management. Here's a tip: you can save space by deleting images after they've gone through OCR, provided you only need the text and not the image. Select a system that will grow with you because you won't want to change systems and waste time converting your system's files to another system.

For more serious document management, you'll want to look for **document management software**, sometimes also called **document image management software**. Some of these programs also have workflow capabilities, such as document image routing, file creation tracking, editing and document sharing.

When document management is more involved with keeping track of records and the use of bar coding, it moves into the area of **tracking software** or **records management software**.

Smeadlink Express File Room is file management software for paper records that uses bar code technology for automated file tracking and quick, accurate data entry. Optional color-coded label printing can reduce filing and retrieval time and virtually eliminate misfiled folders. This software is designed to track file locations and usage and provide file retention management. Smead Software Solutions, 800/216-3832 [MN] or **www.smeadsoftware.com**.

Bringing together document management and records management, **Smeadlink Express** is designed to provide complete control over all documents, both paper and electronic, used throughout an organization. Smeadlink Express offers a package to manage the document life cycle. Smead Software Solutions, 800/216-3832 [MN] or **www.smeadsoftware.com**.

Important tip: Find out just how much time is involved with the various steps in the document management process—initial scanning, running an image through OCR, searching and printing. Determine whether the investment in time and money warrants your use of document management, to what degree and by whom. Do your homework—selecting a document management system takes some research and planning. And ask for references as well as current reviews or awards.

10

For Collectors Only: How, When and What to Save

Quick Scan: If you're an inveterate collector or you're in a profession that simply requires you to save many records, documents or resources, this chapter is for you. Here are some guidelines that will help you save only the essentials. Be sure to also check out the Resource Guide for additional resources, products and services.

I'm convinced the world is divided into two groups of people—those who save and those who don't. And there has to be a Murphy's Law somewhere that says, "If you're a collector, you're probably living or working with someone who isn't."

I admit it. I'm a collector. Not only do I have many interests and avocations (I suffer from the "Da Vinci Syndrome"), but I have chosen occupations that attract collectors. I have been a school teacher, an editor and a manager. Today I am a professional speaker, trainer, writer and consultant and I continue to maintain well-organized resource material.

I am not against collecting. Certain professions demand it. But collecting requires strict guidelines and routines if you ever hope to stay in control.

Consider the degree your collecting habit is taking control over you. Recognize that it can be tamed and turned into a constructive resource that will give you a professional edge.

Types of Collectors

Sometimes it's helpful to see the different kinds of collecting traps we fall into. People with a "possession obsession" like to buy new things and add to their growing collection. And once something enters their environment, it remains for the duration.

"Chipmunk collectors" don't go out of their way to purchase new possessions. Instead, they squirrel away everything for the winter—*every* winter. "Waste not, want not" is their motto. Chipmunks were taught to hold onto everything for dear life. Beware of thoughts like these: "I might need this someday" or "Somebody else might need this" or "This could really come in handy…for someone…someday."

Compulsive hoarding may be a type of obsessive-compulsive disorder (OCD). This type of collecting can result in tall piles of old newspapers, broken items or even trash. There are online and local self-help groups that may help; try contacting Messies Anonymous (**www.messies.com**). And if you suspect OCD, contact the OC Foundation at 203/401-2070 [CT] or **www.ocfoundation.org** for information and support.

People who love the printed word are "information junkies." These are people who love to learn, read, write, improve themselves and find out what the experts have to say. And even if you're not an information junkie per se, you still live in an "information age," where there are more than 1,000 specialized publications every year, 1,000 new book titles each day throughout the world and websites full of useful information that keep growing in number and content. The sum of printed information is doubling every eight years; the billions of computers in the world have greatly contributed to the problem of information overload.

If you can relate to any of these collecting habits (and most of us can), you'll want to keep reading. Any of these habits can become nightmares in short order if you don't put a lid on them. The way you do that is by learning to *make decisions* about paper, possessions and even emails. But as we discussed in Chapter 1 and 2, decisions aren't made in a vacuum.

Making Decisions about "Collectibles"

The secret to making decisions and controlling papers, possessions and info is to know your goals and values. Know what's important to you and what's really worth your time and energy. According to Roy Disney, Walt Disney's brother, "Decisions are easy when values are clear."

Once you're clear about your values and goals, you're ready to establish some stick-to-'em criteria. The problem people have when they're going through their stuff is that they aren't using the right criteria. As a result, every item requires a major decision from scratch.

To Save or Not to Save... That is the Question!

If you're suffering from "Discard Dilemmas," the following two general guidelines (as we discussed in the last chapter) can help you with troublesome *papers*:

1. When in doubt, *save* tax, legal or business items.

2. When in doubt, *toss* resource information, especially information you seldom, if ever, use.

As archiving email has become more of a legal concern, companies are getting legal advice on what to keep and for how long; it's not a bad idea to get legal advice on retention of hard-copy items, too.

When you're in a discard mode (or should we say discard mood), use these simple guidelines along with the following criteria to clear clutter:

10 Questions to Toss Out When Deciding What to Save

1. Does the item significantly enhance your work or life?

2. Do you need it now?

3. Was it used last year? More than once?

4. Will you use it more than once next year? (How likely is it that you will *ever* need it?)

5. Would it be difficult or expensive to replace? Could you get it from someone else?

6. If it's a hard-copy document, can you save it on your computer and is it important enough to do so?

7. Is it current (and for how long?)

8. Should it be kept for legal or financial reasons?

9. Could someone else use it now or make this decision?

10. Is it worth the time and energy to save?

Go back and star each question you could use. Keep them right in front of you as you make your discard decisions. Add any others that specifically fit your situation.

Or follow the "cardinal office rule" of former Los Angeles Mayor Richard Riordan, who advises, "Don't keep it in *your* file if someone else can keep it in *theirs*."

The Sorting Process

Now that you've established your criteria for saving (or tossing), you're ready to begin the actual process of sorting your collectibles. Your best bet is to make it a game with definite time limits. You can spread out your game over a period of time, doing a little this week and a little next week. Or maybe you prefer to dig right in and work for a few days straight, such as over a weekend. Or instead, try this one on for size: pretend you have to move your office in less than 24 hours to a space that is half the size. (Got your adrenalin flowing yet?)

Carve Out Some Uninterrupted Time

Whichever is your style, choose blocks of time without interruptions, as this is real mental work that requires concentration. Block out at least a few hours. Have on hand the necessary supplies—a trash basket (or barrel), a pencil, a timer, empty cardboard boxes (such as Fellowes Bankers Boxes [**www.fellowes.com**] or other cardboard or plastic file boxes with lids are great) and space to work.

Start Small

Tackle a small area at a time—one pile on your desk, a file drawer, a section of a file drawer, etc. Begin where the need is greatest. If your file cabinets are packed to the gills, start there. If you haven't seen your desk in years, there's no better place to begin. It's best to choose something small and be able to work through it. Set your timer to establish a reasonable time limit (an hour or less).

Think Big

Use a macro, big picture approach to get a handle on your things. Begin by sorting through the designated area, deciding what to save, what to toss and what should be stored elsewhere. As you decide which items to save, sort them in categories based on types of items (e.g., books, files, supplies, personal items to take home), as well as *how often* you intend to use them (e.g., daily, several times a week, once a month). **Only things you use or refer to regularly during your working hours should be in your office.**

Use a Plan of Action

The process is not simply willpower, of sitting down and forcing yourself to go through your stuff (although a little willpower won't hurt). What you need is a **plan of action**, particularly if you have "long-term buildup." (Chapter 1 will help you design a simple plan of action.)

Write as you sort. It's helpful to list your criteria and your sorting categories as you do the process. This list, along with a written plan of action, will help you tremendously. Carefully number and label boxes and drawers *as you go*. Keep a written record of any items going into storage.

I use my computer to keep a record of boxes that are stored off-site. It's easy to update my Word document, which is named "StorageFiles." I also keep a printout of "StorageFiles" in my manual filing system. My boxes are labeled alphabetically (I'll double up on letters should I ever get to "Z," heaven forbid!) I share an off-site storage room with my husband, who uses a numbered box system.

An attorney who is a solo practitioner keeps track of open and closed client files with two Word documents: "OpenFiles" and another for "ClosedFiles." Each document has the client names, the number and location of their files and when those files were opened or closed. These documents are regularly backed up as well as printed out in hard copy.

What if you inherited somebody else's clutter? I received a letter from Sharon Lawrence, a student of mine who ran into this problem several months after taking two of my seminars. She had just accepted a position as a financial management analyst in a California county administrative office. She writes:

> I have a new job and a new challenge to being organized. I left my organized office for a complete disaster area. I couldn't believe my new office; when I walked in, my mouth fell open. There were three inches thick of papers strewn over the entire surface of the desk, a bookcase filled with a year's worth of obsolete computer printouts and two file cabinets filled with five-year-old data, which belonged to other analysts. I informed my boss that I couldn't function until I had gotten organized.
>
> It was hard to know where to begin. By the end of the second day, I had shredded and/or recycled four trash cans full of obsolete reports and duplicate copies of letters and reports. I had also managed to clear the desktop. I still faced four piles of paper which had been sorted into broad categories.
>
> Working a little each day for two weeks, I have now managed to organize the piles of information into file folders. I have also given away two file cabinets and distributed their contents to the appropriate analysts. People now walk by my office and say things like, "Wow, what a difference!" I tell them about your classes and how this is the new me.

This is great, you say, if you know what you're going to need on the new job. But what if the job isn't second nature to you? When Nancy Schlegel became a systems engineer for IBM, she waited a year before she tossed out information. "After a year, I knew what I needed and what I didn't and I was in a better position to set up a filing system."

Where to Store It

Deciding where to store your hard-copy records and resources depends on four factors:

1. Up-to-date sorting and purging
2. Frequency of use

3. Size, shape and quantity of materials

4. Proximity to related items

First, have you completed the sorting and purging process before you buy that extra filing cabinet or bookcase? Where to house something should only be considered after you decide *if* you should keep it.

Second, the more frequently you use an item, the more accessible it should be. Identify *prime* work areas in your office—those areas that are most accessible. If your desk top and a desk-side file drawer are the most accessible areas, do they contain items that you use most often in your office?

Third, the size, shape and quantity of your resources will suggest the types of containers, accessories or pieces of furniture you select to hold those resources. If you have 12 inches of file folders you probably won't be choosing a five-drawer lateral file cabinet. If you're a graphic designer or a printer you may need special cabinets to hold large, oversized materials.

Fourth, things that go together should generally stay together. Try to group similar types of books, files and supplies together. Sound like common sense? You'd be amazed to see how many items that are unrelated to each other end up together—sometimes for years.

See the Resource Guide for specific storage products and ideas on art work, blueprints and photographic images; files and records; and literature organizers. For computer files and data, see Chapters 12 and 13. Also see Chapter 8 for turning your paper files into computer files by scanning them.

How to Prevent Long-Term Buildup

Having a philosophy about paper helped Kathy Meyer-Poppe when she was Revlon's Corporate Fleet director. Her philosophy was, "File a paper or toss it out—it's either important enough to be filed right then and there or it's not that important. So throw it away."

Many years ago management consultant Bill Butler shared his philosophy of cleaning one file a day: "One file you can manage."

There are no rules to maintenance. You may like to adopt Butler's "one file a day" or Poppe's "file or toss" routine. On the other hand, once a week or once every six months may work better for you. Or perhaps you want to wait until the need arises—bulging file cabinets or an impending move. Some people tell me the only way they can get organized is by moving—so they actually plan a move every few years!

Computer files can get overgrown, too. For ways to prune computer files, see "A Squeaky Clean Hard Disk" section in Chapter 12.

It can be thrilling to "clear a path" as one client described making headway on her collection. It's also thrilling for me to get letters like the following from Coleen Melton, a California art teacher:

> I'm writing to report to you that my goal is accomplished: 20 years of art placed into retrievable order thanks to your "Positively Organized!" class and your notes of support. I even have my husband wanting to organize his filing cabinet, and that is a miracle in itself.

Even lifelong collectors can learn and use the art of organization.

Giving It Away

The Environmental Protection Agency estimates that 250 million computers will be thrown out over the next five years. The Cellular Telecommunications Internet Association estimates that 130 million phones are discarded each year in the United States.

Instead of either saving or discarding obsolete equipment, *give it away.* Sometimes it's easier to get rid of things if you have someone to whom you can donate items; today there are agencies who refurbish old computers and cellphones and give them to others less fortunate. Often, you can get an income tax deduction through such donations.

Many major computer companies have recycling programs and may give you a trade-in allowance towards the purchase of a new computer.

And here's one caveat: before you donate or trade in a computer or cellphone, think about identity theft. Your computer files and emails may contain sensitive financial and personal information. Get a trace remover software program (see the Resource Guide) to wipe out sensitive information. Better yet, hire a computer pro who specializes in this area. And before you donate or sell a phone, be sure to permanently delete phone numbers, addresses, email addresses and passwords.

To learn about donating to organizations that take used computer or cellphone equipment, see the Resource Guide.

Resource Guide

It's helpful to have a good office supply catalog handy or to be online at an office supply store site while you're reading about many of the products in this guide.

Art Work, Blueprints and Photographic Materials

Artist and Document Storage Files

Artists portfolios, art folios, art cases, presentation cases are all different names of portable containers for storing, transporting or displaying art work. Check out good office supply or art stores as well as catalogs. For storage rather than display, consider the following items available in most office supply catalogs:

For flat storage

Safco has many flat storage solutions in its catalog. Here are some products to look for: the **Art Rack** is a modular, vertical filing system with eight large compartments; the **Safco Portable Art and Drawing Portfolio** is a low-cost, durable file with a handle that comes in three sizes and is useful for transporting art work, film, drawings and large documents (see Figure 10-1); **Safco 5- and 10-Drawer Steel Flat Files** are for serious, professional storage; **Safco Vertical Filing Systems** offer efficient systems for keeping large sheet materials well protected, yet organized and easily accessible; and **Safco Giant Stack Trays**, which stack up to five feet high, are economical alternatives to expensive metal files for art boards, blueprints, film, drawings, drafting paper and other oversized documents you want to store flat. These Safco products are available nationwide through office products dealers, industrial supply dealers and art and engineering dealers. For a catalog or more information, call 888/971-6225 [MN] or visit **www.safcoproducts.com**.

Figure 10-1. Safco Portable Art and Drawing Portfolio

Smead Artist Portfolio is another alternative. **www.smead.com**

For Rolled Storage

Safco Products offers rolled storage solutions that include their **Corrugated Fiberboard Roll File**, an economical way to organize and store large materials that comes in three different tube lengths and in three different compartment configurations (see Figure 10-2); **Safco Tube-Stor KD Roll Files**, which provide an ideal low-cost system for active or inactive storage and include two convenient label areas to list rolls and locations and built-in tube length adjusters; **Safco Mobile Roll Files,** which are good for active rolled materials that you need to move from office to office. (For contact info, see listing under "For Flat Storage" above.)

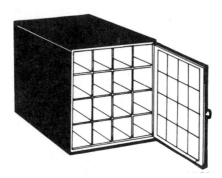

Figure 10-2. Safco Corrugated Roll File

CD and DVD Storage

DVD Library Systems from Pioneer North America organize large collections of CDs and DVDs. 800/421-1404 [CA] or **www.pioneerusa.com**

Also look for **organizers** from Allsop Inc. (800/426-4303 [WA] or **www.allsop.com**) and Case Logic (800/925-8111 [CO] or **www.caselogic.com**

Photographic Storage: Digital Photos

Chances are you have (or will soon have) thousands of digital images and you need a way to organize and share them. Certainly take advantage of the built-in folder system on your computer.

I recommend versatile **Memory Manager** software for organizing your digital photos the way you organize your photo albums. The simple editing tools let you crop and improve your photos. You can also share your photos via email. Creative Memories, 800/341-5275 [MN] or **www.creativememories.com**

As much as I'd like to recommend online photo-storage sites, I need to offer some warnings instead, especially for those so-called "free" and "unlimited" sites. First, some of the "free" sites may have a catch, which is sometimes buried in their terms and conditions clauses and may put your photos at risk. For example, you may be required to purchase products, pay a monthly storage fee or sign in regularly; failing to do so can result in your pictures being permanently erased. **Read the "terms" in the privacy or user agreements carefully.**

Of course, whether or not you use such an online photo-storage and sharing site, **make offline backups of important photos.** CD, DVD or thumb drives work fine—and keep them off-site if possible.

Photographic Storage: Nondigital Slides and Prints

Archivalware Tools for Serious Collectors offers museum quality archival storage for serious collectors, hobbyists and scrapbookers. Search the online (or print) catalog for a wide range of products including acid-free albums, papers and boxes to preserve photos, slides, books, prints, important papers and memorabilia. All products are acid-free, lab-tested and museum quality. University Products, 800/336-4847 or **www.universityproducts.com**

The **"Century Photo Products"** catalog is an excellent source for photo, slide and negative pages and albums. Century Photo Products, 800/767-0777 [CA] or **www.centuryphoto.com**

Creative Memories is a great source for photo-safe albums, album-making supplies and memory preservation accessories. Creative Memories offers a wide selection of albums as well as accessories such as photo-safe page protectors and a compact personal trimmer for cropping photos and small shapes. Creative Memories, 800/341-5275 [MN] or **www.creativememories.com**

Light Impressions is a catalog/website that offers the largest variety of fine archival storage, display and presentation materials for negatives, transparencies, CDs, photographs, artwork and documents. Light Impressions 800/828-6216 [CA] or **www.lightimpressionsdirect.com**

Visual Horizons offers a good selection of media presentation, storage and organization products. Visual Horizons, 800/424-1011 [NY] or **www.visualhorizons.com**

Files and Records Storage

When you have inactive records, look in your office supply catalog or store under the category "storage files." There you'll find a variety of choices.

If you need permanent storage boxes that are moisture resistant, consider plastic boxes with durable construction and snap-tight lids. You can use them for hanging files or for general storage at home, at work or on the go.

Another choice is corrugated fiberboard boxes (see Figure 10-3 for two examples). They usually come with lids. If you'll need access to files, consider getting drawer style storage boxes. Some of these are available with metal reinforcement, which provides greater durability for stacking.

If you have many, many boxes of records you want to store off-site, look in the Yellow Pages under a heading such as "Storage." See also Chapter 9 for more information on filing.

Literature Organizers

Magazine files or **holders** sit right on a shelf or table and are great for storing magazines, catalogs, manuals or reports. Some are made of high-impact plastic. Others are made of corrugated fiberboard, which costs less but still does the job.

Store magazines and catalogs in a three-ring binder without punching holes with Baumgarten's **Magazine Organizer** strip, **www.b3.net.**.

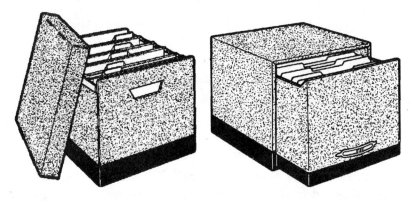

Figure 10-3. Corrugated fiberboard records storage box with lid (left) and storage drawer (on right), which gives easier access to files.

Literature sorters and **organizers** come in many different styles and sizes and are great for catalog sheets, brochures and forms that you use frequently or that need to be assembled into kits. See Figure 10-4. (See also Chapter 8 for systems by Ultimate Office.)

Figure 10-4. Fellowes Literature Organizer with 24 compartments (www.fellowes.com)

Recycling, Reusing & Donating Old Computers, Cellphones & Media

Association of Personal Computer User Groups (APCUG) lists local (and international) user groups, many of which have community service projects dedicated to collecting, restoring and donating computers to schools, churches, senior centers, etc. **www.apcug.org**

CellForCash.com has a mission to help consumers and businesses capture the value of their unused cellphones. Your old cellphone may be useless to you but of great use in a different market or even in a different country. (See also the affiliated fundraising organization, **www.WirelessFundraiser.com,** 800-364-0258.) CellForCash.com, 800/503-8026 or **www.CellForCash.com**

The **Computers for Schools Program** (CFSA) is a non-profit professional association of organizations involved in the management of refreshed (functional systems replaced by up-to-date equipment) computers and their placement into our nation's schools and educational institutions. CFSA offers many local pickups of donations. 800/939-6000 [IL] or **www.pcsforschools.org**

GreenDisk is an award-winning company featured in *TIME* magazine that provides high security recycling and disposal of media from a CD to a PC and most of the technotrash items in between. With more than 12 years' experience, GreenDisk works with both for profit and nonprofit companies to create a national network of service providers, jobs for workers with disabilities and a line of recycled products. Green Disk, 800/305-DISK (800/305-3475) [WA] or **www.greendisk.com**

The National Cristina Foundation (NCF) links corporations and community organizations and public agencies who train people with special needs. NCF encourages corporations and individuals to donate surplus and used computers, software, peripherals and related business technology. NCF directs those donations to prescreened training and educational organizations. 203/863-9100 [CT] or **www.cristina.org**

Phone Fund accepts cellphones, digital cameras, PDAs and laptops as part of a simple fundraiser program you would do for a school or other community organization. **www.phonefund.com**

RIPMobile, a division of **CollectiveGood Inc.**, offers a reward system especially targeted to the young crowd, who have access to millions of used **mobile phones**. CollectiveGood also collects **pagers, PDAs** and **ink jet cartridges** at more than 1,500 locations throughout North America. RIPMobile works directly with the public and CollectiveGood recycles mobile devices (phones, pagers, PDAs) and all of their related accessories, usually in partnerships with charities, companies, and/or governments. 770-856-9021 [GA] or **www.RIPMobile.com**

Share the Technology is a nonprofit corporation that since 1996 has functioned as a public service computer donation database, listing computer donation requests and offers from across the U.S. (and other countries). Online forms allow donors to submit offers and donation seekers to submit requests. recycle@sharethetechnology.org or **www.sharetechnology.org**

Donating excess new inventory or equipment

If you have excess new inventory or equipment to donate, including computer donations, contact one of the following organizations:

Gifts in Kind International partners with businesses and nonprofit organizations to provide quality products and services that improve lives in communities around the world. Started in 1983, Gifts In Kind International is the third largest charity in the U.S. Top manufacturers and retailers, including 44 percent of the Fortune 500 companies, rely on Gifts In Kind International to design and manage the donation process. 703/836-2121 [VA] or **www.giftsinkind.org**

National Association for the Exchange of Industrial Resources (NAEIR) is a nonprofit organization founded in 1977 that solicits donations of valuable, new merchandise from American corporations and redistributes this merchandise to nonprofit organizations, churches, and schools. 800/562-0955 [IL] or **www.naeir.org**

Trace remover programs

Before you donate computer equipment, be sure to use one of the following programs to erase all your data:

BCWipe is designed to securely delete files from disks so that recovery by any means is impossible. BCWipe is fully integrated into the Windows shell. Jetico, Inc., **www.jetico.com**

Window Washer removes data on your Web and desktop activities. For deleted computer files, the program is set up to completely overwrite the files with random characters making them permanently unrecoverable by undelete or unerase utilities—a security feature that exceeds the tough standards of the Department of Defense and the National Security

Agency. Webroot Software, Inc., 866/612-4227 [CO] or
www.webroot.com

Reminder on removing data from mobile devices you're donating

Just as a donated or recycled computer needs to have its data destroyed before coming into the hands of a stranger, the same is true for mobile device data (your phone book, incoming and outgoing calls and text messages, stored credit card numbers, photos, memos and other info).

First, remove your SIM card that has much of your data if you want to transfer that data to another device.

Then you'll need to do a series of manual reset commands to erase other data and settings. Check the manual for your phone for the correct procedure for your model or if you're having difficulty (or want to double check the correct steps), go to ReCellular's site at **www.wirelessrecycling.com/home/data_eraser/default.asp** and click on the manufacturer and model of your device.

11

Mobile, Traveling Offices:
Getting Things Done
on the Road or Telecommuting
from Home (or Starbucks)

Quick Scan: If you travel a good portion of the time, you have multiple or mobile offices, you have far-flung team members, you're a telecommuter with a home office or you're just on the go a lot, you need special time management techniques and work tools to manage your priorities and responsibilities. Discover how to master communications and paperwork from afar or just away locally from your office. See high-tech telecommunications to use in the air, on the road or just on the go. (See also Chapters 4 and 16, the Resource Guide, my new book, *Teach Your Computer to Dance* and updates at www.adams-hall.com.)

More people today have the challenge of a "traveling office," of working in at least one nontraditional office—be it a car, a corner or dedicated room at home, a vacation location, a hotel room, the cramped quarters of an airplane seat or a local hot spot such as Starbucks.

Trends and Changes

Perhaps the most telling work-related statistics are not that over 50 million people work outside their main office on a regular basis (and that figure is climbing) or that more and more people are setting up part-time or full-time home offices or that telecommuting (a term coined by futurist Jack Nilles in 1973 when he was a professor at USC) is an accepted work mode. Rather it's that laptop computers now outsell desktops in the U.S. and there are more cellphone lines than landlines in the U.S.

Working 24-7

More offices are becoming mobile, 24-7 **virtual offices**, which "nomad" workers can locate almost anywhere—their home, a hotel, their car or their customer's place of business. A virtual office is typically equipped with a laptop computer and one or more mobile devices that include cellphone and often PDA capabilities. A mobile office with its equipment is easy to relocate whenever the need arises.

Not all work-related trends get a universal thumbs-up. Setting up a fully-equipped home office in a vacation home can get mixed reviews, especially from a spouse. And when a boss or you have a 24-7 work-week expectation, it may mean that you can no longer separate a weekend from a workday when you're getting and handling emails, instant messages and phone calls on your "days of rest."

But mobile offices give us greater flexibility now as to where, how and when we work—if, and this is an important if, *we are good time managers.*

Remote Access

And the tools are getting better to let us work wherever we want. **Remote access software programs** let you access files and emails (from your laptop computer or even a properly enabled mobile device (such as a smartphone) and **remote control programs** can let you see and actually remotely control your actual main computer desktop and contents. There's more on remote access and remote control below. Or, you may just use file synchronization and file sharing tools. (More on all these tools later in the chapter.)

Devices, Mobility and Capabilities

With greater mobility comes the trend toward making mobile devices as powerful and versatile as computers and turning them into all-in-one devices. Consequently you can reduce the number of devices you carry (and their weight) as well as the number of cables, cords and power adapters.

Even power adapters and chargers are evolving. You may be able to buy a universal adapter to recharge your laptop computer as well as your phone.

Because most adapters are not labeled with even the manufacturer's name of the connecting device, you may feel you're playing Russian roulette when you plug an anonymous adapter into a device. To keep your sanity, work out a system to keep straight what goes with what. For example, you could put chargers and their accompanying cords together in marked plastic bags. You could also label each charger by affixing a piece of masking or duct tape on which you write the name of its corresponding device (using a fine felt-tipped marker such as a Sharpie pen). Better yet, label chargers and cords with the DYMO RhinoPRO handheld label printer discussed in Chapter 7.

To reduce the weight and number of items you need to pack up, more devices are being made that use a USB connection to get power from your computer instead of an adapter that plugs into a socket. Every little extra pound adds up—especially when you're an exhausted traveler. (By the way, if you're traveling internationally, you'll want dual-voltage chargers to avoid buying extra chargers.)

Most of us are unaware of all the potential already built into the devices we own. Do you know that your phone may not need an Internet connection to do some online searching through services such as Google? If your phone can do **text messaging**, you can send a text message such as "weather Chicago" to the phone number 46645 (which is number talk for "GOOGL") and then wait for a reply to see the answer. If you text the word *help* or the word *tips* and send it to 46645 on your mobile device dial pad/keyboard), Google will respond with a number of information options such as directions, movie name, weather, stock ticker, Q&A, Froogle, Google and Calculator.

And your phone may also be able to surf the Net. For example, Google has a Mobile Web search service (**www.google.com/xtml**) that links to pages formatted to display properly on the small screens of devices with a Web browser. Google has another mobile search service for phones that don't have a Web browser but do have WML (wireless markup language).

It used to be that only smartphones could browse the Web. Now there's Opera Mini, a fast and easy alternative that allows users to access the Web on mobile phones that would normally be incapable of running a Web browser. This includes the vast majority of today's WAP-enabled phones. Instead of requiring the phone to process Web pages, it uses a remote server to pre-process the page before sending it to the phone. This makes Opera Mini perfect for phones with very low resources or low bandwidth connections. Opera Software, ASA, **www.opera.com/products/mobile/operamini**

The Challenge of Traveling

Whether you travel 8 or 80 percent of the time for business, keeping up with all your responsibilities in multiple (and mobile) offices can be quite a challenge. As one executive admitted, keeping up is difficult even when you're not traveling. The tools, tips and techniques in this chapter could make the difference for you between exhaustion and exhilaration.

New modes of communication and ways of sharing travel tips and information are blossoming. Before you plan your next trip, see what people like you are sharing online about their travels by visiting online **wikis** where travelers share their experiences, good and bad. (See the Resource Guide.)

Not that many years ago, one association executive told me, "The airplane is the best place to read, think and write because you're away from the telephone." That was yesterday. Today, it's a question of whether you'll use a plane's built-in high-speed Internet connection onboard for email or VoIP (Voice over Internet Protocol). Having said that, don't overlook the opportunity to get some real work done on a plane by avoiding the constant interruptions you face daily on the ground.

Let's take a look next at how you can work most effectively on the road.

Working on the Road

Today, because of computers and technology (especially the Internet), you have more options than ever before in terms of the amount and kinds of work you can do on the road.

Before you leave for your trip, decide how much and what kinds of work you need and have to do. Traveling or working in other locations can be stressful in itself; don't overburden yourself if at all possible.

Wherever you're working on the road, you need the right tools and techniques. These days, mobile devices are becoming so powerful that some people leave their laptop computer at home. However, it's more common to see a double-barreled approach of a laptop and a handheld to make a road warrior fully armed and ready to work. But see what percentage of time you need to have a "traveling office." If it's for a good chunk of your work time, then it makes sense to outfit yourself accordingly; don't use an occasional business trip, however, as a reason for getting the latest electronic gizmo or service.

By the way, before you pack up for your next trip, decide whether you really need to take your laptop along or if a two-inch, one-ounce USB thumb drive with just your working files will be enough of a traveling office this time.

Set Up a Portable Office System

You need to plan a system to organize your work, communications and papers. As with everything else, there's no one right way to organize this system. But having a regular system in place, with the right tools, equipment and supplies as well as the right routines, can help you be more productive and stay in touch and in the loop. As much as possible, have your portable office system model your traditional office system. That way you'll feel more in control and reduce your stress level. And if necessary, there are ways for you to be connected to your main computer through a remote control or remote access program (which are discussed soon) so you can stay in control and be as connected as you need to be.

Traveling Time Management

Just as important as choosing your tech tools and services is making special use of your travel time. Accomplish as much as you can in the allotted time by **consolidating activities** when you travel. Plan ahead all the meetings you want to have and the people you want to see in a particular location.

While on a plane, take advantage of "creative thinking time." One consultant takes a simple sheet of paper and brainstorms ideas in the form of Mind Maps (visual idea outlines) and decision trees (pros and cons) for two or three of his current projects.

Consolidate similar activities while working on a plane, too. For example, group together all your writing work. Because space is at a premium, you're almost forced to work in this linear way. It's harder to jump from one thing to another when you can't spread out all your "stuff." (And if you're one of those people who accomplishes more when you travel, perhaps you should incorporate this one-thing-at-a-time work style into your back-at-the-ranch office, too.)

Traveling Technology

Today's high-tech telecommunications make traveling or working in multiple locations and staying in touch easier than ever and that's why you need to follow two rules.

Rule #1: Determine how much and how often you need to communicate.

Communications is a means to an end; not the goal itself. Too many people are communicating so much of the time that they have no down time, no private time, no thinking time and maybe even no "doing" time.

Many are also making too many routine items urgent—not a very effective use of time—and responding too much, too often and too soon. If you set up a pattern with someone in early communications by responding immediately even to nonurgent matters, you may be creating an expectation that you're always on call, every time, forever. Then a later, more measured, yet reasonably-timed response from you that better fits your schedule may be seen as your ignoring them. An example of a way to better control your time and response rate is restricting who has your cell number so you're not always available.

As a result of this time crunch from having too many work and communication demands, multitasking has become a lifestyle, not just part of your computer's operating system.

Prioritizing is more important than ever before. Good organizational skills let you first see the big picture—your goals and values—and then design your system—the right habits and tools.

Another big problem is trying to decide which tools (or toys) to use. I did some seminar work for one Fortune 500 firm that had a problem with too many communications options without a unified messaging system. Many employees had to check five or six systems several times a day just to make sure they received all their messages. Pity those employees who were less than positively organized and forgot to check every one of them! The more tools and systems you have, the more likely it is that something will slip through the cracks.

In addition, the company, through its strong emphasis on individualism, encouraged people to use communication channels that best fit them. This is a nice idea in theory, but when you have to remember how all of your colleagues like best to communicate and those colleagues are scattered across the country, your communications difficulties can easily multiply. New communications software can remember the preferred mode for you. (See the Resource Guide.)

Unified messaging, as discussed in Chapter 5, can help alleviate this problem by putting the messages in one electronic in-box rather than being stored in many different places. Unified messaging services, however, won't eliminate the increasing volume of messages that you may be receiving each day. That's why you need to use the most effective email, instant messaging and phone techniques (also see Chapter 5).

Rule #2: Use the right communications tools for you and the *least* possible number of tools—keep them simple but effective.

The cost of the tools you select is a consideration, but be sure you measure cost in terms of time, energy and frustration as well as actual dollars. If you can use a quick, low-tech solution to accomplish something, don't feel compelled to spend a lot of time trying to learn a high-tech "solution" that may become part of the problem. Use technology where it really counts. Remember that if you have too many communication tools or the technology is too challenging for you, you probably won't use the tools or the technology effectively.

Traveling with Your Laptop Computer

A **laptop** or **notebook computer** is central to most people's portable office system for handling writing, email, IM, projects, presentations, spreadsheets or Internet work on the road.

A laptop computer can be an invaluable tool transforming your relationship with customers. You can get a real customer service edge by providing on-site analyses and presentations, order taking and complete customer service by being logged into your desktop computer or your network or having a self-contained, complete solution on your laptop. (You may also want to carry a portable printer).

Make sure you have a laptop computer that's suitable for your needs. There are basically two different weight/size configurations: (1) the very lightweight models with smaller screens which can be sparsely or fully equipped (if you pay a lot more) and (2) the heavier, larger screened, possibly less expensive models that can be more powerful than your desktop computer (if you still have one). Note that there are also "ruggedized laptops" that are designed to take more of a beating and new mobile computers will be smaller in size, weight and capabilities.

Your choice may vary whether you occasionally take your laptop on the road with you or it's an everyday companion in your mobile office.

Special considerations with laptop computers

Laptops give you much more freedom but sometimes freedom comes at a cost especially when traveling. Whether you're straining your body by lugging a laptop through airport terminals or straining your patience at airport security, you may think twice about traveling with a laptop. When laptops start to weigh more than seven pounds, traveling with them can be a chore or a back-breaking experience. Be realistic as to what you can transport comfortably by also taking into account the weight of adapters, extra batteries, maybe an external mouse or keyboard and a laptop cooling pad.

Even if you're using your laptop in your mobile or home office, you may be straining your neck, shoulders, arms or wrists because laptops offer ergonomic challenges. With the screen and keyboard attached, what's a good ergonomic distance for the screen, may not be for the keyboard. As with any computer, you want a screen that works for you as well as a keyboard and a pointing device that feel good to you. (For more on ergonomics and solutions, see Chapter 6.)

Laptops have other issues, too. Laptops generate considerable heat which can not only potentially fry your computer's motherboard but also burn you. Why take a chance? Instead, wherever you use your laptop, consider getting a laptop cooling pad (many are inexpensive) to place under your computer. In choosing a laptop, be aware that computer processor chips specifically designed for laptops (mobile chips) generally run cooler (than chips initially designed for desktops and later placed in laptops).

Battery do's and don'ts

Another important concern when you're traveling is whether your battery will last long enough. Although you can bring an extra fully-charged battery along, you may not want to carry extra weight. For air trips, an option may be to book a flight on an airline which offers power ports for your computer.

Whether you're traveling locally or across the country, you have several ways to maximize battery life on the road.

First, since your LCD screen is the biggest energy consumer on your machine, consider reducing the screen's brightness. You might also want to adjust the timing on the computer's operating system power options for when the screen goes blank after not using the computer for a specified period of time.

Because a bigger screen requires more energy, you may decide to get a laptop with a screen no larger than 14 or maybe 15 inches to save on battery use (screens bigger than this also have a tough time fitting in airplane seating space and letting you work on a plane).

Second, remove any devices that don't need to be attached (e.g., USB drives or PC cards that aren't being used).

Third, take a look to see when your hard drive goes to sleep under the power options and power management setting.

Fourth, having more memory (RAM) reduces the amount of work your hard drive does and thus, saves energy and battery life.

Fifth, consider changing the timing for automatic saves on your word processing program and PIMs (personal information manager programs). Remember, the harder you make your hard drive work, the sooner you'll use up your battery life. Hibernation saves more power than the standby mode but it takes longer to wake up your computer.

Finally, when you're looking for your *next* laptop computer, look for: (a) batteries with longer lives that don't have to be drained to maximize their chargeability, (b) the latest mobile processing chips that maximize battery life and also run cooler and (c) some additional memory (RAM).

It can be a good idea to buy any user-replaceable accessories such as batteries close to the time you purchase a new laptop just in case they aren't available later. (See the Resource Guide.)

Protective travel cases for your laptop

Most importantly, make sure your laptop's travel case has plenty of shock-absorbing, air-filled pouches for padding to protect your computer if it's accidentally dropped or knocked. But there's more to consider with a laptop bag. Too small a bag makes it difficult to have enough protection but too large a bag will mean it's not considered carry-on luggage on a plane.

Features to look for include: (1) different-sized outer pockets to hold personal items, business cards, pens, maybe even a PDA or cellphone, (2) wheels or padding in the shoulder straps to ease the work in transporting your laptop, (3) expandable bags for bringing back handouts and briefing books and (4) bags with paler linings that make it easier to see the contents in dim light (such as on an airplane).

The Goldilocks approach

Take care of your laptop computer on the road. Avoid temperature extremes and fluctuations. For example, don't leave your laptop in a hot trunk, which can cook components and screens. An icy cold environment can crack a screen.

Laptop accessories

A number of products and accessories will help to make your laptop more productive such as mini-surge protectors or extra task lighting.(See the Resource Guide.)

Laptop security on the road

Because your laptop computer may be exposed to security risks especially while you're away from your office, you'll want to make your computer more secure by using a software firewall, running antivirus and antispyware software, turning on data encryption and maximizing your wireless Internet protection.

Try to avoid public settings while working on sensitive information and financial transactions. If you must work in a public setting, discourage others from peeking over your shoulder by using smaller fonts, a lower brightness setting on your PC and if necessary, a privacy filter on your laptop's screen.

Another important concern is keeping your computer from being stolen. F.B.I. statistics show that just three percent of stolen laptop computers are recovered.

Although prevention and common sense (don't let it out of your sight even in a bathroom) are the best first line of defense, you may want to take other steps such as encrypting the data on your laptop or mobile device, having a lock on the device and being able to remotely wipe out all the data on it if it's stolen. Another approach is to get track-and-recover software that sends a signal when your computer is logged onto the Internet that can be traced through an ISP (Internet Service Provider). (See the Resource Guide.)

To deter laptop computer theft when you're out in public, make your laptop inconspicuous by using an inexpensive backpack rather than an expensive laptop bag.

In your hotel room, you might try using security cables or locks or a safe in your room, if available, or the hotel safe.

Here are three disaster prevention tips for traveling laptops. First, make sure your laptop is covered by your insurance, no matter where your laptop happens to be. Second, if possible get 24-hour on-site service and/or replacement for your laptop. Third, take your overnight delivery service number with you (and any of their forms) in case you need to ship it back for repairs or an exchange.

Certainly affix a label with pertinent contact information (maybe include the offer of a reward for returning your computer). Put labels on peripherals, if possible, as well. Also use your laptop's password protection feature, which blocks others from even booting up your laptop but may show pertinent contact/reward information on your screen. (Some computers have this feature and others go a step further with fingerprint or retina ID verification for using a computer.)

And finally, be sure you have a clean computer—too many viruses and worms are spread to networks from authorized users accessing a network with a laptop while outside the office or syncing up a laptop to an office computer. To prevent your computer from wreaking havoc, follow as many of the protection and maintenance tips discussed in Chapter 14 as possible.

Connecting to Your Main Computer with Remote Control & Remote Access

Whether or not you take your laptop along, consider these Internet options to stay connected to your data and files while on the road.

It may not be enough to have a mobile device or a laptop computer with you while you're away from the office. What you may need is access to *all* the information, data and programs that are on your main office computer (e.g., your desktop computer). Even if you've synced your desktop data with your mobile device before taking off, while you're away from the office that desktop data may keep changing.

You have a couple of options to stay in the loop: **remote control** and **remote access** programs. These programs may work not only with your laptop computer but also with your mobile device (e.g., PDA or cellphone). Note that each of these remote programs has different capabilities and requirements.

Remote control programs

With this type of program, you don't have to worry about syncing your main (e.g., desktop) and laptop computers because you're actually using your main computer's files.

With a remote control program, it's like you're sitting at your desktop computer with its operating system while you're away from the office. After you type in a remote control password and then access codes using a computer with an Internet connection, you see your own computer's interface and contents pop up on the screen. If you're on the road with your laptop and you want to use all the files and applications that are on your desktop computer, this is the way to do it. These programs also let you copy files from one machine to another.

Keep in mind that your main computer must be turned on and connected to the Internet for this type of approach to work and you need a fast enough connection (this will be less of a concern as bandwidth increases over time). Another potential problem is that remote control programs may not work with every mobile device.

Finally, if you use someone else's (or a hotel business center's computer) to access the data on your main computer, keep security concerns in mind since you may not only be leaving a trail of passwords and other information on the host computer but also exposing all of your online activities if there isn't a secure, encrypted Internet connection. (For more info on Internet and email security, see my new book, *Teach Your Computer to Dance*.)

Remote access programs

A remote access program lets you access your main computer over the Internet with your laptop computer or mobile device in a more limited way. With this approach, you may have access to say, your email, calendar, in-box and file tree without needing as large a bandwidth connection. (See the Resource Guide.)

Web-based remote access services and websites

With some remote control programs, you need to have the software installed on both the host (your main computer) and the computer you're using away from the office. That can present a problem if you're not using your computer on the road. One solution is to use a browser-based remote access service that does not require special software installed on the remote computer (or mobile device); instead, you just need to sign up for the remote service and have an Internet connection.

Mobile Devices

Besides a laptop computer, you may use a mobile device such as the BlackBerry or a smartphone with email capabilities. This may be the way to go if most of your communication is by email and you don't want to lug your laptop.

These devices are taking center stage, especially for mobile professionals. Besides providing the standard time and personal information management features, they may be able to: (a) connect you to the Internet or specially reformatted Web pages called *Web clippings*; (b) send and receive email attachments and instant messages (including *push technology* where emails automatically appear on your screen without having to dial an access number); (c) make phone calls; (d) send and receive faxes; (e) do two-way paging; (f) access GPS (the **g**lobal **p**ositioning **s**ystem that pinpoints your geographical location) as well as all kinds of travel information; (g) have removable plug-in software modules and storage devices or built-in hard drives to greatly expand the capability of the devices; (h) sync your data with your main computer quickly and easily; (i) function as cameras, camcorders, televisions and game machines; and (j) in time, have a capability virtually equivalent to fully-functioning computers. (See the Resource Guide and also Chapter 4.)

Driving and safety concerns

We all know how multitasking can "task" us as we go through the work day. Keep in mind that using any communication tool while driving means you're multitasking.

A year-long study by the National Highway Traffic Safety Administration (NHTSA) found that a majority of car crashes involving cellphones and other wireless devices occurred while drivers were talking and listening, rather than dialing. Another NHTSA study also found that hands-free phones weren't much safer than conventional handheld phones when people were driving. Finally, an Insurance Institute for Highway Safety study found that using mobile phones while driving was just as dangerous whether holding a handset or using a headset.

With over 170 million cellphone subscribers in the U.S., this is something to think about seriously. Some cities, in fact, are trying to ban cellphone use by drivers in a moving vehicle. Since cellphone users spend 40% of their mobile phone time while driving, the safety implications are serious—as are the financial implications, since some juries almost seem to be punishing cellphone drivers who cause accidents by bringing in large civil judgments against them. End of lecture.

Cellphones

While many people have both a pager and cellphone, when given a choice, many more choose the cellphone.

Cellphones let you stay in touch with colleagues and customers, prevent voice mail backlog and may let you hear your email and send and receive text messages and instant messages. Since cellphones give you the option of having the built-in voice mail pick up a call when you don't want to answer, use this feature during meetings or seminars or when a call shouldn't have priority over whatever you're doing at the moment.

Here are some useful digital cellphone features to look for: easy-to-read display; calendar and scheduler; calendar notes; Internet access; email; recalling last numbers dialed; phone number storage (capacity can be 1,000 plus); voice mail alert; caller ID; call forwarding; call waiting; built-in date, clock, alarm, vibrating alert; scrolling keys; conference calling; programmable call timer; email forwarding to a fax machine; and a service that assigns two different numbers to the same phone. If you travel abroad to different continents, look for a phone that incorporates the GSM (**g**lobal **s**ystem for **m**obile communications) digital technology that's used overseas, especially in Europe.

As for carriers, choose one that most closely covers the areas you travel. When you travel outside your carrier's territory, you may have to pay special charges for long-distance or "roaming." If you use an outside area frequently, expand your area coverage with a different program and/or a different carrier or get a fixed-rate cellphone plan with national coverage, free long distance and no roaming charges.

Pagers

Pagers are still a useful wireless device. What's nice about pagers besides their small, lightweight size, is that compared to cellphones (the pager's major competitor), pagers tend to cost less per month, receive signals better in buildings and have broader coverage. A pager may also be a little less "interrupt-driven" and instant than a cellphone; you may be more likely to complete a task before responding to a page.

Pagers come in three main flavors: (1) the simple, easy-to-use, inexpensive one-way numeric pager (which provides only a digital readout of the phone number of the person calling you), (2) the one-way alphanumeric pager (which provides both numeric and text messages and can also receive email) and (3) the two-way text messaging (also known as *interactive paging*) pager. The two-way pager has a mini-keyboard that lets you communicate with another pager as well as a telephone, email address or fax machine; Internet news and information services are available as well. Sometimes you can get voicemail messages on these pagers, too. Two-way pagers can be an adjunct to your existing email system if senders keep their messages short.

Check to see how many messages/numbers your pager will hold, the coverage area for your pager and the cost. One other word of caution: pagers can drop characters when they're used in airplanes, tunnels, trains and buildings with a lot of steel.

Mobile Communications Choices and Challenges

Communication is so much a part of work today whether or not you're traveling that you should give special thought to how and when you prefer to communicate (as well as others' preferences). Be aware, too, if there's a *communication culture* with your colleagues that dictates preferred communication tools and methods.

Unified Messaging

With your time really at a premium on the road, here's where unified messaging can really benefit you. Unified messaging is a service that consolidates your voice mail, email, text messages, instant messages and faxes in one mailbox. For more information, see Chapter 5.

Email Time Management on the Road

Chances are you have several choices for accessing your email on the road (including on an airplane through a high-speed Internet connection). Before you travel, determine the least expensive way to access your email (such as a local access number or an 800 number if you don't have a wireless connection) and whether you need to lug your laptop. Since your time on the road is at a premium, another essential pre-trip step is to get your email management and organization in place before you walk out the door. This includes setting up email filters that help you separate essential email from routine and unwanted email. (For more on this see Chapter 5.)

With the trend towards ISPs (Internet Service Providers) providing more or even unlimited storage of your emails, you may be able to access not only new emails while on the road but also archived ones. You may decide to use your regular email provider or free **Web-based email** to send and receive email from any computer with an Internet connection (at cyber cafes, airline clubs and business centers)—see the Resource Guide.

Keeping Up with Calls While Away

Most business travelers try to respond to calls the same day and to stay in touch with work groups several times a day. Other business travelers rely more heavily on their staff or may use other communication channels/devices such as email or a smartphone.

If you're **a manager in charge of a far-flung** team, you have special needs to keep up not only with phone calls but all communications. "Virtual managers" who manage "virtual teams" need to make special efforts to stay in touch. Because phone calls are more personal, they offer an excellent channel of team-building communication. As *Wall Street Journal* columnist Carol Hymowitz explains it, "Voice time replaces face time as the dominant form of communication." But it's key to utilize instant messaging and email along with your cellphone so responses and communications are prompt and up-to-date.

You need to be especially organized when you communicate by phone with virtual team members. That means planning to spend a little extra time on the phone to develop a more personal relationship and to listen carefully and empathetically.

These days it makes more sense to just use your cellphone rather than a hotel phone system so you have a record of calls and messages on your phone's system. It's probably more cost effective and private, too.

With cellphones, it's easier to stay in touch than ever before. The hard part is consciously managing your cellphone time—deciding how and when to communicate via cellphone and with whom.

A Word on Voice Mail

Why is it you always seem to get even more calls when you're away?

Voice mail systems can work great when you're out of your office. If you have a voice mail system or service at work, find out if you can arrange to have it notify you (or automatically forward the message to your cellphone) when a message is left.

Of course, a voice mail or "voice messaging" system is far preferable to an answering machine because it lets several callers leave messages at the same time, especially important if you receive many calls and don't want to risk the chance of losing a call whenever your machine is handling another call simultaneously.) If you have an answering machine, certainly have one with remote access where you dial a code to retrieve messages and consider also adding a voice mail service to catch those simultaneous calls.

Here's a timesaving voice mail tip if you're traveling and are fortunate enough to have an assistant. Have your assistant listen to and transcribe your voice mail and then summarize important messages for you by leaving one message on your voice mail or simply sending you an email summarizing your calls.

Many hotels now have their own voice messaging systems for guests but be careful when using them because they don't offer as much privacy as other tools. If the hotel voice mail system uses a code (such as your room number and the first four letters of your last name), ask if you can change the code. You could also opt not to use the system at all and revert back to written telephone messages; that will discourage callers from leaving private messages.

Don't discuss any sensitive, confidential or personal matters on hotel voice mail (or on an incoming hotel telephone line for that matter) and maybe not even on your own cellphone or other mobile device especially when you're in a hotel or other public area and/or if you're using Bluetooth technology.

Here is another cellphone security tip: make sure to use a **password** or code to check your **cellphone voice mail**.

Handling Digital Documents and Paperwork on the Road

When possible, eliminate paperwork and use digital documents instead. If you're staying in a hotel, look for one that caters to business travelers with either special business floors or special equipment in the rooms. If you're planning to do extensive work from your hotel room, check the status of their phone system and rooms before you get there. Find out if there's a business center on site, available equipment, hours of operation and fees; if there's no business center, find out what the hotel charges for printing, copying and faxing as well as any special services. Check with the concierge for nearby business or printing centers.

Planning

Planning is the secret to handling all docs when you travel. When you book your hotel reservation, for example, make sure the room has the basic necessities: a table (or desk) with a light, a phone and close access to high-speed Internet and electrical/modem outlets. If needed, see if any hotel-provided in-room computers, printers or fax machines are available or if there is a complimentary hotel business center with such equipment. If you're bringing your laptop, make sure you follow the safety precautions especially for wireless Internet access discussed in Chapter 14 and also in my new book *Teach Your Computer to Dance*. Here are some other ways to plan ahead for docs.

Transporting & Printing Docs

Portable printers can come in handy but if you don't want to lug equipment, there are other options.

A **USB thumb drive** is an excellent way to transport only essential files while on the road. It's also convenient to use **PC Cards**, which are credit-card-sized cards for "plug and play" operations as well as additional portable file storage. Don't overlook online file storage through your ISP (Internet Service Provider) or a commercial service or just sending an email to yourself with a document as an attachment. With these file storage options, you can then use a business center computer or printing service.

If the formatting of the document is important and you don't bring your computer along with you, you may need to save it as a PDF (portable document format) file that preserves the formatting and can be read by any computer that has Adobe Reader. (Note that you need special software to *edit* PDF files.) XML is another file format that will become more widely used as a way of sharing and reusing information and data across applications, platforms and the Internet.

If you travel a lot and need a lot of copies, email your PDFs to printing companies (such as a FedEx Kinko's) in your destination city. Or get recommendations of local suppliers from hotel concierges or from local business contacts. I did this recently for an important leadership conference presentation I did out of town. Besides saving shipping charges, having documents printed and delivered for you in your destination city may save your back.

Faxing

If you plan to send or receive many faxes, you have several options. Using your laptop, you could send and receive faxes via your computer. Fax management software such as **WinFAXPro** by Symantec (www.symantec.com) could be very helpful; you can even send or forward faxes via email to people who don't have fax hardware or software.

Some hotels have faxes sent to an electronic fax mailbox, which guests can retrieve at the nearest fax machine. Some hotels may offer a service that delivers faxes via guest-room TV sets; using a remote control, a guest can either see the fax onscreen or have it deleted. Some airlines now have phones with fax capabilities.

If you need a hard-copy fax when you're on the go, you can print out any fax stored in your modem-equipped laptop via a hotel fax machine or at a public fax station located at a quick printer or commercial mail station. Look in the Yellow Pages for "Fax Transmission Service." If you're traveling by car, it might make sense to bring along a small, portable printer.

And here's a tip if you ever plan to use the hotel fax machine: check the cost first. Hotels sometimes assess high service charges—a flat rate $25 service charge per message or per-page fees of up to $10 for the first page and $1 for each additional page. An overnight delivery service could be cheaper and the hotel will probably have a daily pickup and delivery by such a service. (For other options see the earlier "Traveling Technology" section in this chapter.)

Paperwork Accessories

If your work or trip is paper intensive—such as going to a trade show or conference—select practical accessories to hold and transport paperwork and supplies. Try an expandable, document case that contains different colored folders—analogous to the Daily Paperwork System described in Chapters 4 and 8. Take along a lightweight tote bag filled with reading material; when empty, the bag can be folded inside the document case or used for transporting other items. A large, transparent, plastic folder could hold thank-you and other notes, cards, stamps, envelopes and letterhead. If email with or without attached files doesn't handle your paperwork output, a few Express, Priority Mail or FedEx envelopes may be useful to have on hand if you're going to be gone for a week or more and anticipate processing some paperwork on the trip and you want to mail some of it back, maybe along with dictation tapes.

Speaking of dictation, **Dragon NaturallySpeaking** has been the best voice recognition/dictation solution for years, providing award-winning speech recognition software that works with your computer or various handheld devices (800/654-1187 [MA] or **www.nuance.com**).

Portable file boxes may work for you if your office is in your car trunk or you have many files to take with you on a business trip. File boxes come in all shapes and sizes and can accommodate standard and hanging folders. Check your office supply catalog under "file boxes" or "storage files." (See also "Portable Office Products" in the Resource Guide.)

Categorize Different Types of Paper

Even your reading material for a trip can be organized into categories. One category could be "Business Reading," such as reports, industry newsletters and selected articles. Others could be specific, project related categories. Try to include a "Fun Stuff" category such as the daily paper, *USA Today* and *The Wall Street Journal*, which keep you current and are good sources of conversation starters.

Deciding What Papers to Bring Along and What to Leave

If possible avoid traveling with a very heavy briefcase. Paper weighs a lot and can cause great strain. You may want to ship (rather than carry back to your office) papers you accumulate on a trip, after first sorting and eliminating papers. Or better yet, have all of that information on your laptop, mobile device or USB thumb drive.

Take pertinent resource material with you in a concise, easy-to-carry format. If you want or need to use a hard-copy paper-based system (or a computerized PIM, personal information management program, isn't your cup of tea), you may want to do what one regional sales manager does. He created an alphabetical notebook system that he takes with him when he travels out in the field that contains summaries of clients and prospects, the latest meetings, the types of programs his company is offering and sales materials.

He uses single word phrases, "buzz words" he calls them, so he can see information at a glance. Typical information includes people profile facts such as key contacts and their family members and special interests plus buzzword summaries of problems and solutions that instantly remind him of next actions to be taken. If a client calls when he is on the road, he is prepared to talk intelligently, armed with up-to-date information. When he's in the office, he uses the book there, too. You may prefer to keep such information on your mobile device or laptop computer; but if you're very visual or kinesthetic, you, too, may prefer the "low-tech," hands-on approach. Whatever works for you is what I always say.

One executive has mail and important reading material sent to him via Federal Express when on an extended trip. He says, "Nothing is more depressing than returning from a trip to a stack of papers. When I come back, rarely do I have anything on my desk."

Triaging Paperwork & Business Cards

File your paperwork as you go into active project folders or at the very least, into two colored folders, say, red for "urgent" and blue for "not urgent." If you have papers for an assistant, use a separate folder.

Use different colored Post-it Notes to distinguish paperwork with different priorities or to categorize different types of work. Or you may prefer to type notes in your mobile device (or laptop computer) or dictate instructions for each paper as you read it using a dictating device or a mobile device such as a smartphone that has dictation capability. Anything you can do while on the road will save you time when you return from a trip.

As for all those business cards you collect, follow these four tips, which are especially useful at trade shows and conferences. First, jot down either an "A," "B" or "C" at the top to indicate the importance of this contact. "A" cards usually are ones that will need some immediate follow-up and are grouped together, as are Bs and Cs. If a card doesn't rate one of these letters, it gets tossed as soon as possible.

Second, write the date and event or place of the contact.

Third, if you need to write more background or follow-up information, write "over" on the front and jot notes on the back. (If you learn any personal tidbit, for example, names and ages of kids, write that down, too.)

Fourth, if you ever use the back of your card to write someone else's name and address (because they don't have a card) cross out the front of your card so that you don't accidentally give it to someone else.

You should probably put your notes on the back of the cards you collect. I strongly recommend scanners as discussed in Chapter 8 to scan both the front and back of your cards.

Resource Guide

See **www.adams-hall.com** for periodic updates and also my new book, *Teach Your Computer to Dance.*

Laptop (AKA Notebook) Computers
Accessories

In general, if you're having trouble finding user-replaceable accessories such as batteries or rechargers, try Mobility Electronics, Inc., a leading provider of hard-to-find, model-specific accessories and services for mobile electronic devices (888/205-0093 or **www.igo.com**) or Targus, Inc. (877/482-7487 [CA] or **www.targus.com**).

The ASF **Notebook Computer Light** provides a little extra task lighting when you need it without disturbing others. ASF Lightware Solutions, 800/771-3600 or **www.readinglight.com**

Bags/padded cases

Here are five excellent sources of well-padded cases:

Belkin, **www.belkin.com**

Brenthaven, **http://brenthaven**

Kensington, 800/535-4242 or **www.kensington.com**

Targus, 877/482-7487 or **www.targus.com**

Tekstyl, **www.tekstyl.com**

Battery add-on option

APC Universal Power Battery UPB80 can give you up to eight additional hours of battery life depending upon the power, screen and other settings on your laptop computer. American Power Conversion, www.apc.com

Cables, power adapters and rechargers

AC Anywhere is an adapter that plugs into your car's cigarette lighter or 12V outlet. It turns the outlet into a standard AC power outlet so you can recharge your laptop's or PDA's battery. Belkin, Corp., 800/2BELKIN or **www.belkin.com**

EverywherePower adapters can recharge laptops, cellphones, PDAs, portable printers and more. Mobility Electronics,Inc., 888/205-0093 or **www.igo.com**

Zip-Linq USB cables and power adapters can be plugged into the USB port of a computer to send power to handheld devices or to let the devices get power from a car's cigarette lighter or a 110-volt wall socket. Ideal for mobile professionals, Zip-Linq retractable cables are small enough to carry in a pocket but can expand to over 2 feet in length when fully extended. ZIP-LINQ, 800/609-7550 [CA] or **www.ziplinq.com**

Docking station

If you're looking for a port replicator or a docking station to add connections to your laptop computer for such devices as keyboards, printers, mice, USB drives and Ethernet/other connections, take a look at the **Universal Notebook Docking Station**. Targus, Inc., **www.targus.com**

LCD screen cleaner

Klear Screen Klear Screen is a manufacturer-recommended screen cleaner designed to safely clean screens without scratching them when used with their optical-grade Micro-Chamois or Micro-Fiber Polishing Cloths. Meridrew Enterprises, 800/505-5327 or **www.klearscreen.com**

Security locks

Check out the locks at Kensington Computer Products Group, **www.kensington.com.**

Surge protector

Targus Mobile Notebook Surge Protector helps safeguard your laptop computer from costly damage that can occur during power surges and spikes. Targus, Inc., 877/482-7487 or **www.targus.com**

Track-and-recover software to locate stolen computers

CyberAngel Security Software silently transmits an alert to a security monitoring center if the authentication is breached at login or boot-up. The software identifies the location from which that computer is calling. CyberAngel Security Solutions, Inc., 800/501-4344 [TN] or **www.sentryinc.com**

Stealth Signal software secretly sends a signal to the Stealth Signal Control Center via telephone or an Internet connection, allowing their Recovery Team to track your computer's location when you report it lost or stolen. The software can also delete files remotely. Computer Security Products, Inc., 800/466-7636 [NH] or **www.computersecurity.com**

Mobile Website Content

AvantGo lets you download news and other content from mobile websites through syncing, wireless surfing or a combination of both. With the software, you can get thousands of specially formatted websites on your smartphone or PDA to see news, weather, sports, stock quotes, maps, movie listings and more. iAnywhere Solutions, Inc., **www.ianywhere.com**

Paper-based Portable Office Products

The **Eldon Mobile Manager** looks like a briefcase but acts as a portable filing cabinet. Molded-in rails accommodate hanging files and other documents. A zip-down supply pocket and two oversized pockets store supplies. See **www.eldonoffice.com** for this and other portable office products.

More portable office accessories, shown in Figure 11-1, let you take your office with you. If you need to write while on the road, consider a **storage clipboard** with a durable clip and pencil holder and an inside compartment that stores paper, pens and more small supplies. Look for portable **file/storage boxes** with rails inside to accommodate hanging files and folders. Some have a supply compartment in the lid to hold pens, rubber bands, paper clips and other small office supplies.

For a large number of folders and/or hanging files, look for larger plastic **tote boxes**, which are sturdy and lightweight, provide moisture-resistant storage, often have molded-in rails for hanging folders and sometimes include a transparent, snap-tight lid for easier viewing of stored contents.

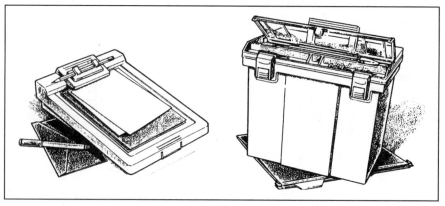

Figure 11-1. Storage clipboard (left) and portable file box with storage compartment in lid

Fellowes Bankers Box Hang 'N' Stor Hanging Folder Storage Box is an ideal product for storing and transporting a large number of letter-size hanging file folders. Plastic channels with a built-in track permit the files to glide smoothly. The file has a separate cover, tote handles and a large labeling area. **www.fellowes.com**

Portfolio cases are convenient tools to transport a note-taking pad and key documents. Some come equipped with a flap pocket or special pocket folders, a business card holder, a calculator and a pen/pencil strap. (These portfolios are not to be confused with the large art portfolios discussed in Chapter 10.)

An **auto clipboard** is a handy note pad. It attaches to a windshield or any smooth surface with a suction cup. It usually features a pen on a retractable cord.

Remote Control and Access Programs

GoToMyPC is Web-based remote control software that lets you see and access your actual main computer desktop and contents and work as if you were sitting right there with access to all your file and network connections. Citrix Systems, Inc., **www.gotomypc.com**

LapLink Gold lets you connect to other Laplink-enabled computers over any connection type to access a PC's critical resources. You can remotely access files and folders; synchronize data between computers; run applications; support coworkers or friends; print files on distant printers; and operate, maintain and even reboot computers. You can access your remote PC even when it's protected by firewalls. LapLink Software, Inc., 800/527-5465 [WA] or **www.laplink.com**

Remote Access Services—Web-Based

LapLink Everywhere is both remote control and remote access software that works with computers and mobile devices. You can access your remote PC even when it's protected by firewalls. LapLink Software, Inc., 800/5275465 [WA] or **www.laplink.com**

MyWebEx offers Web-based remote control of your main computer. Just install MyWebExPC on the host computer. No software is required on the client computer. Access is all done through the browser. WebEx Communications, Inc., **https://pcnow.webex.com**

Sharing and Syncing Files

If you don't actually need remote control or access of your computer and you're just looking to share or sync files, there are services available for you.

BeinSync keeps your files and emails in sync between your PCs so they are always available and easily shared—all without resorting to sending yourself emails or using remote access products. If you're traveling without a laptop, BeinSync also supports remote Web access. BeinSync, Ltd., **www.beinsync.com**

FolderShare automatically syncs file changes between linked computers. It allows you to create a private peer-to-peer network that will help you synchronize files across multiple devices and access or share files with business colleagues or friends. You no longer need to send large files via email, burn them to CDs/DVDs and mail them or upload them to a website. FolderShare allows you to share and sync important information instantly with anyone you invite. Formerly Byte Taxi, Inc., it was acquired by Microsoft Corp., **www.foldershare.com**

Unified Messaging

Your phone company may offer unified messaging. There are also these options:

Office Communicator 2005 is designed to manage, in a single view, instant messages, email, voice and other business communications and allow switching from instant messaging to a video chat or conference call with the click of a button. At the time of the writing of this book, it is being beta-tested. Microsoft Corp., **www.microsoft.com**

Onebox is for fax, email, voice and conferencing services. J2 Global Communications, Inc., 888/588-4600 [CA] or **www.onebox.com**

Part 4

Positively Organized! Computing

Organizing, Finding and Protecting Digital Info

12

Organizing and Finding Your Computer Files

Quick Scan: Gain full value from your computer by discovering more effective, timesaving ways to organize your computer and its files so that you can work more easily, find files and information more quickly and safeguard your valuable work.

The storage capacity of hard drives has increased by more than ten thousand percent in the last 20 years and it is expected to increase at least ten-fold in the next five years. Gigabyte drives will join megabyte drives as dinosaurs and terabyte (trillion byte) hard drives will be the measuring stick.

But one day, despite your computer's speed and all the space on your latest gigantic multi-gigabyte or terabyte hard disk, you may discover you're having trouble getting around or backing up your computer hard drive.

Perhaps you thought your newest computer system would make everything easier and more automatic, certainly easier than dealing with all the paperwork on your desk and the files in your cabinets. But with a larger hard disk plus all those Internet and multimedia files and a workload that just won't quit—well, you just don't seem to have time to tweak your system (or you may be overwhelmed and not know where to begin).

The bad news is that just like paper files, your computer and its files need to be accessible, up to date, properly categorized and regularly maintained. It's not enough to rely on desktop search tools to keep you really organized (there's more on this topic later in this chapter). You and your computer can slow down dramatically and you're less likely to do backups whenever computer file organization and maintenance is poor (or nonexistent).

But the good news is both you and your computer can function better when you organize your folders and files, practice good computer housekeeping and use appropriate backup strategies.

Chances are naming, organizing and backing up all your files and folders just isn't as systematic and automatic as you know it should be. Although finding individual files has gotten very easy with desktop search programs, poor organization means it's difficult to find related files in one place on your computer and to have organized, less time-consuming backups.

When it comes to the data on your computer, you want to be able to:

- Organize it

- Find it

- Back it up

- Protect it

We'll cover the first two in this chapter, backups in Chapter 13 and protection in Chapter 14.

Three Key Steps to Organize Your Computer, Folders and Files

How you organize your computer's hard disk, folders and files goes a long way toward helping you be in more control of your computer's contents and saving you time in backing up your vital information.

Step 1: Partition Your Hard Disk

With hard disks just getting bigger and bigger (your computer may contain hundreds of thousands of files), it makes sense to find ways to minimize how many of those files you must back up each time so backups don't take as long to complete. The quicker a backup is completed, the more likely you are to back up regularly.

The first step is to separate your computer's operating system, software applications and programs from your documents, video files, photos and music by dividing up your hard disk into at least two **partitions** or sections (or parts). This separation allows you to better organize and back up your computer. As you'll see below, you may want to take special steps with your large video files. Partition Magic is the software I recommend for partitioning your hard disk (see the Resource Guide).

The benefits of partitioning

While placing files in folders is a computer organizing tool, having partitions on your hard disk makes organizing folders and files even easier.

Partitions allow you to separate your **data** (what you create) from your computer's operating system and the software programs you buy. Separating them makes it much easier to do backups since it's generally just your data files that you need to put on a *frequent* backup routine. They're the files that are most likely to change from day to day, week to week. If you're also constantly backing up your operating system as well as all of your software programs, that's a needless time drain and that extra time may keep you from doing backups at all. (For more on suggested backup routines, see Chapter 13.)

How partitioning works

The hard disk in your computer is automatically designated by the manufacturer and the operating system software as your "C drive." When you partition your hard disk, the C drive is divided up into partitions such as the C: partition, the D: partition and the E: partition. All of these partitions are located on the one actual, physical hard drive (the C drive). The letters used for the partitions you create, besides the C: partition, depend on what other equipment you have in or attached to your computer such as a DVD, CD drive, thumb drive or other backup or hard drives.

If you partition your hard disk into a C: partition and a D: partition, you could put your operating system and your other software on the C: partition. Then you could have all of the data files you create (as well as music, video and image files) on the D: partition. To do your regular backups of just your data, you would just select the D: partition. That really speeds up the backup process. Also, by having your data files in a separate place, it makes them more organized and easier to locate. By the way, the term **data files** includes but isn't limited to word processing documents, spreadsheets, presentations, images, applications, Web pages, audio/video clips and databases.

Step 2: Set Up a Computer Folder System

Once you've organized your hard disk into partitions you're ready to take full advantage of your computer's **hierarchical folder system**. This system lets you create categories and subcategories into which you can put your application (program) and data files you buy and the data (document) files you create. Using a hierarchical filing system helps you better manage the large numbers of files and folders that come with the increased hard disk storage that's now available.

Such a system lets you group files logically by categories called **folders**. You can also create subcategories called **subfolders** (which are folders nested inside folders). Computer **folders** can hold files as well as other folders and are a great organizing tool.

Said another way, a PC hierarchical system gives you a way to graphically (visually) organize and see different levels and sublevels of the work you do and to group related files together. The big danger is to get carried away and create too many levels of subfolders. **Limit the number of levels of subfolders.** Beware of creating too complex a system that takes too much time to use. In general, you don't want to go more than three levels deep.

You also want to make sure you don't accumulate too many documents or applications in any one folder. When that happens, files can become difficult to find. That's when you may need to subdivide large folders into smaller ones. But if you have too many small ones, your system can become too complex. It's all a matter of balance and good design.

And even if you're using one of the fast desktop search programs, it will still pay for you to organize your files logically for backup purposes and to locate related or similar files.

More folder and file guidelines

To keep your system as simple and as accessible as possible, here are a few more guidelines. Limit the number of documents or applications you keep in each folder, especially ones that you use frequently. One rule of thumb is to create a **new folder** every time you accumulate **more than 20 files** in a folder. The fewer files you have in a folder, the faster it is to find files—especially the files you use most often—and to find related files. And **keep files and folders you use most often, most accessible**. It takes longer to find active files and folders that are surrounded by many inactive ones you rarely use. Get in the habit of moving old or rarely used files to archival or storage folders and disks.

It's all in a name

Consistency and **brevity** are more important than creativity when it comes to personal computer file or folder names. However, if too short a file name means you can't decipher the contents of a file without opening the file, then a longer file name is preferable. Also, it can be helpful to make your paper and computer systems consistent with one other.

As an organizer, I recommend you create a good file naming system that uses simple names and consistent codes or abbreviations. I recommend that you begin each file name with a short, codified, abbreviated version that's followed by a clear descriptive phrase. It can save you time to use this kind of naming system. Even though you may be able to create long, descriptive file names, a shorter, descriptive file name that is part of an organized naming system is better. However, the key is being able to recognize what's in a file and who it relates to by looking at the file name next week or next year. If it takes a longer name to clearly convey the contents, put clarity ahead of brevity.

I use initials followed by a dash and an abbreviation for many of my file names. For example, in my system the "L-" prefix represents **l**etters, the "H-" stands for **h**andout materials for my seminars and "N-" stands for seminar **n**otes.

Have a naming system
that parallels your paper filing system

You may want to use a naming system that's parallel to your paper filing system. Mine are loosely parallel to one another. I generally prefer more subject-oriented naming schemes; I have a PR folder on my computer, for example, as well as a file drawer devoted to that subject. I also use alphabetical client files on paper and on computer.

Save vs. save as

Speaking of file names, here's a tip that just could prevent a headache or two when using programs that give you a choice between "Save" and "Save As." Be sure to use "Save As" if you don't want to accidentally overwrite an old document with the same name as a new document. (Using "Save" automatically replaces the old document.)

Path names

It may be helpful, too, to put the **path name** of a document at the bottom in very fine type so it will print out on a hard copy version. Later on, you'll know immediately where on your computer that document was created and stored. You may be able to have the path name automatically typed in a header or footer by selecting an option to include the path name.

With desktop search programs becoming more sophisticated and instantaneous, this step may be useful but not necessary. Also, for security reasons, you may not want to show a path name on a document. Nevertheless, let's explore just how a path name works.

Just like a person, each individual file has both a name and an address. A **path name** is the name and address of a computer file.

A name alone is not enough. Both a person and a file need more than a name to make them truly accessible. An address is necessary to locate a person as well as to distinguish one person from another. John Jones on Maple Street isn't the same person as John Jones on Elm Street. An address is a path to someone's door, starting with the state, going to the city, then to the street and number and finally to the individual.

A computer file needs an "address," too. A **path name** is the address for a computer file. Your computer locates a file by following a path first from the "drive" you're in (usually the C: or D: partition on your hard disk drive or it could be the letter assigned to your DVD, CD, USB thumb drive or a second hard disk); then on next to the first folder level (and through any subfolder levels) on that drive you're in; and finally to the actual file name.

Generally it's easier to click your way through the path with a mouse to find the right file. If you ever need to type in the path name, here's how you'd do it: (a) type the drive or partition letter followed by a colon and then by a back slash; (b) type the names of the folders and subfolders in order containing the file, typing backslashes before each folder name; and (c) finally type the name of the file with a backslash preceding the file name. Here's an example: D:\ABC Corp\proposals\#1.

Keep your organization simple by reducing the number of folder levels. That will keep your mouse clicking (or the time spent typing a path name) down to a minimum.

To repeat, build consistency and clarity, rather than creativity, into your folder and file names. Try to make folders and subfolders parallel by using the same names and sequence of names. For example, if you have consulting clients, each client might get their own first level folder by their last name with the following second level folder names: Proposals, Correspondence and Reports. Use consistency when naming files, too.

And just as there can be a John Jones who lives on Maple as well as one who lives on Elm, so, too, you can have the same file name (or the same file) in two different folders. The path name lets you locate the correct file at the correct address.

You can't have two folders at the first level with the same name. But with two different first level folders you could have two second level folders as well as files, with the same names.

How to separate your software programs and your data files

Here's an easy way to separate and organize program and data files:

1. Put your software programs in separate folders under a master folder named "Programs" on one partition (such as the C: partition).

2. Then in another partition (such as the D: partition), you could store *files in folders* in four main ways.

First, you could put your data files in separate folders (e.g., one for each client, project or type of work). If any of your software programs are set up to store your data files right along with the program files, you'll need to change the default setting to tell those programs (on the C: partition) that you want data files stored on another partition (such as the D: partition).

Second, you could use the "My Documents" (or equivalent) folder in your computer's operating system. See if the default location for this folder is on the C drive; if so, you may want to designate a different partition (such as the D: partition) for this folder to separate it out from your programs and operating system on the C drive. Then your folders would be placed under "My Documents" in the D: partition. One consultant who is also a speaker and writer has folders under "My Documents" called "Write," "Consult" and "Speak" that are located not on the C: partition but on the D: partition.

Third, you might want to put large video files in their own partition to limit backup time for just smaller data files.

Fourth, if you share your computer with other people, it will probably make sense to have separate folders for each person's data under each name.

Step 3: Do Some Computer Housekeeping

Regular computer housekeeping, especially computer file maintenance, is essential to the health and performance of your computer. Not only can organization make it easier to back up and find files (though desktop search programs can find individual files on even totally disorganized computers), it can also improve the productivity and speed of your computer—particularly your hard disk. If your computer is spending time looking for bits and pieces of a file scattered all over your hard disk, it takes longer to load all of the information in the file.

What's more, if you never do maintenance and your hard disk fills up with files, you're just asking for a computer crash. Preventive computer maintenance can help avoid problems.

Bigger is better, right?

If you've ever been tempted to substitute a bigger hard disk for computer housekeeping chores, think again. You may have also been tempted at one time or another to buy another file cabinet for all your papers and files. Or perhaps you've bought a bigger house to accommodate all the "stuff" you've accumulated.

If you're behind in your computer housekeeping, a bigger hard disk will be harder to organize and just make matters worse. As with file cabinets, you can only tell how much space you need after you have purged your files. Once you've cleaned out your hard disk, see if you have 75 percent or more filled with current programs and files. If so, a larger or additional hard disk may be very appropriate.

By the way, when was the last time you cleaned out your hard disk? Have you ever cleaned it out? Since for most of us, out of sight means out of mind, it's particularly easy for unneeded or duplicate computer files to accumulate. With the availability of larger and larger hard disks, this will continue to be a problem.

Four reasons to clean out your hard disk

There are four reasons to take the time and trouble to clean out your hard disk:

1. To speed up your computer

2. To speed you up (locating files, especially related files, becomes difficult when your folders are full of files you aren't using)

3. To make more room on your hard disk

4. To reduce the time it takes to back up your files (you're more likely to do backups if the task takes less time and a hard disk with fewer files takes less time to back up).

A squeaky clean hard disk

The best computer file maintenance is done as you go—deleting duplicates and out-of-date files, storing inactive files on backup media and having a backup routine that you use regularly. But if you're like most people, you'll probably need to sit down once every six months to a year and do a thorough spring cleaning. Where do you begin and how do you proceed? Here are some useful steps:

- Before you do any "computer housekeeping," go to Windows Explorer or its equivalent so you can see at a glance all the names of your partitions and your first level folders. Make sure you have separated your program/system folders and files from your data ones.

- Go through each main folder and see if you recognize any files you created that you can delete. Use your downtime, such as being on hold during phone calls, to start going through and deleting files. To remove software programs, use an **uninstaller program** (e.g., the add or remove programs feature)—don't just delete program files yourself since certain files may be interconnected with other programs and a do-it-yourself deletion may affect the operation of those other programs.

- Look more closely. Are there any files you're no longer using but you'd like to keep in archival storage? If so, back these up on external hard drives, thumb drives, CDs, DVDs or whatever backup medium you're using. Or perhaps you have a backup device or program that can "tag" these specific files and back them up collectively. For files that are very important, make two archival copies and keep at least one of them off-site.

- Consolidate any files you can—i.e., group separate, related files together in one new file or folder. For example, instead of having every letter to a client in separate files, group all of last year's letters to a client together in one file. This can not only save space on your computer but make it easier to locate information.

- Examine your largest files and decide how often you use them. Perhaps they can be stored elsewhere.

- Look for any folders that only contain a few data files. See if you can move these files elsewhere and then delete these empty folders.

- Print a hard copy of your latest **catalog** (a listing of all the files in your folders) and keep them near your labeled backup media. If you back up your hard disk with a program that contains a catalog feature, print out the catalog when you complete your backup.

- Clean out your **cache** files daily if you surf the Web frequently. Cache files are like snapshots of pages you've visited so your browser can quickly recreate pages you've visited (to save you time). Unfortunately, all these files take up space on your hard disk. You can find your cache files through your Web browser.

Just as with manual systems, try to keep most accessible only the active files you're regularly using. Only these files should be kept in your current, first-level folders. It's so easy to start stockpiling files that you never use. When you do, you'll soon discover you have trouble finding files that are needed.

Make sure you have the latest version of software programs by going to vendors' websites to check for updates. Many vendors provide free, automatic downloadable updates. Make sure your computer always has up-to-date versions of your operating system, browser, firewall, antivirus program and antispyware programs (for more on these programs see Chapter 14 as well as my new book *Teach Your Computer to Dance*).

File Management and Organizing Programs

Your computer's operating system comes with a basic file management program to find, save, copy, move and delete files and perform housekeeping and preventive maintenance chores on your hard disk. You may want to use specialized, third-party programs (as listed in the Resource Guide) with greater or different capabilities that work with or separately from your usual file management program.

Defragment (Optimize) Your Computer's Hard Disk

After eliminating, transferring, organizing and consolidating files, your computer may appear neat and tidy, but chances are that many of the remaining files were and probably still are **fragmented**. Fragmented files have a file's information scattered in different places over your computer's hard disk.

When you save a file to a disk, the disk looks for the first available free space. If only part of a file fits there, that's where the first part goes. Then your disk looks for other places to store the balance of a file. As a result, the more you use your computer's hard disk, the slower it becomes because information for any one file may be scattered as fragments in many places on the hard disk. The more scattered the stored information, the longer it takes for your computer to pull all the pieces together so you can work with a file. Also, disk fragmentation can cause crashes, slowdowns, freeze-ups and even total system failures.

The way to fix this and speed up your computer is to **defragment** (or **optimize**) your disk by using either the computer operating system's built-in disk defragmenter or a separate defragging program. It's a good idea to check once or twice a month to see if your disk needs to be defragmented. I'd suggest backing up your computer before you defrag it since your hard drive's contents are being moved around and rearranged by the optimizing.

Compression

With regard to using **compression**, which removes any extra spaces much like concentrated orange juice removes most of the water, I generally recommend against using it. Even though compression is probably built into your computer's operating system, my recommendation is don't add another level of complication where something else (decompression) can go wrong. Larger hard disks have also come way down in price, as have other media storage devices, making compression a much less needed option (except maybe for sending large email attachments).

Organize and Customize Your Desktop

Unfortunately, clutter isn't limited to your desk; it can also accumulate on your computer **desktop**, the main staging area on your computer screen where you lay out your computer work using windows and **icons**.

Here are some ideas on how to better arrange your desktop so it's more functional for you.

First, check out your desktop's overall appearance. Is it too cluttered or busy for your taste? Can you find what you want easily? Do you have too many icons? Are they logically grouped together? You may want to avoid using busy "wallpaper" (the graphics that cover the background of your screen) because it can add to a more cluttered look.

Group your icons in alphabetical order or using some logical grouping. I prefer using a logical grouping such as all my antispyware programs grouped together in alphabetical order. Play with the spacing between icons and eliminate any unnecessary space. Keep icon label names as short as possible. You can also customize the look of your icons and your desktop.

For programs or files you use constantly, put Shortcuts on your desktop. Shortcuts let you quickly open a program or data file or folder or perform a function using only a few keys. (Here's an example of the latter: to get to your Windows desktop quickly, press the Windows key together with the M key.) You can also add Shortcuts to the My Documents folder or another folder where you store active documents. Make the Shortcuts you use most often the most accessible.

Another option is to use the Start Menu but if it's too cluttered, use the Quick Launch toolbar in the task bar to give you quick access to your computer's desktop screen. Quick Launch can also let you add shortcuts as well as icons for frequently-used programs, disks, folders and documents.(Also see the Resource Guide for desktop customization programs that can help you further organize and customize your desktop.)

Finding Files

Desktop Search Programs

By definition, if you have to search for a file, you don't know where it is. So especially if your files aren't as organized as you'd like and the computer's search tools built into the operating system aren't powerful or fast enough, you may turn to a desktop search program to help you find that needle in a haystack. And with the size of hard drives these days, it may be more like finding a needle in a silo. These programs will continue to evolve to add new features and benefits. (Also see the Resource Guide.)

How different programs work

The various search programs work differently as far as:

1. **What they search**—Some search all of the following and some don't: files, emails of certain programs, email and/or zip attachments, instant messages, calendars, contacts and combining Web-based searches with searches of your computer. With some programs, you can't search your files and your email at the same time. With others, they index the contents of attachments but not the names of the attached files. Some search multiple computers.

2. **How they search**—They vary as to whether they search keywords, portions of words, phrases or Boolean searches, dates or authors of documents

3. **How long it takes to initially index and then search for information**—Some programs need to have the search feature turned on all the time to avoid a complete reindexing of all information to keep the index up to date.

Program features

Among the features to look for in a desktop search program are:

1. Which browsers and email programs it supports

2. Whether it indexes both the subject and content of emails

3. Whether it indexes email attachments and the attachment name

4. Whether it indexes instant messages

5. The types of files it can index (e.g., Word, PowerPoint, PDF, HTML files)

6. Whether it indexes Zip files by content and name

7. Whether it can search all data at one time or separate searches are needed

8. How quickly (or slowly) the initial indexing takes

9. Whether new or revised files and emails are indexed on a real-time basis or at scheduled times

10. The search methods available (whole words, partial words, phrases or Boolean searches)

11. How search results are shown (thumbnails, excerpts, whole files)

12. Whether searched files can be launched from the search program

Once you've determined which program best fits your personal preferences, you'll probably want to use just that one program since multiple programs in this genre can not only slow down computer performance but also interfere with one another.

Keep in mind that while these programs make it quick for you search for information on your computer, they can perform the same function for anyone who gets hold of your computer (in person or over the Internet), even for a little bit of time.

Desktop search programs are not a replacement for organized folders. Although finding individual files has gotten very quick and easy with desktop search programs, neglecting computer organization and housekeeping means (a) it will be difficult to find related files in one place on your computer; (b) your computer will work harder and run slower; and (c) backing up your files will take more time.

Other Organization & Search Options
Virtual file folders with your operating system

Depending upon which operating system your computer uses, you may be able to search for folders and files in a variety of ways and even create virtual folders and file lists (regardless of their actual location on your computer) according to attributes such as the author of documents, date of file creation or keywords. This can allow you to link and reorganize files virtually.

Video and audio search programs

There are programs that search **video** and **audio** content on your computer as well as online.

Photo organizing software programs

More and more, we're saving images on our computers. Without the right software, it can be difficult to organize and locate photos and images. (See Chapter 10.)

Resource Guide

Note: Always check with vendors for the latest version of software products and the compatibility with your existing hardware and software. (Also see **www.adams-hall.com** for updates and also see my new book, *Teach Your Computer to Dance*.)

Desktop Customization Programs

Object Desktop lets you customize your desktop, icons, toolbars and windows. Stardock Corp., **www.stardock.com**

Post-it Digital Notes allows you to put notes on your computer desktop or on multiple, tabbed "memoboards." 3M, **www.3m.com**

Desktop Search Programs

Here are three leading desktop search programs. They will continue to add features to match and outdo one another so be on the lookout for continuing changes, especially in security features.

Copernic Desktop Search is an easy-to- use search engine that lets you instantly search files, emails and email attachments stored anywhere on your computer's hard drive. It executes sub-second searching of Microsoft Word, Excel and PowerPoint files, Acrobat PDFs and popular music, picture and video formats. It can also search your browser history, favorites and contacts. As you add more terms to your search request, search results are narrowed down right before your eyes. As you scroll through the results, previews of the files or emails are shown on the bottom of the screen. Click open and the file or email opens using its native application. Copernic Technologies, Inc., **www. copernic.com**

Google Desktop is an excellent program that searches your computer (and multiple computers) and the Web. It provides a full text search of your email, computer files, music, photos and chats as well as Web pages that you've viewed. Google, Inc., **www.google.com**

X1 is a fast program to search for a particular file, email or other information on your computer's hard disk. As you type in characters, words or phrases, the search results are displayed and refined. With its over 370 built-in file viewers for the most common file formats including Word documents, spreadsheets, databases, presentations, PDFs, graphics and more, you can view files even if you don't have the original software applications that created the files. To increase your productivity, the program can also do typical commands (e.g., reply to email) without your having to leave the program and open up the original application. The program allows you to choose either continual indexing (to always have updated information) or to have indexing done in the background or at scheduled times (which avoids interference with your computer's performance). X1 Technologies, Inc., **www.x1.com**

Disk Defragmenting Programs

Diskeeper is a top-rated program that improves your computer's performance by defragging your files. It offers a Set It and Forget It mode to automate the process. Diskeeper Corp., **www.executive.com**

PerfectDisk is another top defragging utility program. Raxco Software, 800/546-9728 [MD] or **www.raxco.com**

File Compression Programs

PKZip is easy to use with Zip files. PKW Inc., **www.pkzip.com**

WinZip is effective but simple in compressing files. WinZip Computing, **www.winzip.com**

File Management Programs

A file management program shows lists of files and allows the user to move files between folders, make backup copies of files, view pictures, delete unwanted files and perform other housekeeping tasks.

Directory Opus goes beyond the simple file manager metaphor, offering a complete replacement for Windows Explorer and many other utility programs for handling FTP and ZIP, viewing files and images, running slideshows and more. Its multi-threaded design lets you perform multiple operations at the same time; for example, you can Zip one folder while unzipping another, at the same time as you are downloading files from a remote FTP site and copying yet more files between your local folders. GP Software, **www.gpsoft.com.au**

ExplorerPlus can be used with Windows Explorer or as a replacement tool. Novatix Corp, **www. novatix.com**

Info Select is a powerful search and organizing tool. Micro Logic Corp., **www.miclog.com**

PaperPort gives you a searchable index of text in scanned documents (and images) on your computer and allows you to see thumbnails and the content of Word, Excel and PowerPoint files without having to open the applications. Nuance Communications, Inc., **www.nuance.com**

Format Searching Program for Word Files

CrossEyes lets you see the formatting of Word documents in a manner similar to WordPerfect's Reveal Code feature to give you more control over your documents and save time seeing (and fixing) the formatting. Levit & James Inc., **www.levitjames.com**

Partitioning software

Partition Magic by Symantec is a top-rated partitioning software program that is designed to allow you to partition your hard disk without losing data. Symantec, **www.symantec.com**

13

Backing Up
Your Computer Files

Quick Scan: Read this chapter to learn how and when to back up your files using the best methods and media.

A **backup** is a duplicate copy of **computer data** (the files you create as well as the software programs on your computer) that is stored on (a) another medium (e.g., external hard drive, DVD, USB thumb drive or the Web) or (b) another portion of the primary medium you're using (e.g., a second partition of your hard drive such as a D drive). I can't emphasize enough the importance of *up-to-date* backups made on a *regular* basis.

There are four parts to making good backups: (1) getting your computer ready to do a backup (doing the computer housekeeping discussed in Chapter 12), (2) establishing your **backup methods** and **routine,** (3) selecting one or more **backup devices** and (4) actually making up-to-date backups. Incidentally, the backup device or medium you select is only as good as the regular routine you actually use to perform backups.

But don't overlook a simple step you can take during the day, every day, to avoid a loss of data. You may decide to put your computer into standby mode or hibernation rather than turning it off when you're not using it. These are two different states for your computer. **Standby** offers the advantage of coming back more quickly on the screen but it doesn't save your files. **Hibernation** takes longer to come back on the screen but it does save your data to your disk. Either way, it doesn't hurt to save your files before you walk away from your screen.

Why Bother?

You never backed up your filing cabinet; why should you back up your computer files? First, the chances of wiping out your computer data are much greater than losing your hard data. Also, if you're using a laptop computer or USB thumb drive, you may lose it or have it stolen. Finally, it's so easy today to back up. (And why tempt fate anyway?)

Backups are insurance for valuable, current data that would either require more than a half-hour to re-enter or would be next to impossible to re-create exactly as inputted the first time. Whenever I'm producing original, creative material, I not only save it on my hard disk, I also save it on a USB thumb drive and/or an external hard drive.

Besides making additional copies of important information, backups can serve as **archival storage** for less important information that is not being used and is taking up too much space on your hard disk. Once you've backed up this archival information, then you can delete it from your hard disk—*always test that the backup worked before you start deleting files from your disk*. Make two archival backup copies if the information is very important and keep the copies in separate locations (at least one of them being off-site—for example, at home and at the office.

Good backups will let you conduct business as usual even if your hard disk crashes or your computer is in for repair. Don't wait until a crash to get serious about backing up. As writer Wes Nihei observed in *PC World*, "Backing up files is a lot like dental hygiene: by the time you get serious about flossing and brushing, it's usually too late."

Or as Wally Beddoe put it, "There are basically two types of computer users: those who have lost data and those who will."

Malware and Backups

Even if your computer doesn't crash, a computer virus or other **malware** (**mal**icious soft**ware**) may make you wish you had a good backup of your hard drive. Sometimes the only way to remove malware is a clean start by reformatting your hard disk (wiping out everything that's on it) and reinstalling your operating system, other software programs and your data. That's when you'll be so glad you have a good, current backup to reinstall.

Three Options for a Second Chance

Always remember that before you start tinkering with your computer (or some hacker does), have at least **one good backup** on hand in case things go awry. Sometimes installing a new program or getting infected by a virus completely messes up your computer. Life would be good again if you could just undo the installation, the effects of the virus or the inadvertent or unexplainable disappearance of your computer data.

But what do you do if you don't have a recent or good backup on hand or you'd prefer to just wave a magic wand to fix these problems? There are two more ways you may be able to get a second chance. First, your computer's operating system may have built into it a **system restore** function, which if it has been turned on before there is a problem, allows you to put your computer's system back into the state it was in on a prior date (hopefully before the problem arose).

Second, you can get a software **rollback program** that does more and allows you to rewind the clock and go back in time for minutes, hours, or even days (depending on available disk space) to restore files that have been deleted or modified and to uninstall new software. Be aware, however, that not all rollback software programs back up your data files. While rollback software should *not* be your only backup tool, it's nice to have it as another arrow in your computer quiver. (See the Resource Guide.)

Backup Approaches and Methods

You first need to decide *how much* computer data you're going to back up before deciding *how* you'll do it.

Your backup routine should include **selective** as well as **complete** or **full** backups. Complete or full backups are used to copy the entire contents of your hard disk and would be useful if you had a system failure and you had to restore all the data and programs on your hard disk. Selective or partial backups are used to copy individual files, programs or data.

Selective Backups: Incremental vs. Differential

An **incremental** backup is a type of selective backup that copies only files that have changed since your last (full or incremental) backup. If your backup device can do incremental backups, you will save time doing backups—keep this feature in mind when you select a backup device.

A **differential** backup contains all the changes since your last full backup. Although differential backups take longer to make than incremental backups since they create an "all changes in one file backup," they are easier to restore since all of the changes are in one differential file rather than many incremental files.

Another consideration in choosing between incremental and differential backups is that incremental backups save each backed up version of a file. You may want this approach if you ever need to refer to one of these versions or want to have an audit trail. If you don't need to see old versions but only the most current, up-to-date version, use differential backups. Differential backups can save time and space by having one file rather than many files with different versions of the same files. Personally, on important work, I like to have many versions of a document in case a file gets corrupted.

Four Main Backup Methods

You can do backups in four main ways: (1) **image**, (2) **file-by-file**, (3) **online** and (4) **synchronization** or **syncing**.

Image backups

Image backups make a mirror-image copy of your hard disk. They copy your entire hard disk, byte by byte, so they aren't generally used for day-to-day backups. They are more often used for major, complete, periodic backups. They can be very useful when a hard disk crashes and you want backup files that contain an exact copy of your hard disk, including the computer data, operating system and programs.

File-by-file backups

File-by-file backups, while generally slower to make than image backups, are more reliable and make it easier to find backed-up files. You can also restore individual files without having to restore the entire hard disk. Newer technology is aiming for faster, file-by-file backups. File-by-file backups can be used for selective as well as complete backups.

Online backups

If you use an online backup service, see whether you can back up your entire computer's contents or just certain data files. The speed of your online connection will affect how long it takes to do a backup (which affects how likely you are to do a backup). As with anything online, check out the security measures in place. Online backups offer the advantage of off-site storage for your data.

Synchronization with a mobile device

If you have a mobile handheld device as well as a computer where you want the same data on both, you'll want to have another type of backup known as **synchronization**.

With synchronization, all of your electronic devices have the same data (e.g., calendar, customer information, product information, etc.). There are different ways that software programs and websites provide synchronization. Before buying a device, it's important to determine how easy (or difficult) it is to sync all your equipment. Data may be updated on one device at a time or several at the same time or with each device receiving the latest information automatically each time it's turned on.

You also may be able to drag and drop files between the devices without having to go through the entire data synchronization process and possibly utilize wireless (and cradle-less) synchronization through Wi-Fi and/or Bluetooth wireless technologies. This, too, is an area of great change and new approaches will be developed over time to make the process more automatic and effortless.

Backing Up Video Files

There is no one solution that's best for every type of file and every type of device. For example, because of their large sizes, video files may require a different backup solution. You may want to keep these files on a separate partition (portion of your hard drive) or on a separate hard drive. This will speed up backup of your data files that aren't video files since you won't have to back up both types each time you do a backup.

Since video files gobble up hard disk space, you're more likely to be archiving this type of data. With archiving, you're removing noncurrent video files from your computer and putting them in storage. Usually, to have faster and easier access, you'll make an uncompressed file-by-file backup rather than a compressed, image backup of video files.

Backup Software

As for backup software, you may want to use the backup program that comes with your operating system or better yet, a software program that comes with your backup device or a dedicated backup software program.

Important Backup Tips

Your backup routine depends on how often your files change, the number of files you modify a day, the kind of information or applications you use and how easy your backup device is to use. It may also depend on whether you keep any hard copy that would enable you to re-create computer files.

Following these simple backup tips can save you many headaches down the long haul. Check off all the ones you already do; circle those you will incorporate into your routine after reading this section:

- Make an emergency DVD or CD to get you up and running again on your existing computer or another computer (some utilities such as antivirus products create their own emergency disks).

- When you install a backup device, test it out with some junk files before betting your life on it.

- To check if a backup was successful, randomly restore a few files from the start, middle and end of your backup set.

- Each day back up any data, folders or applications you have modified that day.

- Do a full backup of your data every week.

- Keep a backup log of when and what you back up. Printed directories are useful, too.

- Have three complete sets of programs and data: one you're working with on your primary computer and two current backups—one on-site and an additional backup kept off-site (at home, for example, if your office is not in your home).

- Always back up newly installed software, particularly if you made any special installation procedures. Keep a hard-copy record of the answers you gave to installation questions in case you need to reinstall the program.

- Make copies of your customization files, registry and application configuration files.

- Do a full backup of your active program files (as compared to your data files) at least every three months and store it off-site. If all of your program files are grouped together (e.g., in the Programs folder on your C drive), it's faster to back them up from that one location.

- Carefully date and label all backup media.

- Store backups away from magnetic fields (such as power supplies, telephones and monitors) that could corrupt them.

- Make sure you have the original disks or at least a backup of your backup software so you'll be better able to restore files after a crash.

- Once a month check for reliability before you need it by trying to restore at least a few files from a backup.

- Use hard copy as important backup.

- If you're a corporate user and you're on a network, ask your network manager if all data on your machine will be backed up by the network or if you'll need to do your own private backup; also find out if there are any corporate policies regarding transporting any backup data to and from home.

Some organizations keep daily files Monday through Thursday, make a weekly backup on Friday and do a monthly backup every fourth week with copies of weekly and monthly backups kept off-site as well as on-site. My general recommendation is **always have at least one complete, current backup off-site**.

Backup and Storage Devices and Media (Including Online Storage)

There are many kinds of disk devices (extra internal hard drives, external hard drives, DVDs, CD-RWs, CD-Rs, large capacity optical drives, Zip drives, tape, USB thumb drives, keychain or mobile devices, memory cards and online storage) and they all have their pros and cons in terms of capacity, speed, cost, universality and durability. In general, disk devices are generally faster in terms of backup speed than tape devices and can offer a longer life span than CDs and DVDs.

The key with backups is to have **current backups** and **redundancy** (use more than one of these devices and/or places) and to store or transfer them to technology that won't be obsolete in the near future.

Hard Disks

Don't rely on just your computer's hard disk. You'll want a second hard disk (external or internal) for backups. Prices have dropped tremendously on these drives and their storage capacity is ever increasing. I'm partial to external hard drives. Besides offering large capacity and the capability of being stored off-site, they can be used with several of your computers, including laptops.

Combining two external drives that you alternate (keeping one off-site) or using one external hard disk plus Internet backup storage (see later on in the chapter) can make an ideal backup solution. Some computers come with a slot for a removable hard disk (this can also be a good way to store sensitive information overnight by locking up the removable hard disk in a safe or taking it with you).

Another less optimal option is backing up to another partition on the same drive. The risk here is that if the drive fails, the files on both your main drive and the extra backup partition may be unusable.

Optical Media (CDs and DVDs)

Depending upon the type of optical media and the size of your file backup needs, optical media may work for you as a backup medium. With any kind of optical storage, check with the manufacturer to determine how long your data will remain usable.

CDs

CDs can only meet minimal backup needs because they hold about 700MB—less than three-quarters of one gigabyte. Although you can back up your hard disk to multiple CDs, inserting and removing the disks can become old and labor intensive after a short while. There are two types of CDs. A **CD-RW** (readable/writable/erasable) can be used over and over again, generally up to 1,000 times—check with the manufacturer. But if you need a backup to be nonerasable (for example, for archival purposes) you may prefer **CD-R** (readable CDs). In general, CD-RWs aren't designed for long-term storage needs.

DVDs

DVDs may be a better fit for you. Although the disks cost more than CDs, a regular DVD can hold 4.7GB (nearly seven times as much as a CD) and dual-layer disks can hold around 8.5GB. The newer second generation high-capacity DVDs can hold 15 to 25GB in a single-layer capacity and 30 to 50GB in dual-layer capacity. In the future, holographic disks may be able to store far beyond the current capacity levels.

Be aware that there may be compatibility issues with any DVD so you'll want to get a DVD burner and drive that meets your needs and does not present a compatibility problem.

USB Thumb Drives and Flash Memory

I'm partial to the very small USB thumb drive. It's easy to use; just insert it into a USB slot on your computer and copy files or folders that can take up to multi-gigabyte capacity. The key is for your computer and USB thumb drive to have a fast USB connection (USB 2.0 connection is 40 times faster than USB 1.1) and then you almost have your computer in your pocket. In fact, in time it will be standard for these drives to also include the software applications that were used to create the data so they may actually function as a mini-computer. Make sure such a thumb drive doesn't leave traces on the host computer on which the drive is used— especially important if you want to maintain privacy when using someone else's computer.

To get the portability and backup capacity in such a small device is remarkably handy and worthwhile. Another advantage of this format (unlike CDs or DVDs) is that you don't need to burn in the information.

However, be sure that all of this information doesn't fall out of your pocket or purse and into someone else's hands. Also, be careful removing these drives from computers—**click on the safely remove hardware icon** and follow the steps so you don't harm the data on the disk upon removal.

Flash drives that fit in a slot in your computer are popular for many uses. See if the capacity and speed are sufficient for your needs.

Online Backup and Storage

Online backup may end up being your only, or better yet, an additional backup option. Your ISP (Internet Service Provider) may offer free storage for you (or additional storage at a reasonable price). Provided you have a fast enough Internet connection and the storage/backup charges meet your budget, the Internet can be a great way to have an off-site backup that's also accessible when you're out of your office.

Make sure the Web storage site you're considering has a secure connection and enough storage space for your needs. Look for two signs of better security: (1) a small **lock icon** that appears at the bottom right next to the browser icon and (2) if the Web address of the page you're viewing starts with **https://** (the "s" stands for "secure"). Ask about any encryption that is done. Find out the backup capacity size, whether files are compressed and how many versions of files are retained and for how long on their servers. (See the Resource Guide.)

Selection Criteria for Backup Devices

Before you select a backup device, consider the following criteria:

- Capacity (be sure to match or exceed the capacity of your computer—how much do you need now and in the foreseeable future?)

- Ease of use and convenience (if it's not easy to learn and use, you won't bother with it)

- Whether you can set up regular, automated scheduled backups

- Internal vs. external

- Portability/physical size (are you going to be removing and transporting the device frequently and if so, how far?)

- Speed—How much of your time will it take; how fast is it in different modes of operation—with or without compression, with or without verification (error checking)?

- Reliability/verification (what kind of "error checking" does it have?)

- Security

- Ability to share with others (e.g., a USB connection or the Internet are probably your most universal choices) or for you to take on the road or use at home

- Compatibility (with other office computers and/or your network)

- Additional hardware required (the cost factor aside, what kind of space do you have for more hardware?)

- Cost of the device and backup media

Resource Guide

Note: Always check with vendors for the latest version of software products and the compatibility with your existing hardware and software. Also check www.adams-hall.com for updates as well as my new book, *Teach Your Computer to Dance.*

Backup Software Programs

Acronis True Image is an imaging program that can also do incremental backups. Acronis, Inc., **www.acronis.com**

BounceBack Professional is a cloning program to make a copy to a second hard drive. CMS Products, Inc., 800/327-5773 [CA] or **www.cmsproducts.com**

Norton Ghost is an imaging program that performs well, especially on faster computers. Symantec, **www.symantec.com**

Retrospect is a traditional backup program that is flexible and powerful. Dantz Development Corp., **www.dantz.com**

SyncBackSE is a powerful but easy to use backup program. 2BrightSparks Pte Ltd, **www.2brightsparks.com**

Cellphone Phone Book Backup

Cell-Stik lets you easily back up, enter, edit and transfer cellphone contacts between cellphones and/or your computer. I use this great little product, which looks like a USB thumb drive. Check compatibility for your phone(s). Spark Technology Corp, **www.sparktech.com**

Migration Software: Transferring Data from an Old PC to a New PC

Computers don't last forever. In the past, it has been difficult to transfer easily all of your data, programs and settings from the old to the new PC. **Migration software** fills this need. The programs differ; some just move data files, some can also move application settings and some can move data *and* applications.

Alohabob PC Relocator moves not only data and settings but also applications. Eisenworld Corp., **www.alohabob.com**

Online Backup Storage

Here are several online services that may meet your needs.

Atrieva Service, Xdrive, Inc., 800/287-4382 [CA] or **www.xdrive.com**

@Backup, SwapDrive, 619/455-3500 [CA] or **www.atbackup.com**

Connected DataProtector, Connected Corp., **www.connected.com**

IBackup, Pro Softnet Corp., **www.ibackup.com**

Streamload, Streamload, Inc., **www.streamload.com**

Rollback Software

Norton GoBack by Symantec monitors both data files and system files so it can restore deleted files or deleted drives. Symantec, **www.symantec.com**

Retrospect is a top-rated program that does rollback restores as well as traditional backups and more. Dantz Development Corp., **www.dantz.com**

14

Protecting Your Computer,
Your Information, Yourself
and Your Colleagues
On and Off the Internet

Quick Scan: For most of us, our computers are our lifelines to the work
world. If your computer goes down or your data or information is stolen, it can
spell disaster. If you're looking for strategies to help prevent viruses, worms,
spyware, keystroke loggers, Trojan horses, phishing, pharming, evil twins and
other malware attacks on you and your computer, this is the chapter for you.
Although this is the most technical chapter in the book, don't skip it—it has
important info for you as well as your colleagues. (Also see www.adams-
hall.com for updates and my new book, *Teach Your Computer to Dance.*)

S ome days we love our computers and other days we're ready to throw
them in the trash–but be sure you first remove all traces of your data
from your computer and then recycle your computer if you ever carry
out this threat.

Part of the reason for our mixed feelings is that our computers can
be invaded (and sometimes taken over) by outsiders without our
permission. However, you can and should take steps to better protect
yourself and your computer.

There are virtually no online activities or services that guarantee
absolute privacy. But to give it some perspective, there's no absolute way

to keep someone out of your home. That doesn't mean you should never leave your home. It does mean that you should make it difficult, very difficult, for someone to enter without your permission and you shouldn't leave enticing attractions in plain view.

Similarly, on the Internet, what you're striving for is an extreme degree of certainty that your Internet connection is secure and that you have safeguards, software programs and barriers in place to help prevent your computer from being infected with **malware** or to minimize its effect. Malware programs can not only make your computer sick but also possibly let hackers see every keystroke (and password) you type as well as have access to all of the data and information on your computer (and maybe on your computer's network).

There are many kinds of malware. For example, a **virus** is a computer program that is spread through human interaction such as running an infected program. The most common way of getting a virus is by downloading an infected file. A **worm** is like a virus but it is self-replicating and it can spread without human interaction once it's on a computer. A **Trojan horse** looks like a useful program but it isn't. Ordinarily, it is not self-replicating and it does its mischief just on the computer where it's located.

You need a variety of defenses to withstand the many different and changing types of attacks since there is not just one solution that will take care of all of them. And since new attacks and new threats become the latest malware du jour, vigilance is not a one-time effort.

13 Low-Tech Solutions to Lower Your Profile

Some solutions are low-tech. Start by lowering your profile—to make yourself less of a visible target— and have enough defenses and remedies in place to help you prevent and, if necessary, counter an attack.

1. Remove data hidden in your word processing and other files. It's not just the Internet that can affect your privacy. You may have hidden data (**metadata**) in your spreadsheet, word processing or other files that other people can view unless you remove it. What is this metadata? It can include deleted text, revisions that were made, comments and other collaboration data, your name and your email address. So, for example, if you are "recycling" a document, agreement or presentation for another client, that other client's name and information may still be hidden in the new document unless the metadata is removed. There are programs to remove sensitive information (see the Resource Guide).

2. Think about security issues with a desktop search program. A desktop search program can allow you to quickly search for virtually anything in your computer files. But it also allows someone else to search your information quickly if they get hold of your computer (in person or online via a hacker) for even a very short time. If you want to use this type of program, find out whether the program also transmits any of your information to the company supplying the software. (For more information on desktop search programs and security considerations, see Chapter 12.)

3. Get a good shredder. All of the pages you print out from your computer and throw in recycling (and hopefully, not the trash!) could yield valuable information about you and/or your company. Get a good shredder that cross-cuts into small strips, which provide more privacy than straight-cut strips.

4. Have a fast enough computer. This may be the most overlooked item on anyone's security checklist. To keep your computer protected, you need to use antivirus and antispyware programs regularly to check your computer. This checking is very intensive work for your computer. Since it can take a bit of time to perform these functions, you don't want to have too slow a computer, which may discourage you from running these programs.

So, when purchasing a computer, don't just take into consideration the speed you'll need to handle word processing, spreadsheets, presentations or the Internet. Also consider the speed of a computer's hard disk and processor as well as the speed and size of the computer's memory (RAM) so you have a computer that is fast enough to encourage you to perform, on a regular basis, all the necessary safety checks on today's very large hard disks.

5. Get a privacy filter. If you're concerned about people looking at your laptop computer while you're on a plane or train, get a 3M privacy filter that reduces the viewing angle.

6. Lower your profile on the Net. If you have an "always on" connection to the Internet such as through DSL or a cable modem, you're increasing the chances that someone will find your connection and attack it at that time or at their leisure since your connection is always sitting there. Disconnect your high-speed modem when you're not on the Internet.

7. Choose and use your passwords with care. It's important to give some thought and use some imagination in setting up your passwords because there are software programs known as **password crackers** that can easily decipher primitive passwords.

So instead, use more complex passwords (a combination of at least eight upper and lower-case letters, numbers *and* keyboard symbols) to give greater security to your passwords. Passwords should not contain real words, actual names, addresses, phone numbers or birth dates. Change your passwords at least several times a year. Use different passwords for different sites and programs. To make your computer more secure, you can set up a login password (make sure you don't lose it!) and even have your screen saver require password protection upon resuming your work at the screen.

Make sure you keep passwords in a place accessible only to you. You may want to consider a **password manager** program (to track and store all of your passwords). Although many password manager programs get good reviews from independent sources touting them as a secure way to store your online passwords, I still worry about having all of your passwords in one place. Do your own due diligence if you decide to utilize a password manager program.

If you don't want your Internet browser to have your passwords come up automatically at websites, change the **auto-complete settings** so all your passwords are cleared out (and not stored) on your computer. This will also give you more protection if you lose your computer or someone gets hold of it.

Mobile devices can offer password protection, too.

8. Be careful as to what you download or open up. In general, it's a good idea to avoid opening up files attached to emails from senders you do not know. Those files are a great way to infect your computer. But even if you receive an attached file from a person you *do* know, don't download or open up a file that has an extension in the name, especially **exe**. Also, don't open or download files with two extensions. Use your common sense—if an email looks and smells like trouble or you have an uneasy feeling, don't open it up. If people you know start sending you emails with unusual subject lines, call the sender to confirm whether they sent it or malware did. (Or send a separate email asking about the unusual subject line—but *don't* reply to the actual email with the unusual subject line!)

9. Don't go phishing or pharming. Phishers try to trick you by sending you an email that looks like it's coming from a known company and then giving you a **link** to what looks like the company site. It isn't. It's a fake site designed to get you to divulge personal and sensitive financial information. The way to have the phishers go home empty-handed is to avoid clicking on any links in emails (especially where they're asking for personal or sensitive information or requesting that you edit information that's on the screen). In some cases, phishing sites have even been able to reproduce the onscreen lock symbol that signifies a secure site.

In another twist, if your computer has been infected, then even if you type in the correct address for a website, you will instead be directed to an imposter website. This is known as **pharming**. Since the form of attacks is continually growing, so is your need for protection as discussed throughout this chapter.

10. Keep from getting burned at hot spots and other spots away from your office. You may use a wireless (e.g., Wi-Fi) connection at a hot spot (e.g., coffee shop) to connect to the Internet. Remember that Wi-Fi is a shared network. Be aware that fellow customers may be more interested in your information than a caffeine buzz. With their laptop computers, they may be trying to monitor the Wi-Fi radio waves from your computer to capture your information, passwords and credit card information. Even some hard-wired connections (e.g., at some hotels) may be hackable.

Some hot spots have better security protection than others. That's why as a first line of defense, try to minimize your use of hot spots, especially if you're dealing with sensitive information. In particular, try to avoid using instant messaging at hot spots since this is not the most secure method of communicating. When not in use, turn off your wireless card.

Another step is to get a **trace remover** program designed to erase any of your passwords, temp files and surfing history during a Net session at an Internet cafe, library and public computer (see the Resource Guide).

If you're using a USB thumb drive on someone else's computer, be aware that some of these drives offer higher levels of security including password locks and software that leave no traces of your activity (including emails) on the host computer.

Don't cause an accidental breach of your company's computer system. Although companies spend a lot to prevent computer attacks from the outside, many of the attacks come accidentally from insiders. Sometimes computer networks get infected when someone (a) inadvertently syncs up using their infected computer or (b) logs on remotely from a hot spot with poor security.

11. Don't have an itchy clicker finger. As you maneuver through the Web, from time to time you'll see pop-ups or buttons with a message asking you to click them. If you do, you may end up installing a program you'd rather live without. You may also be unknowingly giving permission to have spyware installed when you click "I accept" to those licensing agreements when new software is installed. Next time, read through the agreement before you agree to its terms.

12. Be careful how you answer security questions. Some websites (including non-financial websites) require answers to security questions to verify your identity in the future if the need arises. Be careful how you answer questions such as your mother's maiden name, your birthplace or your birth date. Correct answers may expose your vital identifying pieces of information to website hackers by allowing someone to pose as you for other purposes. Of course, there are certain sites where you want to provide correct information.

13. Prevent theft. Whether leaving a mobile handheld in a recharging device or a laptop sitting on your desk in an office cubicle environment, you can take steps to prevent theft. You can lock up your laptop to your desk or use a tether; have an alarm installed; or install **tracking software** to call or email you if the laptop has been taken. Tracking software can disable a stolen computer and/or delete or encrypt files until the computer is recovered. (See the Resource Guide.)

One Dozen Medium-Tech Solutions

Whether your computer is brand new or showing its age, you'll want to be sure you've taken care of as many of these essential steps as possible *before* you connect up to the Internet for the first time or the next time. If you think it's too much work to even read through these steps, consider the alternative of maybe having your identity, computer data or privacy stolen by computer interlopers. Some of these protective steps only need to be taken once so the task of protecting your computer may not be as daunting as it first appears.

1. Permanently erase files with a trace removing program. Be aware that when you delete files from a disk or computer, those files may not, in fact, be gone. It's often possible to restore those so-called "deleted files." To permanently remove the files, use a trace remover program. Some programs substitute random characters to overwrite files that are deleted and others take protection a step further and also overwrite all unused hard disk space for additional undeletion protection. (See the Resource Guide.)

2. Update your computer's operating system. The operating system that came with your computer will need security updates from time to time to help keep you protected. Get the latest updates to your operating system by going to the software company's site to download fixes and security updates. You may need to go back to the site more than once in one session and run additional checks because sometimes not all the updates and fixes are downloaded to your computer at one time. Keep checking until you are told on the screen that your computer is completely up to date. To keep your computer as secure and current as possible (and with the least effort), enable automatic updates from the software manufacturer.

3. Update your Internet browser and other software. Go to the website of your Internet browser and the providers of your main software applications (word processing, spreadsheet and presentation software) periodically to make sure you have the latest updates on your computer to prevent security breaches.

4. Maybe change your browser. You may also decide to change the **browser** (program) you use to surf the Internet. (See my book *Teach Your Computer to Dance* for more on this subject).

5. Set up your Internet security and privacy levels. Your Internet browser will let you select the level of security and privacy you want to have while you're surfing the Net. You can also take other steps such as blocking third-party cookies.

6. Also use antivirus, antispam, antispyware and pop-up blocker programs or possibly a security suite to protect you. Besides your hardware and software firewalls (see the Higher Tech section below), you'll also want to have one antivirus program, one antispam program, one pop-up blocker and several antispyware programs. You need to decide whether you are going to buy separate programs from different companies where a product may be optimized to deal with a particular issue (e.g., antivirus) or one **security suite** program that contains all or most of the components you want. Note that security suites differ as to the types of programs they contain and even if you buy a security suite, it may contain products from different companies that have been combined together. Since you will probably want to have more than one antispyware program, you will in any event be mixing and matching programs from different companies together. (See the Resource Guide.)

7. Install and activate one antivirus software program. Having an antivirus program on a computer doesn't necessarily mean that it has been activated to protect you. Make sure the program is active and then go to the software manufacturer's website to get updates at least weekly. Better yet, once your antivirus program is up to date, **enable automatic updates** from the software manufacturer. Use just **one antivirus program**; with more than one, the software programs may conflict with one another.

I'm going to get a little more techy here but this is the medium-tech section. Since viruses can lurk in many places including incoming and outgoing email and instant message attachments, get all the protection you can. Run a **full system scan** with the program at this point to scan all files, not just certain types. Scan for every option possible such as all executable file types and **heuristic scanning** (to look for patterns that indicate a previously unknown virus is present).

Sometimes malware can hide from antivirus programs when you do a scan. To get the maximum searching and deletion power with an antivirus program, run a full system scan at least every week in **safe mode**. Safe mode is a special way of booting up (starting or restarting) your computer that minimizes which programs (including malware) are loaded up. To get into safe mode, turn on or restart your computer and you'll probably tap the F8 key every few seconds until the screen (at the top) tells you that you are in safe mode (click *Safe Mode* at the top of the screen). Then follow the screen instructions (or better yet, get someone who's familiar with safe mode to walk you through it the first time). Once you're in safe mode, then run your antivirus program.

8. Install several antispyware programs. Although having only one software firewall program and one antivirus program is recommended, it is a different story with antispyware. No one antispyware program is going to catch everything. Having and running two to four antispyware programs is probably the optimum number. (See the Resource Guide for suggestions.) Update these programs regularly, too.

Here's an interesting situation. Your spyware program may find an infection, zap it and then say that it has been removed but the malware is still there when you run another spyware scan to double-check the removal. Why? The spyware may still be on your computer if your computer is set to automatically create a **system restore**. This backup feature (discussed in Chapter 13) allows you to put your computer's programs into the status from an earlier date. The problem may be that your current system has been cleaned by the antispyware but one or more of the older restorable versions are still infected. You may need to restore an earlier clean version, or if there are none, to turn off system restore and run the antispyware programs again.

Run your antispyware programs at least every week—in safe mode. Run each program another time if spyware is still on your computer until it is removed by the antispyware program. Why? Sometimes spyware reinstalls itself and you may need to remove it again. By the way, if an antispyware program allows **real-time monitoring**, turn the feature on so your computer can handle and help prevent attacks as they occur and not just after the fact.

9. Install a file viewer program. With a file viewing program, you can see the contents of a file such as an attachment to an email without opening up the file. Since opening up an attachment is one of the main ways to get viruses and worms, this type of program helps protect you by allowing you to look at what's in a file without really opening it up.

10. Look for danger signals. On a taskbar on your computer screen, you should see icons for your firewall, antivirus program and those of your antispyware programs that are always on. Take a look at them at least twice a day to see whether they're flashing a warning signal to you that something is amiss.

11. Back up your computer. Once you run your antivirus and antispyware programs and your computer is free of viruses, worms, Trojan horses, spyware and other detectable threats, back up your "clean" computer. This is also a good time to make sure the system restore is turned on so you have a clean date to go back to if you need to restore your computer's system (send yourself an email with the subject line "Clean computer date" so you'll know later on when your computer was cleaned up and safe).

12. Think about privacy with a browser search toolbar. A browser search toolbar is a convenient way to have a search engine's or portal's search capability on your computer screen at all times. Be aware that using this type of toolbar may allow the search site to track your online activity. In finding the right browser search toolbar, find out whether the search site actually does track and record your searching.

Two Dozen Higher-Tech Solutions

For any of the following steps that seem too technical to you, consider hiring a professional to get them installed or activated. And if you're farming out this work to a specialist, you can use these steps as a checklist to double check what's being done and to question why any step is being left out.

1. Install a router that has a built-in hardware firewall. If this lingo makes you feel lost already, stick around. This is important information and you'll get the gist of it in just a few paragraphs. A **router** is a piece of hardware. Your computer's modem gets plugged into it. A router that's part of your Internet connection acts just like a high fence that's around your home. Just like a fence, it can make it more difficult for a stranger to see what's behind the barrier (your computer) and to go after what's being protected. Some fences are more protective than others and some do a better job of completely concealing what's hidden behind the fence. Routers are like that, too.

Although a router is ordinarily used with a computer network to connect up several computers, no matter how you connect up to the Internet (e.g., dialup, DSL or a cable modem), you'll want to connect up through a router. Routers can be used with modems from many computers at once or with just one computer.

A router can have a built-in **hardware firewall** that will give you an extra layer of protection and anonymity on the Internet. If your router is like a fence around your home, a firewall is like a bouncer at the door who decides who comes in.

You'll want to configure your router with its most secure settings and have one that uses **Stateful Packet Inspection** and has **NAT,** Network Address Translation. You'll also want to have a software firewall, too, as you'll see below.

2. Change the password on your router. Routers have a pre-set factory installed password to allow modifications to the router's settings. You'll want to change the factory default password to maintain control over your router. Otherwise, a hacker who can find your router may be able to get control of your router by typing in the factory-installed password and then do a "router rooter job" on your computer.

3. Disable remote control of your router. If your router's settings allow remote management, your computer could be attacked. Disable the remote management setting unless this is absolutely needed.

4. Disable your unused wireless features. If your router (or your computer) has wireless capability but you're not going to use this function (e.g., you use hardwire Ethernet cables to connect up computers), disable it.

5. Make your wireless router and network more secure. Routers can be hard-wired or wireless. With computers, wired connections are generally more secure than wireless connections. Many **wireless (Wi-Fi)** routers come with no security features made active. The default setting can leave you defenseless.

So, if you have a wireless network, you'll want the security settings activated at every access point and at the highest level (e.g., WPA security is more protective than WEP security and WPA2 should be more protective than WPA). Have a secure **passphrase** (password), too.

Change the name of your wireless network rather than using a default name familiar to hackers.

Restrict the strength of your wireless network's signal. The stronger your wireless signal, the greater the likelihood that outsiders can tap into it. Adjust the signal strength so it's just enough to reach each access point and no more. Locate access points in central locations away from windows and outside walls. Keep in mind that your Wi-Fi may use the same technology as 2.4-GHz cordless phones so to minimize interference, keep your phone base and wireless access points apart (also make sure your microwave oven isn't within 10 feet or you may get cooking interference).

For additional security, you may also decide to change the security settings to restrict access and to specify a list of approved computers that can be on your network by using MAC address filtering.

All parts of the network (the router/access point and the user/clients on the network) should have the same encryption key.

My feeling is that it is worth the money to get professional help to set up a more secure wireless network.

There's another reason to be concerned about unsecured networks. Some criminals have begun to use the unsecured Wi-Fi networks of unsuspecting consumers and businesses to help cover their tracks in cyberspace. Failure to secure a network can allow anyone with a Wi-Fi-enabled computer within about 200 feet or so to tap into your Internet connection. Make your network secure so you don't face the task of proving to legal authorities that you had nothing to do with criminal activities that used *your* network connection.

6. Create extra layers of access. Access your network through a VPN (virtual private network) that has its own encryption and authentication methods.

7. Be a tech plumber and look for leaks. There are tools to discover leaks and available ports (entry points) in your system. (See the Resource Guide.)

8. Install one software firewall. A **software firewall** is a software program that, like a hardware firewall, helps protect what goes in and comes out of your computer. How many software firewalls are enough? **One**. With more than one, the software programs may conflict with one another.

Which software firewall program should you use? Your computer's operating system may come with a software firewall. However, you may want to use a more robust, specialized software firewall program instead. If so, be sure to have your operating system's firewall program turned on while you download the more robust software firewall.

Make sure your firewall is **bidirectional** so you get protection on what comes in *and* what goes out of your computer.

Keep your firewall up to date by installing updates, as needed. In some cases, the update will be downloaded to your computer and installed automatically.

Once your software firewall program is installed, it will probably pop up a message on the screen asking your permission before allowing each application (software program) to access the Internet. (Usually, you can give permanent permission for a program you want to use repeatedly so you only have to give permission one time for that program.) Recognize that this is an important matter to consider. If you don't recognize a program, type in the program name in Google (**www.google.com**) to see if you can determine whether it is a legitimate program. When in doubt, just say no.

9. Know where your firewall stop button is. There may come a time when you see that your computer's security is being compromised. Your software firewall should have a button on the screen or a setting that stops all Internet traffic. The time to locate the stop function is before there's a problem. And don't overlook simply unplugging your modem or turning off your computer to brings things to a halt.

10. Don't be so quick to turn off your software firewall for tech support. There may be times when your computer isn't running quite right and a software technical support person will tell you that the problem must be a conflict between the software program and your firewall. You may then be encouraged to turn off your firewall to do some troubleshooting which can extend over quite a period of time. Don't be so quick to turn off your firewall while you're connected to the Internet. In many cases, it's something else that's causing the problem, not a firewall conflict. If you turn off your firewall, you may be making your computer a sitting duck for attacks by hackers. Five years ago, it was estimated that it took 15 minutes for an unprotected computer to become infected. Now, some say it takes 15 seconds. If you decide to turn off a firewall program that isn't part of your operating system, then reactivate the firewall that came with your operating system so you have something in place to protect you during the troubleshooting process.

11. Reinstall your operating system. In some cases, viruses and other intruders are just too crafty to catch and totally remove. The only cure may be to reinstall your operating system and wipe out all data on your disk (that's another reason why it's important to have regular, multiple backups so you can at least go back in time to a clean copy). Be sure to have a couple of current, good backups before doing this. A reinstallation should get rid of any viruses or spyware that have been too persistent to remove any other way.

12. Prepare an emergency recovery disk. If disaster strikes your computer, have on hand a disk with the latest version of your operating system, the drivers for the hardware on (or attached) to your computer and your backup software.

13. Be prepared to go back in time. Another approach that may work for your circumstances is to use your operating system's built-in system restore function. If it has been turned on, it allows you to put your computer's programs back into the state and shape it was on a prior date. As an alternative, there are **rollback** software programs that let you go back in time to undo the mischief done to your machine. **(**See the Chapter 13 Resource Guide.)

14. Be careful when you set up your IM (instant messaging). Make sure you restrict users to just your buddy list. Unless absolutely needed, keep it simple and disable advanced features, file sharing and the file transfer features. Also, since instant messaging in general is not the most secure way of communicating, you may want to have a program to help keep your instant messages confidential and provide protection against unauthorized inbound and outbound IM traffic. (See the Resource Guide.)

15. Block instant messages security leaks. Instant messaging can be a great communication tool. It can also be an entry point to harm your computer or your network.

16. Fine-tune your file sharing. When possible, restrict unnecessary file and folder sharing so if a networked computer gets infected, the rest of your computers are less likely to catch the bug.

17. Restrict remote access and control. If your only off-site uses are email and surfing the Net, then you don't need to set your computer to allow remote access to your data files and software programs. (For remote access and remote control programs, see Chapter 11.)

18. Run only what you have to. Disable communication programs that may be on your computer, but not used, that can open up **ports** (access points to your computer).

19. Surf the Net more anonymously. There are Internet surfing programs that help keep your surfing more private. Your browser may also offer private browsing so you don't leave a trace as your surf the Net. Other programs remove traces of where you've been on the Net. (See the Resource Guide.)

20. Data encryption. Data encryption can protect the contents of your computer. There are also encryption programs to keep outsiders from reading your files.

21. Email encryption. Most email isn't encrypted. There are encryption programs with varying levels of security and methods to encrypt emails.

The **electronic** or **digital signature** can be another valuable security tool. It tells the recipient with certainty who "signed" the document and guarantees that nothing was changed. The electronic signature is a typical feature of encryption programs. However, be aware that nothing is foolproof. Electronic signature encryption has been cracked by hackers from time to time.

22. Tighten up macro security in your everyday software applications. A **macro** is one computer instruction that carries out a series of computer instructions. Some viruses hide within macros. You may have macros within your word processing, spreadsheet, presentation or database programs. You can change the security setting for macros usually through choosing Tools and then Options, clicking the Security Tab, clicking on the Macro Security button and selecting the desired level of security.

23. See all the files that are really there. When you look at your folder and file organization with your file manager, you may not be seeing every file. To see hidden files in Windows, open up Windows Explorer, choose Tools and then Folder Options; click on View; then uncheck Hide Extensions for Known File Types; and click OK.

24. Take out the cache each day. When you surf the Net, your computer stores **files** and **cookies** from different sites. If you don't erase all these files and cookies, they can slow down your computer. Go to your browser, select Tools and then Internet Options; click to delete Files (including offline content); and click to delete Cookies. This is probably a good step to do once a day. Your browser may have different menu options to perform this task.

Disaster Prevention

Good organization, computer housekeeping, backup and using the tips in this chapter can help prevent disasters. Here are a seven more tips that can help.

1. Before you upgrade your operating system, check out the compatibility of everything you intend to run. After you upgrade your system, avoid, if possible, adding more than one thing at a time. Most importantly, wait until whatever you add, be it a new software program or some new hardware, works well for you. Adding anything new can create problems and it becomes difficult trying to unscramble problems and affix any responsibility to a particular product (or a company). **Never do an operating system upgrade without first having a full, complete backup of all programs and data files**. Also make sure you have on hand all your installation CDs or DVDs for all your software as well as for the previous operating system.

2. It's a good idea to do a backup before you install *any* new software.

3. During a power outage, don't just turn off your PC; unplug it and all the attached peripherals.

4. Never reformat your drive without first testing your backup files.

5. Be careful about movement. Don't move or bump a drive while it's in operation (and wait a minute for a hard drive to stop spinning before you move it). Carefully transport a removable drive in a padded case to prevent harmful movement.

6. To protect your files from unauthorized use (just as you wouldn't give a house key to just anyone), limit access to your computer files through password protection.

7. Smoking may be bad for a computer as well as for someone's lungs. Smoking around a computer may damage its circuits and contacts (remember how computers are built and assembled in very clean rooms—the need for good air quality doesn't stop at the computer assembly room).

Disaster Recovery

Oops. Sometimes you need help restoring a file, a drive or an entire computer's contents that have been accidentally deleted. For companies in the business of restoring data, see the Resource Guide. There is also software that can do this to a more limited degree.

Resource Guide

Also see **www.adams-hall.com** for periodic updates as well as my new book, *Teach Your Computer to Dance.*

Note: Always check with vendors for the latest version of software products and the compatibility with your existing hardware and software.

Antispam Programs

Cloudmark Desktop helps stop spam, fraud and phishing attacks. There are different ways to block spam. This product's approach is to block spam with zero false positives. In the context of work productivity, the classification of even one good email as spam can be devastating (i.e., an invoice that gets thrown into a spam filter and it's ignored). With antispam products, what you are looking for is high accuracy so workers can minimize the time to review spam emails by having to scan through their spam folder, which is highly inefficient. Cloudmark, 415/543-1220 [CA] or **www.cloudmark.com**

iHateSpam for Outlook is a great spam filter that can greatly reduce the junk email you find in your mailbox. Sunbelt Software, 888/688-8457 or **www.sunbelt-software.com**

MailFrontier Desktop is designed to start working immediately to block and remove junk email from your inbox. There are no rules you need to create, no lists to populate, nothing—the program does it for you. As you use MailFrontier Desktop, it continues to learn about the email that you don't like in order to provide better protection for your in-box. You can change the aggressiveness of the spam detection settings, update your own allowed/blocked lists, use a challenge/response system, and even block all email in a specific language. MailFrontier, Inc., 866-366-7726 [OR] or www.mailfrontier.com

Antispyware Database and Forum

Spyware Warrior is a website with tips and articles on spyware and antispyware, a forum to discuss spyware issues and solutions and a ready source for the latest developments in this area. Spyware Warrior, **www.spywarewarrior.com**

Antispyware Programs

Since no one antispyware program catches everything, here are several to consider:

AdAware offers free and fee versions. LavaSoft, Inc., **www.lavasoftusa.com**

PestPatrol is a popular program. Computer Associates International, Inc., **www.my-etrust.com**

Spybot offers immunization against known threats; removal of spyware infections; and real-time protection to prevent changes to your computer's settings. This popular free program asks for voluntary donations. Spybot, **www.spybot.info**

Spy Sweeper can block attempted spyware installations before they can infect your computer with its always-on presence; remove existing spyware infections; and help prevent changes to your computer's settings. Webroot Software, Inc., **www.webroot.com**

Spyware Doctor can provide three-way spyware protection for your PC through real-time threat blocking, advanced system scanning and immunization against known browser infections. PC Tools, **www.pctools.com**

Data Encryption

PGP Desktop Home is designed to be an easy-to-use desktop security solution that protects confidential communications and digitally stored information with strong, broadly accepted, encryption technology. It was created for individuals who want to secure private email, selected files and AOL Instant Messenger (AIM) traffic. It can be used by both casual and power users. **PGP Desktop Professional** includes all of the functionality of PGP Desktop Home plus PGP Whole Disk Encryption for users of Windows XP. PGP Whole Disk Encryption provides data encryption for an entire hard disk drive including the operating system, software applications and user data. PGP Corporation, 650/319-9000 [CA] or **www.pgp.com**

Steganos Security Suite not only encrypts data, it also hides files and drives from outsiders. Steganos GmbH, **www.steganos.com**

Data Erasing Programs

BCWipe is designed to securely delete files from disks so that recovery by any means is impossible. BCWipe is fully integrated into the Windows Shell. Jetico, Inc., **www.jetico.com**

Window Washer removes data on your Web and desktop activities. For deleted computer files, it is designed to completely overwrite the files with random characters making them permanently unrecoverable by undelete or unerase utilities—a security feature that exceeds the tough standards of the Department of Defense and the National Security Agency. Webroot Software, Inc., 866/612-4227 [CO] or **www.webroot.com**

Disaster Recovery Programs and Services; File and Disk Repair

DriveSavers, in the business of data recovery since 1985, rescues data from crashed and broken hard drives and other storage media. DriveSavers Data Recovery, Inc., 800/440-1904 [CA] or **www.drivesavers.com**

File Restore can undelete and restore files cleared from the Recycle Bin. Winternals Software, LP, **www.winternals.com**

Search and Recover is designed to recover files even after the Recycle Bin is emptied; recover data from formatted drives even after Windows is reinstalled; recover data after a virus attack, partitioning error or computer crash; recover data from hard and floppy drives, CD/DVD media, cameras, music players and memory cards; and on the other side of the coin, securely delete any file or folder, overwriting it up to 100 times. It can work with video, sound and image files, too. Iolo Technologies, LLC, **www.iolo.com**

SpinRite is a stand-alone program designed to refurbish hard drives, floppy disks and recover data from marginally or completely unreadable hard drives and floppy disks and from partitions and folders which have become unreadable. Gibson Research Corp., **www.grc.com**

Undelete replaces the Windows recycle bin and intercepts all deleted files, no matter how they were deleted. It can even restore your earlier, saved over versions of Microsoft Office (Word, Excel and PowerPoint) files. It also includes **SecureDelete**, an electronic shredder to completely erase confidential files. Diskeeper Corp., **www.executive.com**

File Viewer Program

Quick View Plus is designed to allow you to see the contents of a file without opening it up and being exposed to any viruses or worms inside the file. Avantstar, Inc., 877/829-7325 [MN] or **www.avantstar.com**

Firewall

LeakTest is a free testing program to determine whether your firewall is working. Gibson Research Corp., **www.grc.com**

ZoneAlarm is a top-rated software firewall program. Zone Labs, Inc., www.zonelabs.com

Instant Message Security Program

IMsecure Pro helps secures IM inbound and outbound communications, even across multiple clients. If all parties to an IM conversation are using the program, it is designed to also encrypt all sides of the conversation. Zone Labs, **www.zonelabs.com**

Internet Protection, Privacy and More

Acronis Privacy Expert Suite is designed to remove traces of your Internet activity, shred files on your computer you don't want recovered and be real-time antispyware. Acronis, Inc., **www.acronis.com**

Anonymous Surfing helps shield your IP address and protect you from online tracking, pharming attacks and snoops with its always-on 128-bit SSL (Secure Socket Layer) encryption. The goal is to let only your computer view any data being sent to or from it over a wireless or wired connection, especially when you're in public places such as the local coffee shop. It works silently in the background, without slowing down your Internet connection. For more complete protection on the Net, take a look at **Total Net Shield**. Anonymizer, Inc., 888/270-0141 [CA] or www.anonymizer.com

GhostSurf is a very useful Net surfing tool designed to provide an anonymous, encrypted Internet connection and erase traces of your surfing. Tenebril, Inc., 800/790-9060 [CA], **www.tenebril.com**

P.I. Protector Mobility Suite software, loaded on a USB flash drive, creates a portable computing environment providing access to a wide range of applications such as private Internet browsing, portable Outlook email, portable Outlook Express email and file synchronization. With P.I. Protector software, when you search the Web or just access your email, the product is designed to maintain your privacy by diverting your Internet activities to the flash drive and leaving no trace of your activities on the computer hard drive. P.I. Protector does not require installation or additional setup on the host computer. imagine LAN Inc., 800/372-9776 [NH] or **www.imaginelan.com**

ShieldsUP! is a quick, popular, free Internet security checkup and information service. Gibson Research Corp., **www.grc.com**

Metadata and Hidden Words

When you distribute a Microsoft Office document, the document may contain information that you do not want to share publicly (that might not be immediately apparent when you view the document in your Microsoft Office application) such as change tracking, comments, collaboration data and the location of files on your disk.

With the free Microsoft Office add-in, **rhdtool.exe**, you can permanently remove the hidden data and collaboration data from the Windows XP 2002 and 2003 versions of Word, Excel and PowerPoint. Go to www.microsoft.com and search for rhdtool.exe.

Speaking of hidden data, if you're looking for a way to see the hidden formatting codes in Word similar to what WordPerfect shows, try **Crosseyes**. Levit & James, Inc., **www.levitjames.com**

Security Suites

If you decide to go the security suite route, look at the **ZoneAlarm Internet Security Suite** from Zonelabs which contains a software firewall, an antivirus program, an antispam module, an antispyware program and *spim* protection. (Spim is IM spam.) Zone Labs, Inc., **www.zonelabs.com**

Theft Prevention

Carrying your laptop in a bag that isn't ordinarily used for laptops, such as a daypack, can offer more security in airports.

But if your computer is ever stolen, there are some programs that will disable the laptop or delete or encrypt files until the computer is recovered. As a last resort, follow Mike Hogan's suggestion in *PC World*—have an OWNER file (or maybe one called LOST & FOUND) in your laptop and desktop computer. Think about adding the offer of a reward if your computer is "found."

CyberAngel Security Software silently transmits an alert to a security monitoring center if the authentication is breached at login or boot-up. The software identifies the location from which that computer is calling. CyberAngel Security Solutions, Inc., 800/501-4344 [TN] or **www.sentryinc.com**

Stealth Signal software secretly sends a signal via telephone or an Internet connection allowing Stealth Signal to track your computer's location when you report it as lost or stolen. The software can also delete files remotely. Computer Security Products, Inc., 800/466-7636 [NH] or **www.computersecurity.com**

Cellphone phone book backup

If you ever worry about losing your cellphone phone directory should you ever lose your cellphone, **Cell-Stik** lets you easily back up, enter, edit and transfer cellphone contacts between cellphones and/or your computer. I use this great little product, which looks like a USB thumb drive. Check compatibility for your phone(s). Spark Technology Corp, **www.sparktech.com**

Part 5

Positively Organized!
Collaboration

Working, Communicating and
Computing with Others

15

Working Collaboratively with Others

Quick Scan: If you have customers, coworkers and/or staff, you need to read this chapter. Mastering the other chapters without mastering this one may leave you organized, but working in a vacuum. When you're Positively Organized, you maximize not only the ways you work by yourself but also use leadership to bring others into the fold by building a more human, caring, "emotionally intelligent" work environment with teamwork while fostering quality and customer service.

The first 14 chapters focused largely on what you as an individual can do in the workplace. But for dramatic results, you need to spread the word so that everyone with whom you work has a chance to be their best and make valuable contributions toward helping your organization— whether it's your work group/team, department, supplier base or company—reach its goals. This chapter covers the human elements of working with and bringing out the best in others so your organization can produce quality products/services with caring customer service.

Why Everyone You Work with Is Your Customer

You have probably heard about the importance of customer service and customer satisfaction. You may not, however, realize the extent to which it applies to you and your work. No matter what kind of work you do or organization you work for, customer focus needs to be your bottom line.

To compete and be profitable in today's world economy, your organization can no longer be doing "business as usual." The old maxim, "if it ain't broke, don't fix it," isn't true any more. Change is the name of the game and to stay competitive in business, you need to continually innovate and improve to provide **quality** goods and/or services for your **customers**.

External and Internal Customers

"Customers" need to be your primary focus and remember, there are two kinds of customers for every organization: external and internal. **External customers** are typically considered to be the most important. They're the ones who are paying for your goods or services. They're the ones most organizations try to satisfy first to stay in business.

Internal customers are the team members with whom you work to provide the goods or services for your external customers. They could be office coworkers, contacts in another department or division or part of your supplier base.

For many organizations, internal customers, come in second. That wasn't so, however, for Hal Rosenbluth, when he was CEO of one of the largest travel management companies in the world. Rosenbluth, who called his internal customers "associates," said, "We don't believe our customers can come first unless our associates come first. If we have happy people here, then they're free to concentrate only on our clients." Stated another way, *if your internal customers aren't happy, chances are good your external customers won't be either.*

Customers and Quality

So in a very real sense *everyone* with whom you work or interact is your customer (and vice versa). Even if you're a sole proprietor, you simply don't work in a vacuum. Once you recognize that we're "all in this together," you start to appreciate the importance of teamwork, service and quality.

"We are in the Quality Revolution and it's every bit as critical as the Industrial Revolution," so said Lloyd Dobyns, writer/narrator of the PBS program "Quality...or Else."

Even 99.9 percent quality isn't good enough; the following would result if organizations in the U.S. abided by only 99.9 percent quality: 1,314 phone calls would be misplaced in the next minute; 22,000 checks would be deducted from the wrong bank accounts in the next hour and 20,000 prescriptions would be written incorrectly this year.

Focusing on quality products and/or services can lead to and increase customer satisfaction—external as well as internal. To be on a quality team can provide a real sense of pride and accomplishment.

Quality is more than a buzzword or a fad; it's a way of doing business that permeates every aspect of a business **by focusing on both the customer** *and* **the work process.**

Customer Focus and Retention

To focus on the customer means to provide service and quality *as the customer sees them.* You stay close to your customers (both external and internal) by listening to them, asking them questions and working diligently to meet their needs. Customer focus means following through, doing what you say—which all involves good organizational skills and systems.

Oddly enough, some companies seem to provide just the opposite of customer service and satisfaction, especially if a "problem" arises. Not admitting any wrongdoing coupled with no apology and no genuine attempt to resolve the problem is a good way to lose old customers and reduce the number of new ones. Too often in our era of downsized, cost-cutting operations coupled with exclusively online "customer support," it's impossible to reach live, responsive, responsible human beings; I call this kind of customer support "invisible (virtually nonexistent) customer service."

And that brings us to the importance of **customer retention**. It costs six times as much to attract new customers as to retain existing ones. A study cited in the *Harvard Business Review* said that customer retention has a substantial impact on profitability, with the increase in dollar value of repeat customers ranging from 25 to 85 percent. Customer retention may, in fact, account for the biggest source of future sales growth.

By the way, only 30 percent of customers with problems complain (they just take their business elsewhere) and only two to five percent of complaints ever get voiced to the headquarters level. However, more and more unhappy customers *are* voicing complaints via Internet sites, blogs and wikis.

The Work Process & Customer Service

Focus on the work process— the main focus of this book— is an important means by which you provide customer service. It's examining the effectiveness of your organizational skills, tools and systems to check whether they're the best means for providing goods and services on time, within budget and to the customer's satisfaction.

Identify and eliminate inefficient work processes, especially those that stick out like a sore thumb. I remember many years ago standing endlessly in a hotel checkout line, while the woman ahead of me noticed one particularly inefficient hotel clerk. She commented, "He never gets anything right. And it takes him a long time to get it wrong."

There has to be a better way of doing things such as hotel checkout (and of course, hotels have now routinely implemented "express checkout" systems that save valuable customer time—both the internal and external customers' time). And as someone once said anonymously, "It takes less time to do something right than it takes to explain why you did it wrong."

Make sure you evaluate your existing work process. There may be steps that shouldn't be done at all. Get involved with **work simplification** if possible. For example, one major American automaker developed an automated system to track sales, inventory and production because of a complex system that gave consumers options in some 40,000 possible combinations. A foreign manufacturer, on the other hand, didn't need such a complex automated system because it created only 32 possible combinations. Try to eliminate the need for a complex automated system in the first place.

But what about customer service? Some might argue that 40,000 combinations give the customer more choice; others would argue that having too many choices overwhelms most people. Look, too, for a balance between serving the external and internal customers.

A quality work process depends on the genuine commitment by everyone in an organization, especially those at the top, to quality, innovation, customer service and internal customer support. Openness to change and continuous quality improvement is evident at all levels of such an organization. In a quality-conscious organization you'll see a strong emphasis on training, communication, innovation, flexibility, employee involvement and teamwork—all driving forces in an "emotionally intelligent" organization.

Emotional Intelligence and the Internal Customer

According to a two-year Labor Department study, companies that train workers, involve them in decisions and give them a stake in the business are more profitable than those that do not. The Secretary of Labor said the study indicated the "surest way to profits and productivity is to treat employees as assets to be developed rather than costs to be cut."

It would be good to see the emphasis shift more to "human capital"—the worth of individuals and how to maximize it in a very human, caring sense. And there needs to be a greater emphasis on what people need in the workplace (and their lives) to help them thrive and ultimately contribute more in terms of the quality and quantity of their work.

Some workplaces do offer more to meet the needs of their people including "Family-friendly" programs. Flexible schedules, telecommuting, video and web conferencing and special nonmonetary rewards and perks acknowledge that people have a life outside of work. Some companies give work balance days to handle personal or family business.

At the same time, people are working harder and longer than ever. But when they're working in collaborative, high-functioning teams to develop a quality product or service, they experience a sense of belonging, purpose and meaning—which, in turn, can raise the levels of quality and customer service.

Look at where you work. See if there's a culture that cares about quality, service and both the external and internal customers. If so, you're probably seeing **emotional intelligence (EI)** in action. EI (sometimes called "EQ" for emotional quotient) consists of about two-dozen people skills that you develop personally for yourself and socially with others you manage or work with. In his books Daniel Goleman cites extensive research showing the correlation of EI to workplace and career success and performance by EI organizations.

In short, if organizations use EI practices to develop their internal customers—their people—they will be better able to serve their external customers. This chapter will show some EI practices you can use to help develop yourself and your internal customers—be they coworkers or staff.

Positively Organized! Leadership

In order to provide exemplary external customer service and produce quality products and services, develop the organization internally (the internal customers) through Positively Organized! leadership.

Such leadership encourages each participant at every level in an organization to play a **leadership** role, which I define as *supporting, inspiring, guiding and/or managing others to be as productive and successful as they can be.*

Generally, the higher up a participant is, the greater the impact a participant can have. But let's look at how Positively Organized! leaders *at all levels* can use cooperative, emotionally intelligent methods of working with and leading others to bring out the best in each person and the output of their organization.

Building Empowered Teams

Positively Organized! leaders promote empowered, cooperative, cross-functional teams in flattened hierarchies.

A **cross-functional team** is when people from different departments or those who perform different functions work together as a team on a specific project or problem. Such teamwork breaks down barriers between people who work in different work groups, departments and even different companies. Cross-functional teams naturally develop in **matrix organizations**, which focus on project work and bring together different departments that work together in more of a "flattened hierarchical" structure.

A **flattened hierarchy** (unlike a traditional, hierarchical "functional" organization) brings internal and external customers closer together more quickly as problems come into the foreground faster and demand immediate attention.

A flattened hierarchy only happens, however, if your organization has a pervasive, empowered work climate that fosters trust, teamwork and recognition—a climate that famous humanist psychologist Abraham Maslow termed "enlightened management." He also used the term "synergy" to describe the cooperation that such a climate creates.

One *Wall Street Journal* story said it concisely: "Teamwork is in." The story described a study focused on 4,000-plus teams in more than 500 companies and found that performance and advancement were being measured not only by individual achievements but also by the ability to be a team player.

Team leadership

Increasingly almost everyone will need to assume at some time the role of **team leader and coach** who facilitates employee participation and teamwork.

Team leadership is replacing old, autocratic, traditional management styles of "do it my way," which rarely work. And team leadership is more about *facilitating a collaborative work process* rather than "managing people."

As for the latter, foremost management expert Peter Drucker said the term "manager" isn't particularly useful anymore because in today's progressive organizations, managers increasingly work with "colleagues," rather than dominate "subordinates."

Interesting enough, I saw a study that showed that women more naturally exhibit the kind of nontraditional traits needed in today's new, enlightened leaders—the ability to share information and power, encourage employee participation and demonstrate how both individual, personal goals may be reached while attaining organizational goals. But whether or not such traits come naturally, they can be trained and coached.

Today's leaders would do well to embrace the following statement by John McDonnell of McDonnell Douglas about operating with a "fundamental belief that everyone wants to do a good job and that overall performance will be greatly enhanced if people are assisted, coached, trained and supported rather than controlled."

The 95% rule and giving authority to make decisions

According to management consultant and author Lee Cheaney, today's managers should also "manage on the behavior of 95 percent of employees and not on the five percent who cause problems." He suggests dealing with that five percent promptly and fairly, spending the bulk of your time developing your team.

To develop the 95 percent, today's manager needs to help form work teams that have real authority to make decisions and to act. When one

General Mills cereal plant gave such authority to its work teams, it realized a 40 percent higher productivity rate compared with traditionally managed groups.

We're seeing this kind of shift taking place in manufacturing circles as well as in service areas and in the office. Research indicates that workers are happier, too, with more involvement. Studies indicate that workers want open communications; more opportunities to contribute and to have their work and innovative contributions recognized; and the chance to develop skills.

Leaders today have the opportunity to address these factors through open communications and a participatory management style that gives more responsibility to workers and work teams. Participatory leaders encourage their people to make decisions and come up with solutions of their own. When I presented a seminar to a credit union group in Portland, one manager shared his policy, "Don't come to me with a problem unless you have at least two solutions."

In today's business climate, effective leaders need to be proactive, embrace change and innovation, be passionate about their work, provide training and development opportunities and genuinely care about their people.

We need leaders who roll up their sleeves and work collaboratively *with* other team members in a highly charged, optimistic, pioneering spirit. Teams who work collaboratively can experience meaning, purpose and even joy as they pull their know-how and ideas together and discover that in the words of playwright Noel Coward, "work can be more fun than fun."

Actively Involve Employees

Teams have a better chance of thriving if leaders at all levels encourage and promote employee involvement. Research indicates a direct correlation between high employee involvement and motivation, quality, productivity and profitability.

For starters, make sure there's a genuine *culture of caring about people* in place. Without this culture or context, many of the ideas in this section could be perceived as insincere, phony and manipulative.

The top two employee involvement motivators

Employee involvement needs to begin with caring about the individuals who make up an organization. Such caring should relate to what motivates people at work.

Contrary to popular belief, the top motivator for employees is *not* money. Research shows that money is not a main motivator (although not having enough of it can be a *de*motivator).

The number one motivator is **achievement**. A small achievement can qualify as well as something new or something done even a little better than before. Even *degrees of less failure* can qualify.

The number two motivator is **recognition**, which can be as simple as genuine words of praise from someone else, especially a leader, who recognizes the achievement.

These two motivators go hand in hand and outstanding leaders care about and foster these motivators on an individual and organization level. Reinforcing these motivators creates true employee involvement.

Incidentally, other important motivation factors include honesty and ethical behavior of management as well as open communications. If these factors aren't present, then recognition will probably feel false and will cease to motivate.

Performance management

Performance management in which employees set and evaluate their own performance objectives is an important way to involve employees. Be sure to build in recognition and reward for good and/or improved performance.

As a part of their performance management process, one company has each employee complete a thought-provoking, two-page, self-evaluation form for past and future performance. The form asks employees to list their performance objectives for the coming 12 months, any necessary behavior changes they'll need to make and significant achievements during the past 12 months. In addition, employees are asked to "stretch" themselves—to make a special effort to accomplish something in the next 12 months and identify what that effort will be. There is also a chart for listing strengths, weaknesses, problems and opportunities.

Train to see a real gain

Get involved in your own training and encourage others to do so. Assess areas where you could use some additional training. Help create and facilitate a culture of continual learning.

Notice whenever you feel uncomfortable in doing new work or taking on a new responsibility. Don't pretend you know something when you don't. Don't worry about feeling inadequate. Let it be a signal that it's time for you to learn something new, and whenever you do, there's usually some feeling of discomfort that's natural.

Progressive organizations offer many training opportunities that emphasize both "hard" (technical) skills as well as "soft" (EI/people) skills training, such as team building and coaching.

Remember training pays off. One economist found that even short-term, company-sponsored training brought higher wages and better performance reviews.

Capitalize on cross training

One way to get training, aside from a formal training department, is to take advantage of **cross training**. This kind of training lets you see, and in some cases lets you do, other people's jobs. There are many advantages to this kind of training. First, you have a chance to learn new skills or new aspects of your company. Learning additional skills could add to your marketing and career potential. Second, it can be helpful from an operations standpoint to have someone else fill in for you if you're out sick or on vacation.

Third, when you can see what procedures are followed by other people or departments, you have a chance to see why these procedures are necessary. You may be more cooperative when you're asked to fill out a form, for example, because you've seen firsthand, just how important it is to another department. (Or perhaps, you'll offer some suggestions for improvement because you're looking at the procedures from a different perspective as an outsider.)

Building a real sense of cooperation is a major reason to cross train. One major company has a chart that reads:

~~Y~~OUR PROBLEM
Cooperation is spelled with two letters: "WE."

Describe what you do and how you do it

Your department or office should develop its own **training manual** that describes all of the different positions and responsibilities in detail. Everyone should write a description of their responsibilities, functions and processes. All of the information should be checked, tested and updated from time to time.

Normally, training for a new position is handled by one other person, often a predecessor. When the training isn't in some written format, vital items can become omitted.

It's important to document in a manual all that you do in your position. Such documentation might even justify why you need an assistant (or a raise!). Plus it's a real help when you train someone else to do your work—temporarily, when you go on vacation, or permanently, when you get that promotion.

Incentive and recognition programs

Many organizations today have a whole variety of employee incentive or employee recognition programs that encourage and reward employee-generated, innovative, cost-saving ideas; a superior work effort; surpassed performance goals; and employee longevity.

There is a difference between "recognition" and "incentive" programs. An incentive program is designed specifically to motivate employees to perform, whereas a recognition program shows appreciation and recognizes achievement after the fact. In your organization, it may be more appropriate to use one type of program alone or to use a combination.

Mission and guiding values

To further reinforce individual achievements and recognition, tie them in with the mission of your company, organization or work group.

Begin by giving everyone a copy of your organization's mission statement, as well as the guiding values. Share them with external customers, too.

If you don't have a mission statement and guiding values or if they're buried in long-range documents, have a meeting or two devoted solely to exploring the relevance of mission and values. Compare mission and values statements of other organizations. Suggest that an action team be formed to develop (or revise) them. This group could have representatives from all different levels or departments in the organization. This is a great way to build participation in the organization.

Even if you're in charge of a small team, it makes sense to have your team identify and adopt the mission and values.

The benefits of camaraderie

Building camaraderie is a fun way to encourage employee participation, teamwork and creativity. Many companies are finding that the group that plays together, stays together.

Get to know one another

You may spend at least eight hours a day at work, yet know very little about your coworkers. One organization has a voluntary Employee Profile form that asks about such areas as hobbies, outside interests and children. These forms are compiled and published periodically in an employee directory. They could also be published on an intranet or a *wiki* (a kind of giant online bulletin board to put photos, articles and other items) to help employees become better acquainted.

I developed my own profile form when I was president of a professional association. It was a useful tool for board members to get to know one another. I included such items as "family members or significant others," "pets," "education/Alma Mater(s)," "activities, hobbies, interests, charities, etc." and "special goals, dreams, aspirations." I encouraged my board members to answer any of the items that felt comfortable or appropriate for them.

Leading by organizing

An important part of leadership is organizing yourself so you can work more effectively with others. Being organized puts you in a better position to positively influence others. And as an organized member of your work group, you have a special ability to lead. Another way to say it is, "As you organize, so shall you lead."

As an organized person, you're a doer but you can also be a leader if you master the art of delegation, which has an important training and coaching component. We'll be discussing delegation as well as other tools to share work with others. When you're organized, you have a good view of both the macro and the micro—the big picture as well as the details. You can see more clearly what needs to be done, when and how.

How to delegate successfully

Delegation, used correctly, may be another tool to help you increase your work output and your team's and provide a way to build up the skills of team members. Effective delegation means, for the delegator, giving people not just things you don't want to do, but more often giving things you *do* want to do.

In fact, according to Ben Tyler, past Burlington Industries Transportation Division president, "It's giving up things you enjoy to someone else and recognizing that not only can they do it, but often they can do it better." For the delegate, delegation is an opportunity to grow, develop and shine; for the delegator, delegation is a chance to develop, coach and mentor others.

Effective delegation requires four steps: (1) organize, (2) communicate, (3) entrust and (4) follow up and evaluate.

Organize

First, organize yourself. You need to see the whole picture in order to make delegation decisions. Think through the process. You'll also need a good personal organization system in order to follow up later. Top designer and entrepreneur Calvin Klein says he organizes himself first so he can delegate effectively to others.

Communicate (if necessary, train and/or coach)

Second, communicate the specific details of the delegation and if necessary, train your delegate. The amount of training and direction will vary according to the delegate's abilities and the nature of the assignment. You may need to take time yourself to clearly teach the delegate how to do something or identify someone else to provide the training.

In addition to (or instead of) training, you may need to coach your delegate to improve performance through motivation, discussion, diagnosis and feedback (for more on coaching, see the book *Coaching for Improved Work Performance* listed in the Resource Guide.)

Entrust

Third, entrust your delegate with the assignment. Resist the temptation of peeking over shoulders (unless the delegate is a rank beginner and truly needs such an intervention). By the way, the dictionary definition of the verb "delegate" is "to entrust to another."

Follow up and evaluate

When you follow up and evaluate, *praise a job well done.* Of course, you can't do this step if you haven't mastered step number one. So we've come full circle, back to organization.

If you find it tough getting people to follow through and give you things on time, do what Kathy Meyer-Poppe did when she was a director at Revlon. She told her staff, "This is what I need and this is the date I need it by." Then she put it on her calendar and her staff knew she had done so. They also knew she would ask for it if it wasn't done. But usually she didn't have to ask. She said, "They knew it was truly important when I said, for example, 'I need this by next Friday'—that I'm not just blowing in the wind." She stayed flexible, too; if her request was unrealistic, her staff told her and together they selected a new deadline and agreed on it. At times she suggested they reprioritize their work.

Reverse delegation

In my experience I've identified two types of what I call "reverse delegation."

In the first type, you may want to try **reverse delegation** when someone higher up delegates something to *you* for which you don't have time. When Meyer-Poppe's staff came back to her to negotiate work assignments or deadlines, they were practicing a type of reverse delegation. This tool works best when you're organized and can clearly see the important things you have to do, how long they will take and how they relate to the goals of your delegator, your department and yourself.

This type of reverse delegation occurs when a person gives the delegated task back to the delegator. It requires great tact, diplomacy and communication skills. It also requires a thorough understanding of goals and objectives for the company or office and for the delegator. There has to be a real benefit for the delegator whenever you reverse delegate.

When I was the communications manager for an aerospace company, my boss wanted me to get involved in coordinating one of his new pet projects—the creation of a historical aviation museum. Since I had no interest in his project and saw no connection either to my job or my career, I suggested that he involve someone else who was far more qualified than I. Coming up with the name of someone else was an easy task; the company historian worked right next door to my office and was a natural for this project. I didn't know it at the time, but I was practicing reverse delegation.

There's one other type of reverse delegation that you should practice when you're given an assignment or project through which you want to shine and/or learn new skills. Take each of the four steps of effective delegation—organize, train, entrust, and follow up/evaluate—and make sure *you* are doing them. Organize yourself, get any necessary training or information, secure the trust or authority to do a job and finally, follow through on evaluating the job with your boss. This type of reverse delegation is a marvelous communication and self-marketing tool; it can show your boss not just how well you work, but how dependable and organized you are!

How to organize others

A question I'm often asked by well-organized individuals is how they can organize a boss or a coworker. Impossible as it may seem, there are a number of steps you can take.

Broaden your definition of "organize." Make sure it goes well beyond clean desks to incorporate the importance of goal setting, prioritizing, working more effectively and the notion of process improvement. Make sure it also complements your "corporate culture" or the philosophy and mission of your organization as a whole.

In addition, recognize that organizing others is usually a communication, coaching and training issue. The communication/coaching aspect focuses on how to *motivate* others to *want* to be better organized. Begin by answering the following question that others are asking themselves: "**What's in it for me?**" Remember the acronym for that all important question: **WIIFM**. There have to be real benefits for them in terms of achievement and recognition or whatever is a real motivator *for them*. They have to clearly see a connection between getting organized and any benefits that are motivators.

Once you can show a positive connection, you have a good shot at helping them begin the organizing training process. As with most training, this is a process that takes place over time. There are skills to learn and habits to practice. If you yourself are organized and are a patient teacher who acknowledges and reinforces small successes, you have a chance to see some exciting results. If you're a team player, not a dictator, you could even transform your entire organization.

But even after all your efforts, you may at times need to recognize the limitations of certain individuals who just can't seem to grasp certain "basic" organizational skills. In those situations, you may just need to take more control, insist on a daily meeting (in person or by phone) and intercept certain details or projects that simply shouldn't end up in that person's hands.

Getting involved in training others requires you to look for and apply a variety of approaches, depending on the needs of the individuals involved. Look, too, for books, videos, cassettes, CDs, DVDs, in-person and online training classes and seminars and consultants to teach organizational skills and processes. In some cases, you can be the trainer yourself if you take various tasks and activities, write out the steps involved ahead of time and then teach those steps to someone else.

Review this chapter, as well as the rest of the book. Look for ways to improve how you and your coworkers can get things done. Sometimes it's the little things that can make a big difference. I suggest, for example, that a manager/assistant team take five to 10 minutes daily to meet and discuss the day's schedule, projects and priorities.

Or use a well-designed work request form to help organize and prioritize work flow. Such a paper-based or online form should have a checklist section for routine work, the time frame or deadline for completion (see the work priority slip discussion coming up in this chapter) and a "special instructions" area for writing additional comments, requirements or notes.

If you're not in management, don't be afraid you won't have enough impact. An organized person with vision, creativity and drive can accomplish miracles. But don't do it alone. Look for other like-minded individuals who are open to change, quality improvement and innovation.

If you are in management, you have a special responsibility to influence and inspire others. That does not mean, however, having others do it your way. It means facilitating change, teamwork and an exchange of ideas and information.

Managing multiple bosses, projects or priorities

It's a real challenge trying to work with multiple bosses or coworkers and juggle different projects and priorities. The key word here is "priorities" because that's where you'll need to start.

Begin by setting up a work priority system. First, define priority levels, get agreement on these levels from coworkers and bosses and incorporate these levels into the project management or other software programs you're using or in a paper-based system onto a work priority slip. You could use the following codes, for example, and have them printed onto Post-it Notes or included in email subject lines:

A-1 Drop everything—this requires immediate attention!
A-2 This is a hot priority to be done ASAP.
A-3 Handle this by the end of the day.
B-1 Complete by the end of the next work day.
B-2 Complete by a specified day, from two to seven days out.
B-3 This is an important but long-term project, due in more than a week's time up to several months.

Note that priorities can and will change; what was a B-1 yesterday may become an A-3 today, unless, of course, the task is reprioritized.

You also need to set up some guidelines along with any agreed-upon priorities. One guideline could be to work on all urgent priorities before going on to the next level. Another should offer suggestions on how to handle conflicting priorities (it's best to do this before the actual conflicts arise). Still another should provide for setting aside set blocks of time every day or week to work on long-term projects. Ideally, have your team meet to formulate codes and guidelines and reach consensus.

You could also use different colored preprinted Post-it Notes or Flags by 3M for different paperwork priorities or Post-it Digital Notes for online work. Color has a way of really jumping out, especially with the new, bright colors that are available.

Resource Guide

See also **www.adams-hall.com** for periodic updates.

Books and Other Learning Resources

American Productivity & Quality Center is a nonprofit organization that works with business, labor, government and academia to identify best practices and to discover effective methods of improvement. It issues a variety of publications. 800/776-9676 [TX] or **www.apqc.org**

Coaching for Improved Performance by Ferdinand Fournies (McGraw-Hill, 2000) is a practical guide for effectively coaching all levels of employees to raise quality, productivity and career satisfaction.

Conquering Chaos at Work: Strategies for Managing Disorganization and the People Who Cause It by Harriet Schechter (Fireside, 2000). This wonderful book offers help, hope and humor for people in all different work places. **www.MiracleOrganizing.com**

Pilot Vision and Other Pilot Secrets to Succeed in the Business World (Adams-Hall Publishing, 1999) by John Michael Magness is a great little leadership book.

Working with Emotional Intelligence (Bantam, 2000) by Daniel Goleman provides stunning research and case studies that demonstrate outstanding business leaders and performers are not defined by their IQs or even their job skills but by their "emotional intelligence": a set of competencies that distinguishes how people manage feelings, interact and communicate.

16

Collaborative Communication

Quick Scan: Discover positive, effective communication skills as well as tips on making your meetings more meaningful and productive. Be sure to also check out the Resource Guide.

In this chapter we'll explore communication skills that help build strong, collaborative working relationships, meetings and teams.

Eight Communication Secrets

People in the workplace often take communication for granted and assume that enough of it goes on. There's plenty of email, instant messaging, texting, phone calls and certainly meetings. But the sheer quantity of communication that takes place doesn't insure quality nor caring in the communication. Here are eight strategies for developing collaborative communication.

One: Keep People Informed

Someone once observed, "When you don't keep people informed, you get one of three things: rumor, apathy or revolution."

You'd be surprised how frequently people in work groups really don't communicate with each other to keep one another informed—even of their simple comings and goings. It's especially important to keep a receptionist, assistant or office manager informed, particularly if they have any dealings with external customers. Lack of basic, up-to-date information about the availability of key personnel can create a credibility gap in the organization. Decide *who* needs to know *what* as well as *how* and *when* they will get that information.

Traditional in/out boards and wall charts are a low tech solution. There are also dedicated "in-and-out board groupware programs" accessible through a mobile handheld device or computer that are available, which can let every user in a company know where colleagues are and the details of their schedules. Whichever tool you choose for keeping tabs on people's whereabouts, use it consistently.

Two: Communicate Clearly & Positively

Ask yourself as you begin any communication, what's the key question, its deadline and/or time frame—and be as **specific** as possible. Try to use numbers to add clarity to convey how much time you have ("I have three minutes to talk"), how much time you'll need, how many things you want to discuss, etc.

Don't forget to **compliment** key colleagues you work with, ideally at least once a day. But of course, you must be sincere. The power of a compliment can help transform a working (or personal) relationship. I have seen it happen in my consulting work.

Be positive and open-minded about possibilities rather than negative and close-minded. Instead of saying, "I don't know" and leaving it at that, you might add, "But I'll find out." Instead of saying, "We can't do that" or "we never have done it that way," try "Let's see what we can do."

If you have to give some "constructive criticism," approach it positively as a way to help someone else grow and develop. Become aware, too, of different communication styles and preferences. Communications research indicates that people like to receive communication in the way they're most likely to deliver it.

Three: Use Multiple Channels

Multiple channels can make communication more interesting and less likely to fall prey to distortion or bias from information that's conveyed through only one channel or source. Such channels can include any of the following: email, instant messaging (IM), text messaging, telephone calls, meetings, Web conferencing, video conferencing, memos, faxes, company publications, intranets, wikis (a kind of giant online bulletin board), coworkers, higher-ups, the "grapevine" and customers.

Include at least one personal channel of communication such as the phone, face-to-face meetings or Web or video conferencing, especially if you're relying heavily on a less personal channel, such as email or IM. This is especially important for team members or customers who are scattered all over geographically. **Remember, the purpose of communication includes not only the sharing of information but also the development of relationships.**

Be on the lookout, also, for communication channels that are innovative, creative or humorous. Use color-coding whenever possible to flag or categorize messages. One U.S. president used color-coding on a "message calendar" to highlight key topics to discuss with his aides; he had different colored bars on each of the calendar's days, for example, purple for foreign policy, orange for the economy, blue for social policy and green for government reform.

Four: Avoid Too Many Channels

To avoid information overload, **beware of using too many channels or communication tools**. Most of my bigger corporate clients provide each employee with several means by which they can communicate with others inside and outside the company. The problem is workers spend a lot of time checking *all* of these communication channels several times a day (and night). They may also spend time finding out the communication channel preferred by the receiver. It gets very complicated and time-consuming. (Consider using **unified messaging** where several modes of messages are accessible through one source; see Chapter 5 for additional information.)

I developed a survey for a large corporate client where I had all members of one department indicate their preferences, both when sending and receiving communications. Then I charted them all out so everyone could see one another's preferences. You could do such a survey within your work group, maybe even agreeing to reduce or eliminate certain communication channels. Groupware software can help determine and utilize each person's favored mode of communication (see Chapter 17).

Five: Get Feedback

Keeping people informed is only half of the communication story. To complete the story, **ask people what they think**. This needs to happen regularly for both internal and external customers. Be prepared, however, that once you ask people what they think, you must really *listen*, take the information seriously by *responding* and *acting* on it.

Conducting a survey, such as the one I just described, is an excellent way to see what's on people's minds. Keep surveys as simple as possible. Design a major benefit into the survey—why should anyone want to take the time to complete it? Tell survey participants *what's in it for them*.

Companies are surveying both their external and internal customers. Some companies are involved in a "360-degree feedback" process to see how they're doing, which may include surveys by external customers, employee performance appraisals, "upward appraisals" (subordinates' evaluations of their superiors) and "peer appraisals." The latter are more typical of companies with a leaner, flattened hierarchical structure.

Insurance agent Don Gambrell created a clever, two-sided, Farmers Insurance form/response letter to encourage customers to renew their policy and/or communicate with him about why they haven't done so. The left half of the page had a brief, friendly letter called "This is My Side" asking for the customer to respond to the other half, called "This is Your Side," which has six different quick responses to check off. An SASE was also enclosed. He used this form for over 20 years because it worked.

"The President's Luncheon" is one way a federal credit union asks employees what they think. Every month, six or seven employees are chosen at random to have lunch with the president and discuss any topics they feel are important to them, to the credit union or to management.

One CEO has a dedicated phone line for employees to call him. The line rings directly in his office and isn't screened by anyone. Whenever it rings, the CEO picks up the phone and speaks openly and confidentially with employees.

Another company set up a toll-free number for employees to leave messages, which are then transcribed anonymously by an outside company.

The suggestion box can be a good way to get feedback but one department discovered a new twist. This was a busy call center where phones rang off the hook and ten disgruntled employees didn't work well together. The department replaced the suggestion box with a "Gripe Box," and employees completed "Gripes and Complaints" cards anonymously. Though the Gripe Box sounds negative, it worked because it reflected how people were feeling and gave them a chance to vent those feelings. Gripes and complaints were handled openly but anonymously at department meetings, solutions were generated and today everyone gets along very well.

One organization asks employees to bring one to two suggestions to improve the work process every time they go to a meeting. Ideas are later evaluated and rewarded.

One small business owner I know of offers an open dialogue for her employees every other month over pizza. She takes them out for pizza and then they meet for two hours. The first hour is an open gripes session about anything and anybody, including management. The second hour is spent on positive comments and solutions to gripes.

Just staying close to your customers and having your eyes and ears open can be a very effective way to find out what people think; convey that information back to your customers and you have real two-way communication. That's just what a local caterer-restaurant owner did. Zabie Vourvoulis published a beautiful, two-color brochure for her customers, in which she affirmed her "commitment to quality" and acknowledged customers' contributions.

> We struggle constantly with the issue of service and how best to fill your needs. Many times, small suggestions or comments from you have led to big changes (paper biodegradable disposables for instance). We've also purchased new, more comfortable and sturdier stools, and we've developed an interesting, reasonably priced dinner menu...Your support has been wonderful. It's encouraging to know that effort and caring have a place in this fast-paced world of ours. We certainly appreciate yours and we hope that ours shows every day.

Many businesses are using email to stay in touch with customers. You can do a lot of market research this way (but make sure you comply with antispam laws), although email customers, who are often shrouded in some anonymity, can be rather blunt. Some businesses are using email for their internal customers as well; one company lets employees disguise their identity and posts replies daily on an electronic bulletin board.

Appreciative Inquiry

One positive approach I've found particularly helpful as a management consultant when soliciting feedback from an organization is **Appreciative Inquiry (AI)**. A compelling, collaborative methodology, AI frames questions positively and encourages thinking outside the box that goes beyond the level of the problem. AI is also a great problem-solving tool that incorporates Albert Einstein's advice: "The significant problems we have cannot be solved at the same level of thinking with which we created them." For genuine, positive change and development to occur, a positive model such as AI works at a level above problems because we can't solve a problem at the level of the problem.

Six: Standardize Communication

See if you have any specific routines you're currently using in your own office, your work group and/or your company concerning communications—e.g., how the phone is answered, by whom and when calls are returned; how visitors are greeted and by whom; and how email is prioritized and managed. Do you have any procedures in writing? If not, now's a good time to start!

Seven: Practice Good Listening Skills

Listening is crucial to good communication skills and customer service. Yet recent studies show that 75 percent of what we hear is heard incorrectly and of the remaining 25 percent, we forget 75 percent of it within weeks or days. The average listener has an immediate retention level of only 50 percent; within 24 to 48 hours, the retention level drops to 25 percent.

It's not easy to listen. It takes great concentration, in large part because we hear four to five times faster than we can speak. We may become bored and think about other things to fill in the gaps when someone else is talking or even worse, interrupt people to complete their thoughts. To be an "active listener," which is the most effective kind of listener, requires the ability to slow down and concentrate, absorb information, put yourself in someone else's shoes, restate accurately what you've heard, ask clarifying questions and evaluate the whole process objectively. Listening is a skill to be learned and practiced, a skill especially hampered by our fast-paced world.

Eight: Personalize Communication

There are certain words people can't hear enough: their own names and "thank you." Take time to thank people for their thoughtfulness, hard work or good ideas. Sitting down to write a thank-you note is such a simple, but very powerful method of communication. It shows that the recipient is worth your time and you're organized enough to make time for it.

Since writing thank-you notes is becoming something of a lost art, you can really make an impression on coworkers, customers and your boss. It's a really tangible form of communication. Sending an email thank you is good, too. And if you thank customers or others who complain, you also have a chance to turn around a bad situation.

Learning and **using people's names** can have a big impact on opening up communication. I had a dramatic example of seeing that it's "all in a name" a number of years ago. Around 4:30 every afternoon, a postal carrier made the last pick-up at several boxes near our office. Occasionally, I'd go out to the boxes right at 4:30, when the postal truck arrives and hand my final mail to the carrier.

Over the years, there had been several carriers, each of whom was very friendly. When a new carrier assumed the route he seemed very different. He was very serious and wouldn't look up when you handed him mail. He appeared almost upset that you were breaking his routine. He seemed, in a word, antisocial. Normally, I would have introduced myself and made small talk but I figured that was a real waste of time with this guy.

Weeks went by and I avoided making any contact with the carrier. Being normally a very outgoing individual, I decided one day to simply introduce myself. Much to my surprise, when I told him my name and learned his was Richard, he really lit up and began to talk. Every time I saw him, he called me by name and had something pleasant to say.

Until I moved my office to a different location, Richard was an internal customer who was part of my supplier base. The service he provided made it possible for me to be of service to my external customers. Because he was a part of my team, it was important to be able to communicate with him.

When I teach my "e-writing" and email workshops I always emphasize using the recipient's name at least once and preferably twice (assuming the mail is not going to a group). Using names really warms up emails (see also Chapter 5).

Meaningful Meetings

Traditional meetings, as someone once put it, are all too often a place where minutes are taken and hours are lost.

Meetings have also been a place where, according to another survey, many participants feel uncomfortable freely sharing their opinions and believe that most meetings are dominated by hidden agendas.

Participatory team meetings on the other hand are an important way for workers to develop their skills and make innovative contributions. They're also important for dealing with problems, making decisions by consensus, promoting communication, developing leadership, building commitment, sharing information, setting goals and improving operations.

Unfortunately, many meetings aren't as productive as they could be. Some professionals spend between 25% to 60% of their time in meetings. Many meeting-goers feel that up to 50% of meeting time is unproductive.

To improve your meetings, why not have a brief meeting on meetings? Have your work team come prepared to share at least one idea on how to make more productive, participatory meetings.

Consider having a training session on meetings. I conduct such sessions and like to use an entertaining, informative video called "Meetings, Bloody Meetings" starring English actor/comedian John Cleese (see the Resource Guide).

Most importantly, before scheduling a meeting, decide whether a meeting is really necessary.

Ten Tips for Face-to-Face Meetings

In a nutshell, here are the ten tips I teach about effective face-to-face meetings (also see Chapter 17 for special tips on Web and video conferencing meetings):

1. Every meeting should have a stated purpose or goal that is determined in advance of the meeting and that is defined in a **prepared agenda** to which participants have had a chance to contribute. The agenda should be distributed far enough in advance so participants can prepare (at least one day's notice, preferably more time). Each agenda item should be as specific as possible; should ideally include the individual who's introducing it and should cite the purpose of the item at the meeting, e.g., "For Discussion," "For Information" or "For Decision"; and should have a time limit.

One company I know distributes a memo/survey before each staff meeting that solicits two agenda items. It reads in part, "Please write down two things that you would like to hear talked about, questions that need answering, topics of interest, etc.," and participants are asked to leave the completed sheet in a specific person's in-box.

2. Limit the size of the group. Include only those who really need to be there. Four to seven people is an ideal number of people for a planning or problem-solving meeting. (A training session or informational meeting could handle many more.)

3. Pay attention to the physical logistics. Ideally arrange participants in a circle to encourage more participation and if appropriate, provide refreshments to create a more inviting atmosphere. As a professional speaker, I pay close attention to meeting room logistics. I avoid long, narrow rooms and cavernous rooms. I love well-lit spaces. I always find out where the heating and air-conditioning controls are in advance (or who is responsible for controlling them). Whenever possible I place myself opposite the entrance to the room. I prefer a round table but if I get stuck with a long, rectangular one, I place myself at the head if I wish to present more of an authoritarian, expert position and in the middle on one side, if it's a more informal, participatory meeting.

4. List start and end times for the meeting on the agenda and stick to them. It may be helpful to use a countdown timer to stay on schedule or have a clock in your meeting room.

5. Each meeting should **have a facilitator who keeps the meeting moving**, clarifies and summarizes key points, acknowledges contributions of participants by name and ends the meeting on time. The facilitator can provide a quick verbal summary at the end, reviewing the goals of the meeting and how participants contributed to reaching those goals. To build leadership, use a "rotating facilitator," a different person from the work team to lead each meeting.

6. Have a scribe take minutes that reflect key points, decisions, action items and the responsible participants. Minutes should be prepared and distributed to attendees within a few days of the meeting. Electronic whiteboarding and software programs make the process of recording and distributing minutes (via email or on a wiki) very easy. Underline, boldface (or use colors for) action items, deadlines and names of responsible individuals so that they stand out. Have a different scribe at each meeting.

7. Use visuals. Graphics are important. One Wharton School of Business study showed that the average business meeting with graphics was 28 percent shorter than those without graphics. Maybe a picture is indeed worth a thousand words (and can make a meeting that much shorter). Visual tools also can help improve retention of the information by 50 percent.

Have either the facilitator or someone else use a flip chart, a whiteboard, a computer, an LCD projector and a projection screen or an overhead projector to record key ideas and make them visible to everyone at the meeting. Such an ongoing record serves as a "group memory," is useful reference for the scribe when preparing minutes and can be used at future meetings. **Drawing** simple cluster or Mind Maps (as described in Chapter 4) along with simple images can perk up on-the-fly visuals. (See *Beyond Words: A Guide to Drawing Out Ideas* by Milly Sonneman.) **Post-it Easel Pads** can offer all the benefits of Post-it Notes in a large size, letting you easily and safely post and remove these self-stick sheets; this product also doubles as a flip chart pad that attaches to most easel stands and transports easily with a convenient built-in handle. Also check out **digital whiteboards** that connect to your computer, which can save whiteboard notes and drawings digitally on your computer that can be printed out or emailed. (See the Resource Guide.)

8. Include **follow-up** during and after each meeting. Send **minutes** after every meeting summarizing **key decisions, delegations and action items**. Several **standing agenda items** should appear on each regular meeting agenda. Action items, decisions and delegations listed in the minutes should be brought forward to appear on the next meeting's agenda for a status report follow-up. Always include time on the agenda for **successes and accomplishments** that have occurred since the last meeting as well as an opportunity to present **suggestions and ideas**.

9. Be flexible and creative with your meetings and **use different formats** that are appropriate. For manager/assistant teams I recommend **short, but frequent daily meetings** that take no more than five to ten minutes. Certainly a formal agenda for such meetings would be inappropriate but a "standing agenda," that covers routine items, such as the day's schedule, emails and other correspondence, telephone calls and certain ongoing clients/projects, would be a good way to standardize and streamline this business meeting.

10. Keep meetings confidential. Confidentiality breeds trust and encourages participants to open up more fully.

Techniques for Problem-Solving and Decision-Making Meetings

If your team is highly collaborative where it welcomes a free flow of ideas and it isn't too dependent on one strong leader, use a variety of different techniques that involve team members in problem-solving and decision-making meetings.

Such meetings involve ideally four to 12 participants plus a facilitator, have a time limit and typically include four parts:

1. Identification and definition of the challenge or problem—because as Charles Kettering once said, "A problem well-stated is a problem half-solved"

2. Brainstormed ideas (by each participant in round-robin fashion) that include suggestions, alternatives and solutions without discussion

3. Discussion and evaluation of the brainstormed ideas

4. Selection of one to three ideas for implementation

Number 4 can be done by a simple show of hands but a more effective way is to use a preprinted voting card that includes a place to indicate your choice, as well as your priority ranking or the weight you assign to your choice. For example, you might vote for idea D and give it a priority ranking of only 2 (on a scale of 1 to 5, where 5 is high) because you don't feel so strongly about this particular idea.

Another way to do a problem-solving meeting is to have each participant zero in on one key problem area and generate some solutions *before* the meeting. Use a simple survey with three questions:

1. In the coming year (or any other designated period of time), what would you most like to see changed here at this company (or substitute department or other workgroup designation)?

2. How can that change come about? (List specific solutions and steps that need to be taken.)
3. How much time will you contribute to make this change happen and what exactly will you do to help bring about this change?

A solutions-orientation to any meeting keeps the energy on a more positive and focused level. You may even want to avoid using the word "problem," substituting instead the word "item," "issue," "idea" or "challenge." Try to encourage participants to state comments, ideas or questions as positively as possible and discourage negativity or criticism. It's an effective way to run a meeting.

Other useful problem-solving and decision-making techniques to use include flow charting, cause and effect diagrams, decision trees, Pareto charts, force field analysis, pro/con charts, alternatives charts, forced choice charts and multivoting. I teach these and other techniques.

Resource Guide

(Also see Chapter 17.)

Meeting & Other Communication Tools

Crucial Conversations: Tools for Talking When Stakes Are High (McGraw-Hill, 2002) by Kerry Patterson, Joseph Grenny, Ron McMillan and Al Switzler covers key leadership communication skills for handling high stakes and emotionally risky disagreements among individuals, teams, and organizations.

EIOBoard (Electronic In/Out Board) has the potential to let every user in a company know where colleagues are and the details of their schedules. This electronic in/out board solution is available in Web, application, Palm, and telephone interfaces and it replaces traditional magnetic/cardboard in/out boards. Savance, 877/728-2623 or **www.savance.com**

"Meetings, Bloody Meetings" starring English actor/comedian John Clease is available from Coastal Training Technologies Corp., 800/725-3418 or **www.coastal.com**

17

Collaborative Computing

Quick Scan: Read this chapter to discover workgroup computing solutions to conduct meetings and share documents/info online. Check out the Resource Guide for additional resources, products and services.

Computer technology, especially the Internet, is improving how people work together, communicate and share information. With information no longer in the hands of a few individuals and with the trend toward nonhierarchical, cross-functional teams, we're seeing new teamwork possibilities where people can come together online to solve problems and create new business opportunities. Geographic barriers are being removed, too.

Collaborative computing is an ever-evolving process. What seemed exciting and a leap forward in progress yesterday (sending files along with emails) pales with the current possibilities of working together.

Today we have online file sharing, calendaring, scheduling, intranets, extranets, document management, meetings, project management, groupware software solutions and more. Just as cellphones and other mobile devices are morphing into one another, so are the collaborative computing programs and vehicles.

You can't tell what a program does just from the name of it. Whether it's a groupware, project management, collaborative calendaring or file sharing software program, it may do some or all of the following: web conferencing, file sharing, application sharing, screen sharing, printer sharing, multiple screens, file transfers, VoIP, text chat, video,

305

animation, polls, surveys, whiteboarding, meeting controls, passwords and security controls, waiting rooms for participants waiting for permission to join the group, ways to mute or eject participants, integration with other software programs, creation of notes/action items/minutes and wireless or wired connections—all at a wide range of costs. It's exciting that options abound for working collaboratively; however, with whatever technology you choose, make sure it offers a secure connection and any needed encryption.

There are two big collaborative computing areas we'll be looking at: (1) online meetings and (2) online sharing of documents, files and information via email, instant messaging, groupware and project management programs, intranets and other evolving tools (such as wikis and blogs).

Virtual and Web Meetings

As travel costs become more expensive, traveling to a meeting is more often seen as a drain on productivity, time and the bottom line. Using technology for distance meetings has become more comfortable and more advanced and face-to-face meetings are being cut back.

Videoconferencing and web conferencing are stepping in to become more of a fixture in the collaboration process. These types of conferencing go under many names including virtual meetings. Whatever you call this type of collaboration, what you want is to be able to collaborate, share and discuss projects, policies, sales approaches, documents, files or whatever in *real time*.

Web conferencing refers to holding live presentations or group meetings over the Internet with each participant at a computer. Usually, participants see what's on the presenter's screen and use a telephone conference call, VoIP or text chat. **Video conferencing** uses close circuit TV technology and telephony. It is two-way communication and meant to simulate all persons being in the same room at the same time. With more web conferences using webcams (cameras), the distinction between web conferencing and video conferencing is blurring.

The good news is that with desktop sharing features presenters and participants can see one another by using cameras and interact with one another (which can include giving remote mouse control to participants). But make no mistake. These two-dimensional conferencing tools are not the same as the three-dimensional feedback of being there, whether it's to pick up on nuances and body language of other participants or to feel and feed off the response of a live and present audience. Perhaps the biggest loss with non-face-to-face conferencing is the loss of direct eye contact which is so important in communication.

Whatever software you select, make sure it works with your presentation and word processing program as well as having the capability of functioning with the maximum number of attendees you'll have for presentations. Other features to look for include providing security and the ability to resize any printable document without losing picture quality.

Web Conferencing/Virtual Meetings Services and Software

This is a growing area that lets you make real-time presentations and collaborate across the Internet via text-based chat, companion telephone conference calls, integrated audio conferencing or VoIP (Voice over Internet Protocol—using the Internet to make telephone calls). Some offer whiteboarding (see below) and meeting recording services. Always look to see what you really need so you're not paying a premium price for services you won't use or don't need to use.

As web conferencing evolves, look for lower costs, easier and more flexible use by presenters and participants, easier installs and higher quality collaboration and presentations that do not require specially trained organizers to run the services for the meeting.

These services let you bring a presentation, word processing document, websites and much more in a Web-compatible format and include chat windows, annotation tools, ad hoc audience polling and *whiteboard markup* or **whiteboarding**. (A digital whiteboard lets multiple users collaborate on a document or image with participants' comments clearly identified and allows meeting notes to be instantly recorded, saved and shared in real-time over the Internet). In some cases, participants can cut and paste information from the presenter's machine onto their local clipboard. You may want to see pop-ups or icons when someone leaves the meeting or when someone has a chat message. Integration with IM (instant messaging) is becoming increasingly important.

Virtual meeting software will become ever more important in the coming years.

Instant Messaging (IM)

Your IM program may offer audio and video conferencing. Whether it's useful depends upon the quality of the audio and video output, whether video feeds can expand to full screens and its ability to work with network firewalls. Over time, improvements will be made to the business conferencing capabilities of IM.

20 Ways to Improve Online Meetings

These changes in technology means it's necessary to develop new communication tools and skills. Although many of the tips on face-to-face meetings discussed in Chapter 16 also apply, here's what you need to keep in mind with virtual meetings:

Before the meeting:

1. Make sure a Web meeting is appropriate. Especially for an initial contact with someone, a face-to-face meeting may be more appropriate. How else will you really be able to read body language and facial expressions? Maybe just a telephone conference call is enough. Think about the ramifications before setting up a web/video/virtual meeting.

2. Determine how you'll initiate a Web meeting. Meetings are usually started by invitations via phone calls, instant messages (check for compatibility with your instant messenger program), emails or URL links. Some services are more flexible for starting spur-of-the-moment, ad-hoc meetings. Some can determine whether you're online and send an invitation automatically.

3. Use the correct technology and the correct connection. Bandwidth is very important. If some participants have a dial-up connection, the software may not work well. See whether your firewall will allow the connection and technology you're using. Some programs allow presenters and participants to have multiple meeting-content panels on the screen at one time and to be able to move, resize or minimize them—this can mean a smoother presentation since there is less screen switching. If you're using VoIP (**V**oice **o**ver **I**nternet **P**rotocol) as the telephone connection, check to see how secure the connection is.

4. Make sure the presenters know how to handle messaging and polling and design computer slide presentations. (Consider incorporating these Web slide design principles: simple graphics and flat colors will work better and more quickly over the Internet; photographs and detailed graphics can cause lags and delays; dark colors on slides broadcast better than red, orange, yellow or light blue; avoid yellow for fonts or graphics; fonts need to be sized adequately, usually no smaller than 24 point—ideally headings would be 40 point, body text at 30 to 36 point and fine print at 24 point; sans serif fonts such as Arial or Helvetica work better; keyboard text transmits better over the Internet than handwritten text). Prep presenters to look into the camera and to be aware of where the "off" switch is on the microphone. Make sure a dress code is followed—avoid white or light-colored shirts or blouses as well as plaids or small checks.)

5. Do a pre-flight check for the links and phone numbers for the event, the microphone location and audio transmission, the camera placement and the appearance of slides for video transmission to make sure everything works correctly.

6. Plan out the goals and agenda for the meeting, set time limits, distribute the agenda to participants and have action items for follow-up after the meeting.

7. Security is important. Built-in session encryption is available in some cases.

During the meeting:

8. Make it easy to enter meetings—avoid complicated software installations.

9. Have an effective presenter. You can have the greatest software and connections but your weak link may be the presenter. An effective presenter can clearly communicate objectives, provide supporting information and visuals and interact with participants. Be sure to engage participants with desktop sharing, interactive polls, whiteboard slides and Q&A sessions (always repeat questions that are asked).

10. Usually, head and shoulders shots of a presenter are the best main shot. The eyes of a speaker should usually be in the top-

third of a shot. Make sure the background area of a shot is clean and there is not glare on a whiteboard or other demonstrating tool. Have a second camera so there's some variety in the shots.

11. Make sure it gets off to a fast start. With an in-person event, it can seem to take forever for the introductions to occur before the main speaker starts the real program; this delay will be amplified with a live Web presentation.

12. Have an agenda so no one gets sidetracked.

13. Make sure the presentation doesn't last too long—from 60 to 90 minutes is ideal for the Web.

14. Keep the presentation computer techniques simple. To start with, you might want to combine teleconferencing (for the audio portion) with web conferencing (for the video portion). You might want to then go to Internet audio the next time. Until you've mastered the basic technologies, hold off on application sharing, whiteboarding and streaming audio. If there is conversation or other audio interaction during a presentation, turn the audio mute button on while listening to avoid talking over someone else.

15. Have two computers for the presenters—their presentation computer and one that shows what the audience is seeing.

16. Make sure your presenter has prepared patter to fill time when slides load too slowly or the wrong one is accidentally called up.

17. Once the meeting has started, have one window that shows the meeting console, chat, participant information and screen-sharing. Separate groups or teams may want to be able to share their own screens and presentation rights. Flexibility and smoothness of control-sharing features is important because you may want presenters and participants to be able to transfer features such as screen sharing to other participants. Some presenters only want to share parts of their screens.

After the meeting:

18. Follow up a meeting with a concise summary, copies of presentations and content and chat logs.

19. Get feedback about what worked and what didn't. Also, sending a thank you for participation never hurts.

20. Make notes while it's fresh as to what you'd do differently next time.

Sharing Documents and Information

If you're communicating across the world or to an office down the hall and you want everyone to be on the same page—literally, and at the same time—that means using document sharing software that shows the same document on both screens and seeing onscreen editing and changes by each other in *real time* (as compared to emailing versions as attached files).

You can do document sharing with specialized project management and groupware software products but you may want to start with your more familiar word processing and spreadsheet programs. These everyday products are becoming more collaborative and Web-based to allow you to easily share documents. Since there's always a learning curve with new software, it may save you time and aggravation if you can get the result you want from a program you already know and use. So let's start with the document sharing capability of word processing programs and then see other options for sharing information and documents.

Track Changes

On its simplest level, your word processing program (and possibly other programs) probably has a **tracking changes** collaborative tool. Called "Track Changes" in Word, this feature is located on the Tools menu. This feature will track additions and deletions you or a colleague make to a document. These changes will be spelled out in the resaved file along with whoever made the changes (in Word make sure you use the "Save As" command when you save the original file so you don't overwrite the original). Then you can email the revised file and the receiver can review, accept or reject your changes and then make additional changes. Your word processing program may also have an option under the file menu to "send to" an email recipient or online meeting participant.

Simple tools have their limits. The Track Changes tool can become cumbersome especially as the number of collaborators increases. Even if everyone remembers to turn on the track changes before making edits, it can be difficult to work with a document that has been touched by too many hands. If that's the case, look for *worksharing software* to use with your word processor. (See the Resource Guide.)

Online Document Sharing Systems

With this type of system, you can share documents that are stored, retrieved, distributed, managed and archived over the Internet. The documents might be available to every employee in your company or permissions might be set up for individual files or certain storage areas. Check out the security of this type of system (including whether there are multiple levels of security), the number of tiers of security for storage areas, the file types supported and the version control system so you can keep track of who changed what.

Online Calendars

Another approach to sharing information on appointments, meetings, events, and tasks is with an online calendar such as Outlook that shows individual and group calendars. These calendars include many features such as email reminders, notifications, next-step responsibilities and comments. (See Chapter 4.)

Groupware, Intranets, Extranets, Wikis and Blogs

All of these collaborative computing options help work groups do one or more of the following: (a) communicate with each other, (b) share information and (c) improve work process(es) for better quality products or services that satisfy customers—both external and internal.

Many smaller organizations (as well as large) are opting for the collaborative features of **Web-based groupware services** (sometimes referred to as **team groupware**), which include three core functions:

1. Project management through shared calendars, schedules, meeting scheduling, task tracking and allocating resources
2. Idea management through threaded discussion groups/forums and real-time communications
3. Document sharing, protection (with passwords), storage and management that includes routing of documents and "versioning."

Web-based collaboration groupware is especially good for project or work teams that are scattered in different locations who want to share information through the Internet, intranets and extranets. Groupware helps people communicate, collaborate and save time and money, too. Groupware varies in its cost and the need for extensive installation and maintenance support that includes data backup, staff and end-user training. (See the Resource Guide.)

Whenever you mention "groupware," Lotus Notes immediately comes to mind because Notes pioneered this category. Notes is not only groupware software but also a groupware application **platform** used for building and delivering a wide range of customized applications. Programmers and other highly technical people can use Lotus Notes directly to build custom, corporate or groupware applications. Notes helps keep critical information (in a variety of different formats) moving to everyone in an organization who needs it, *when* they need it. (See the Resource Guide.)

Intranets

An **intranet** is an internal, corporate computer network that uses Internet features such as email, Web pages and browsers to build a private communications and data resource center for a specific company or organization. Built within its own secure firewall, an intranet is only accessible to the employees of that organization. Good intranets include specialized sites for different types of workers; for example, marketing and sales people would have some of their own sites, administrative people could have their own, etc. An effective, user-friendly intranet will also have simple keyword search functions. It should facilitate information sharing but not add to information overload.

There is specific intranet software designed to provide easy ways to post information, add, share, manage and edit documents. Besides ease of use and security (encryption) features, see how well it works with your existing word processing, spreadsheet and presentation programs. With some programs, there is no need for a central computer or server to share information—you just install the software on the workstations or computers that want to collaborate and then share documents and data via the Internet or an office network. With this type of software, everyone sees changes made as they happen. (See the Resource Guide.)

Extranets

An **extranet** is an intranet that's connected directly to a company's top customers and suppliers. Because it allows information to flow more freely between companies, efficiency and communication can be improved.

Wikis

In the work environment, a wiki is a website that allows many people to easily add and revise information almost akin to a gigantic company bulletin board that is in essence an online whiteboard. It's a flexible tool that can be used as a company repository of useful information about products, customers and trouble-shooting solutions; it can also reduce the amount of email sent and received. Employees can click on the edit button to add their input. Wikis are collaborative efforts so it's important to have ways for the posted information to be reviewed by peers and edited regularly to keep the information accessible and on point.

Blogs

Weblogs (more commonly known as **blogs**) started out as individual diaries on personal Web pages. Now some companies are hiring professional bloggers to write copy on company sites that presents information and news in a more personal, interesting and informal way. Some websites are interactive and allow comments while others are noninteractive. The format of blogs varies and usually includes links to other useful information.

Resource Guide

Also see my book *Teach Your Computer to Dance* as well as periodic updates at **www.adams-hall.com**.

Digital Whiteboards

mimio Xi (a portable device that attaches to any whiteboard) and **mimioBoard** (a 4' x 6' whiteboard with digital whiteboarding technology built in) both let you capture and share whiteboard notes, collaborate in real time over the Internet and control projected presentations from the board, away from your computer. Virtual Ink Corporation, 877/696-4646 or **www.mimio.com**

3M Digital Wall Display from 3M that allows collaboration with an interactive whiteboard display that lets you share the content of meetings and discussions with associates at any location. Changes you make to presentations can be seen by remote users as you make them. The digital whiteboard lets you write notes in virtual ink and then send them to colleagues via the Internet. 3M, **www.3m.com**

Email, Fax and Telephone

Documents To Go Total Office lets you synchronize and work with your Microsoft Word, Excel, PowerPoint and Access files along with your Outlook data using a Palm-powered handheld or smartphone (such as the Treo 650 smartphone) or the LifeDrive mobile manager. DataViz, Inc., 800/733-0030 [CT] or **www.dataviz.com**

Eudora is a top, award-winning program that allows users to send, receive, sort and manage email and it has great filtering features to help manage and centralize several different email accounts. 800/238-3672 [CA] or **www.eudora.com**

Yahoo! Groups is a free Web-based service that lets you stay in touch with people, keeps an address file, shares files with everyone on your list and provides daily or digest-style emails. **www.groups.yahoo.com**

Groupware

Online collaborative efforts have traditionally been facilitated with groupware applications over a network, such as IBM Lotus Notes.

Other programs or services to look at are:

Colligo enables any laptop or Pocket PC to instantly network to one or more computers using a 802.11 wireless connection. You can create an instant network with one click. Once connected, you can share files, send messages, share an Internet connection, share a printer, compare calendars, replicate databases and more. Colligo offers a personal edition, a workgroup edition and a workgroup edition with a Lotus Notes plug-in. Colligo Networks, Inc., **www.colligo.com**

HotOffice stores files in one central online location for remote access, revision control and keyword search. In addition, the software lets you share ideas on private company bulletin boards. Emails and calendars can be consolidated or kept private and reminders and meetings can be scheduled. Thruport Technologies, Inc., 703/914-9700 [VA] or **www.hotoffice.com**

IBM Lotus QuickPlace (formerly known as *IBM Lotus Team Workplace*) lets users instantly create secure team rooms or workspaces on the Web, providing them with a "place" to coordinate people, tasks, plans and resources; collaborate; and communicate on any project or ad hoc initiative. IBM, **www.ibm.com**

IBM Lotus Sametime (formerly called *IBM Lotus Instant Messaging and Web Conferencing*) allows real-time collaboration over the Internet. You can see, in advance, whether a person or application is available to collaborate; use instant messaging to converse in real time through text, audio and /or video; and conduct Web conferences to share presentations, applications or an entire desktop. IBM, **www.ibm.com**

Intranet Software

Groove is one of several programs that allow groups of workers to share information and files; collaborate over intranets and the Internet; have conversations; post questions and get answers about files and projects; receive notifications when files change and see changes to open documents as they happen; and hold meetings. Microsoft Corp., **www.microsoft.com**

Web Conferencing/Virtual Meetings Services and Software

GoToMeeting is a Web-based online meeting service that has just about all you could want. Citrix Online, **www.gotomeeting.com**

Microsoft Office Live Meeting is a hosted Web conferencing service that lets you hold virtual meetings with anyone, anytime, anywhere with just a phone, a computer and an Internet connection. Microsoft Corp., **www.microsoft.com**

NetMeeting is an Internet conferencing solution for Windows users with features that include remote computer control, multiple program sharing, multi-point data conferencing, text chat, whiteboard, and file transfer, as well as point-to-point audio and video. Microsoft Corp., www.microsoft.com/windows/netmeeting/

WebEx Meeting Center is a leading online conferencing service. It is flexible and powerful. WebEx Communications, **www.webex.com**

Wikis

SocialText Workspace software can set up an enterprise wiki. SocialText, Inc., 650/323-0800 [CA] or **www. Socialtext.com**

Worksharing Software Used with Word

If it becomes difficult to work with a Word document that has been touched by too many hands, a program such as **Workshare** (Workshare, Inc., 415/293-9809 [CA] or **www.workshare.com**) can help you while you're working with Word. It collects user edits and comments and is designed to make it easy to work with them.

Author Bio

Susan Silver is the recognized organizing expert and bestselling author of the award-winning bible of organization, *Organized to Be Your Best!* Susan is a knowledgeable, entertaining and hands-on training, coaching and speaking professional who heads the consulting firm Positively Organized!

Susan's **Positively Organized!**® **Programs** inspire audiences to be their best by showing them essential organization skills and systems to control today's information and communications overload, accomplish more high-value work, build teamwork and reduce stress. Susan also presents leadership, management and supervision programs as well as a variety of business writing and communication skills programs.

A Personal Note from the Author

I want to hear from you. Please e-mail me via the Adams-Hall Publishing Web site (**www.adams-hall.com**) with your results from this book as well as any comments or suggestions for future editions. You, too, could be in print!

Upcoming editions of *Organized to Be Your Best!* could feature your contributions and will keep you up to date on the latest organizational tools and techniques. You'll see how others are dealing with the challenges we all face. What's more, you'll be part of an ongoing process that's on the cutting edge of quality, innovation, performance and achievement.

You can also be part of that process even more directly. Work with my company, Positively Organized!, through a consultation or a customized training program designed to produce positive results for you or your organization in a variety of skill areas. You can find out more about Positively Organized! Programs and Services by clicking on "Susan Silver" at **www.adams-hall.com**.

Index

319

Also by Susan Silver
(and Don Silver)

Teach Your Computer to Dance:
Make Your Computer, Mobile Devices and the
Internet Perform for You

Praise for
Teach Your Computer to Dance

"I learned something new on almost every page. This book is crammed full of valuable hints and tips on everything from avoiding viruses to partitioning a hard drive."
—Andrew Blackman, Reporter, **The Wall Street Journal**

"I like this book a lot. It's written by people who know what they're talking about and who are up on the latest PC and Internet technologies."
—Jonathan Zittrain, Professor of Internet Governance and Regulation, **Oxford University** and Co-Founder of **Harvard Law School's** *Berkman Center for Internet & Society*

"*Teach Your Computer to Dance* is chock full of useful tips. You can pick any page at random and find yourself saying, 'That's a good idea.'"
—Andrew Kantor, Technology Columnist, **USA TODAY**

"*Teach Your Computer to Dance* goes beyond simple 'how to' advice. It's a great guide on how your computer can make you more productive."
—Phil Windley, Associate Professor of Computer Science at **Brigham Young University** and Contributing Editor, **InfoWorld**

"Highly recommended for *all* computer users, *Teach Your Computer to Dance* is full of practical tips and sound advice presented in an easy-to-read format."
—Suzi Turner, Spyware researcher and consultant, owner of SpywareWarrior.com and writer of the *Spyware Confidential* blog, **ZDNet.com**

"Great book for the computer genius or novice. Don and Susan Silver provide the reader with clear-cut advice in an easy-to-read style, guiding you through our technology-crazed world. It's a must-have book for people of all professions."
—Rochelle Stewart, Reporter and *Online Living* blogger, **The Boston Herald**

"This book will save you time and money by teaching you better ways to use the full power of your computer. You'll find plenty of tips, tricks and new sites to increase your productivity and decrease your frustration."
—Liz Pulliam Weston, Personal Finance Columnist for **MSN.com**, nationally syndicated columnist (including the *Los Angeles Times*) and author of *Your Credit Score*

"Unlike many computer books, *Teach Your Computer to Dance* is quite easy to read and understand. The tips are very useful and easy to implement."
—Steven D. Strauss, Small Business Columnist, **USATODAY.com** and author of *The Small Business Bible*

"*Teach Your Computer to Dance* is a great resource for anyone who spends time online. Although there are plenty of manuals around on how to work a computer, this is a terrific resource on how to get the *most* out of your computer and online experience and at the same time practice 'safe computing.'"
—Fran Maier, Executive Director and President, **TRUSTe**

"*Teach Your Computer to Dance* has dozens of expert tips for securing your computing experience. It also contains a ton of great advice for readers of any level."
—Roger A. Grimes, Security Adviser Columnist, **InfoWorld** and author of four books on Windows computer security including *Professional Windows Desktop and Server Hardening*

"*Teach Your Computer to Dance* is a pleasure to read. It's a fun, easy-to-use reference book with straightforward, friendly language to cover the what, where and how of computers."
—Charles P. Pfleeger, PhD, CISSP and coauthor of *Security in Computing*

"*Teach Your Computer to Dance* is well written, well organized and filled with gems."
—Paul and Sarah Edwards, authors of 16 books including *Making Money with Your Computer at Home* and columnists for **Entrepreneur, Costco Connection** and *Homeofficemag.com*

Book Description of
Teach Your Computer to Dance

By

Don Silver and Susan Silver

Life is getting more complex and so is technology. Whether it's your computer, a mobile device or the Internet, you need to know the right steps to control technology.

So take the lead and make technology dance to your tune. Loaded with the best tips and the latest advice on products, programs and websites, this book will show you how to be more secure and:

- ☐ Protect yourself, your computer and your mobile devices—on and off the Internet

- ☐ Control communication overload—email, instant and text messaging as well as cellphone/VoIP calls

- ☐ Discover better ways to search the Web to get quality, not quantity

- ☐ Find your digital notes, info and files easily and organize your computer

- ☐ Make the most of remote and collaborative computing

- ☐ Choose and use the right computer and mobile devices

Drawing on 20-plus years' experience each has with technology, husband-and-wife coauthors Don and Susan Silver have teamed up for the first time to share their knowledge after writing 10 books separately. Readers will recognize the Silvers' clear, concise and clever trademark writing style combined with accessible, well organized, up-to-date information.

And the experts agree. Turn back a page to start reading the outstanding reviews that *Teach Your Computer to Dance* is getting from *The Wall Street Journal*, *USA TODAY*, computer publications and technology/security authorities around the world.

Available from
www.adams-hall.com